9급 공무원 영어 시험대비

박문각
공무원

기 본 서

괜찮아, 잘될 거야! 쉬운 영어, 장DAY 영어

IMAGE로 중요 문장 찾기 / 전개 방식 보기 / 두 문장의 연결 이해

직역이 아닌 흐름을 파악하는 Graphic 독해!

장대영 편저

# 장대영 영어
# Graphic 독해

애듀윌 강의 www.pmg.co.kr

박문각

# 이 책의 머리말

## 이 책을 내면서

수험생들이 공무원 영어를 공부하면서, 제일 먼저 접하게 되는 파트가 문법 파트입니다.
그리고 이 문법 파트는 암기에 대한 부담감이 있지만, 순조롭게 진행됩니다.

그런데, 문제는 많은 수험생들이 독해를 공부하다가 어려움을 겪는다는 것입니다.
우리 공무원 영어 독해가 어렵다는 이야기를 하는 것이 아닙니다.
독해 공부에 대한 방향성의 실종과 잘못된 독해 공부 방법이 문제점이라는 것입니다.

문법은 기본 개념 수업을 수강한 후 어느 정도 자기주도 학습이 가능합니다.
즉, 문제를 풀고 틀렸을 때, 해설을 보면 바로 납득이 되고 틀린 이유를 알게 됩니다.
하지만, 독해는 풀고 틀렸을 때, 해설을 봐도 납득이 안 되는 경우와 틀린 이유를 정확하게 알지
못한다는 것입니다. 그래서 단어만 정리하고 그 문제를 덮게 되는 것입니다.
이 모든 것이 독해 공부에 대한 방향성의 부재에서 나오는 것입니다.

**독해 공부에 대한 방향성**을 올바르게 잡는다면 독해 문제를 풀고, 분석할 수 있게 됩니다.

독해 공부에 대한 올바른 방향성이란
**1. 문장을 넘어서서 글을 볼 수 있어야 합니다.**
**2. 해석을 넘어서서 독해를 할 줄 알아야 합니다.**

**독해 문제의 분석이란**

위에 제시한 독해 공부에 대한 방향성이 설정되면, 문제를 풀고 다음과 같은 순서로 분석이 가능해집니다.

**1.** 답 도출 근거 문장이나 부분 찾기 분석

**2.** 글의 전개 방식 분석

**3.** 문장구조 분석 (구문 독해에서 다루는 영역)

이 독해의 방향성을 위해 이 **Graphic 독해 교재**는 다음과 같이 구성되었습니다.

**1.** STS – 중요 문장 찾기

**2.** MDTS – 글의 전개 방식 찾기

**3.** CLUES – 문장 간의 연결고리 찾기

**4.** READING SKILLS – 유형별 접근법 & 답 도출 근거 찾기

아무쪼록, 이 교재와 수업이 여러분의 합격이라는 목표에 조금이라도 도움이 되었으면 하는 간절함을 담아 짧은 글을 마무리하겠습니다.

'괜찮아 잘 될거야, 장DAY영어가 있잖아'

– 박문각 공무원 장대영

# 이 책의 구성과 특징

## 1 IMAGE로 개념 설명

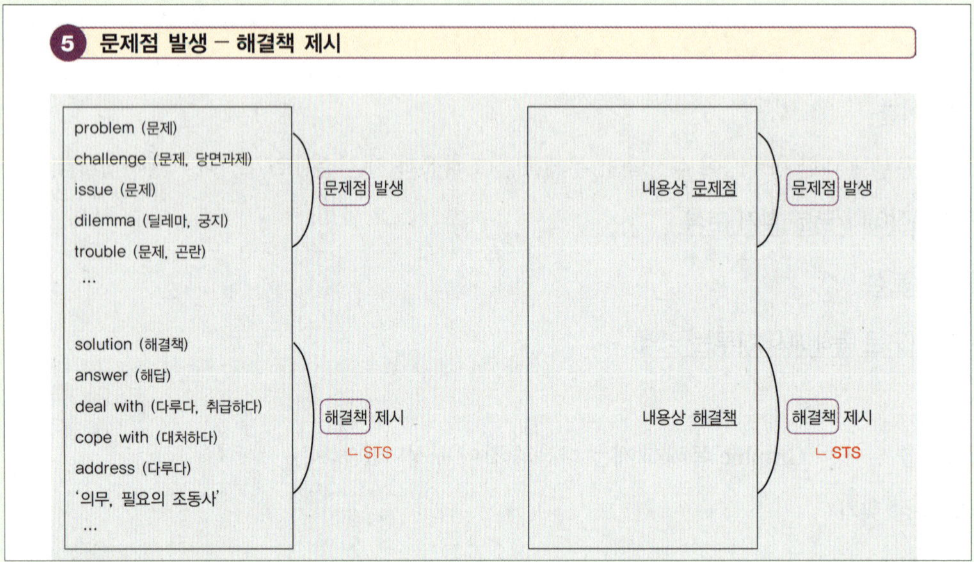


독해개념을 IMAGE로 설명하여 개념을 빠르게 파악하여 글의 구조를 이해할 수 있도록 하였다.

## 2 예제 적용 연습

**예제 1** 다음 글의 요지로 가장 적절한 것은?

Mass political opinion can be sort of like guessing the number of marbles in a glass jar. Most people's guesses will miss the mark, but the average guess of a large enough crowd is generally very accurate. The idea that the masses generally come up with good overall decisions is sometimes referred to as the "wisdom of crowds," and it really does work amazingly well for some things. The problem is that in politics we don't see the glass jar for ourselves — we view it through the lens of the media, and the media show us a distorted view of politics. Thus, we should be aware of such media biases in order to minimize the likelihood that they'll throw off our political judgment, even though there's no way to permanently "fix" them.

① 정치적 판단의 혼란을 최소화하려면 미디어의 편향을 의식해야 한다.
② 편향되지 않은 정보를 습득하기 위해서는 다양한 매체를 접해야 한다.
③ 정치적 견해는 소수보다 다수에서 더 정확할 수 있다.
④ 미디어의 발전으로 대중의 정치 참여가 확대되어 왔다.

IMAGE로 학습한 독해개념을 예제에 적용하는 연습을 함으로써 정답을 찾아가는 방법을 확실히 이해할 수 있도록 하였다.

## 3 펜터치 + 자세한 해석과 해설

### 5 문제점 발생 − 해결책 제시

**예제 1** 다음 글의 요지로 가장 적절한 것은?  　　　　　정답 ①

Mass political opinion can be sort of like guessing the number of marbles in a glass jar. Most people's guesses will miss the mark, but the average guess of a large enough crowd is generally very accurate. The idea that the masses generally come up with good overall decisions is sometimes referred to as the "wisdom of crowds," and it really does work amazingly well for some things. The problem is that in politics we don't see the glass jar for ourselves — we view it through the lens of the media, and the media show us a distorted view of politics. Thus, we should be aware of such media biases in order to minimize the likelihood that they'll throw off our political judgment, even though there's no way to permanently "fix" them.

① 정치적 판단의 혼란을 최소화하려면 미디어의 편향을 의식해야 한다.
② 편향되지 않은 정보를 습득하기 위해서는 다양한 매체를 접해야 한다.
③ 정치적 견해는 소수보다 다수에서 더 정확할 수 있다.
④ 미디어의 발전으로 대중의 정치 참여가 확대되어 왔다.

**해석** 대중의 정치적 견해는 유리병에 담긴 구슬의 수를 짐작하는 것과 다소 비슷할 수 있다. 대부분 사람들의 짐작은 빗나가지만 충분히 많은 수의 사람들의 평균 짐작은 일반적으로 아주 정확하다. 일반적으로 대중이 훌륭한 종합적 결정을 내놓는다는 생각은 종종 '대중의 지혜'라고도 일컬어지며, 어떤 경우에는 정말로 놀랄 만큼 잘 맞는다. 문제는 정치에서는 우리가 유리병을 우리 스스로 보는 것이 아니라는 것이다. 즉 우리는 미디어의 렌즈를 통해서 그것을 보고, 미디어는 우리에게 정치에 대한 왜곡된 관점을 보여준다. 그러므로 우리는, 그러한 미디어의 편향을 영구적으로 '고칠'방법은 없을지라도, 그것이 우리의 정치적 판단을 혼란스럽게 할 가능성을 최소화하기 위해서는 그러한 미디어의 편향을 인식해야 한다.

**해설** STS '문제점에 대한 해결책 제시'에 해당하는 문장 − Thus we should be aware of such media biases in order to minimize the likelihood that they'll throw off our political judgement, even though there's no way to permanently "fix" them.
이 문장이 답 도출 근거 문장이다.

**어휘** mass 대중　likelihood 개연성　throw off 벗다

펜터치로 글의 중심 문장을 빠르게 복습할 수 있도록 하였고, 유형에 따라 글의 구조를 도식화시켜 다시 한 번 답의 근거를 생각해 볼 수 있도록 하였다.

# 이 책의 **차례**

## Chapter 01　STS(중요 문장 찾기)



## Chapter 02　MDTS(글의 전개 방식)

## Chapter 03  CLUES(문장 간의 연결 관계)



## Chapter 04  TYPES(유형별 접근법)



## Chapter 05  실용문



## 정답 및 해설

# 장대영 영어
## Graphic 독해

# 01

# STS
# (중요 문장 찾기)

# STS(중요 문장 찾기)

## 1 STS

STS | Strategies for Topic Sentence
　'필자 생각'이 들어간 문장임을 보여주는 표현들

### STS 1 의무/필요

**1. 조동사**

must
= have to
should
= ought to
need (to)

* S 의무, 필요 ㉛
└ *You 〉 We 〉 일반 S

**2. etc**

compulsive (강제적인)　← compel (강요하다)
obligatory (의무적인)　← oblige (강요하다)
necessary (필요한)
necessity (필요성)　　← need (필요하다)

**예제 1** 다음 글의 주제로 가장 적절한 것은?

> The New Shorter Oxford English Dictionary defines a market as "a meeting or gathering place of people for the purchase and sale of provisions or livestock" and as "the action or business of buying and selling" But markets aren't merely meeting places or a series of transactions; they are social institutions that must be built up and maintained. Initially markets may be thrown up spontaneously, but in the end they are socially sustained; all markets depend for their operation on a complex of social, cultural, and legal institutions. In order for exchanges to constitute the structure of a market many elements have to be in place: property rights need to be defined and protected, rules for making contracts need to be specified and enforced, information needs to flow smoothly, and people need to be induced through internal and external mechanisms to behave in a trustworthy manner.

① problems with the modern market economy
② controversy over the role of markets
③ strength of the modern market economy
④ elements of a market as a social system

**예제 2** 다음 글의 요지로 가장 적절한 것은?

> If the listener is to appreciate the form and beauty of symphony, it is imperative that he should understand such the structure of symphony. A symphony has normally four movements. The opining movement of the symphony takes the sonata form, and has at least two important themes. Each theme is usually introduced early in the introductory section. While the first movement of a symphony is usually the most important, the other three may be equally beautiful. The second movement is slow. This is in contrast to the quicker tempos of the first. The third movement is traditionally faster; in classical symphony it was a minuet. The finale is the fourth movement of the symphony and usually balances the mood and pace of the first movement.

① 심포니는 일정한 구조를 이해하는 것이 그 감상을 위해 필요하다.
② 심포니는 다른 무엇보다도 각 악기들의 조화와 균형을 가장 중요시한다.
③ 현대의 심포니는 고전적 심포니의 형식과는 완전히 다르게 발전하고 있다.
④ 심포니는 대체적으로 보통 사람들이 이해하기 어려운 음악 형식으로 되어 있다.

## STS ❷ '중요한'의 의미를 가진 형용사

**1. '중요한'의 의미를 가진 형용사**

important

significant

vital

crucial

critical

**2. etc**

(동사) matter, count → 중요하다

(명사) importance, significance, consequence → 중요성

* of + 추상명사 = 형용사

of importance

of consequence ⎫ 중요한

of significance ⎭

---

**예제 1** 다음 글의 주제로 가장 적절한 것은?

> More and more parents believe that their children don't have to participate in physical activity if they don't want to. However, physical education (PE) is an important part of holistic schooling. It is about educating the whole person, a holistic education betters us in an all-round sense, rather than a merely academic experience. Some aspects of physical education are vital for future well-being, for example, being able to swim and learning to lift heavy weights safely. Arguments about cost seem petty when compared to this aim and also misguided, since PE departments would continue to exist to serve those that chose to study PE voluntarily, even if the subject were no longer compulsory. I believe that PE is a crucial element of all round schooling and our society's well-being.

① 체육 교육 예산을 다른 과목에 투입해야 한다.

② 체육 교육이 중요한 만큼 지속적으로 실시되어야 한다.

③ 부모들은 학교의 교육 방식에 관여하지 말아야 한다.

④ 교내 체육 활동은 세분화되고 다양성을 확보해야 한다

## STS **3** 결론/요약

### 1. 결론 유도 장치

( '그래서', '그러므로' )　　　　　　　　　　( '결과적으로', '따라서' )

| | |
|---|---|
| So | in conclusion |
| Therefore | to conclude |
| Thus | as a result |
| Hence | consequently |
| That's why | in consequence |
| | accordingly |
| | for these (this) reason(s) |

* <u>That's why</u> → 그래서, 그러므로

　<u>This</u>

　<u>Which</u>

　cf) That's because → 그것은 ~이기 때문이다.

### 2. 요약장치

( '요약하자면' )

| | |
|---|---|
| in short | in brief |
| to be brief | in a word |
| in sum | to sum up |
| to summarize | |



*L.S : Last Setence(마지막 문장)

**예제 1** 다음 글의 제목으로 가장 적절한 것은?

The challenges for us today are the same as they were during the days of the Romans; we just have more advanced methodologies and technologies to apply to the water loss problem. We can look back at past efforts and smile and think that we are so much better, but to be honest we just have better tools. An open mind, an unwillingness to accept existing inefficiencies, and a wish to improve are the basic skills that we need to have today. The rest can be obtained as work progresses. Water loss control programs will only be successful if we are willing to accept what we find and act on it openly. Therefore, it is critical that we understand the extent and impact of water loss, and the control of water loss holds a priority of paramount importance.

① Understanding the Steps of Water Loss
② What Needs to Be Done to Decrease Water Loss?
③ The Occurrence and Bad Influence of Water Loss
④ How Much Water Are We Wasting in Our Daily Lives?

## STS ④ 역접장치

( '그러나' )
· But ________________________.

· However
________, ________________.
________, ________, ________.
________________, ________.

· though
________, ________, ________.
________________, ________.

cf) Though S V → 비록 S가 V한다고 할지라도

· Yet ________________.
  Still

( '반면에', '대조적으로' )
in opposition
on the other hand
in contrast
on (to) the contrary

( '그럼에도 불구하고' )
nevertheless
nonetheless

T.S (Topic Sentence) + Middle ← ________ +Middle
= 중요 문장

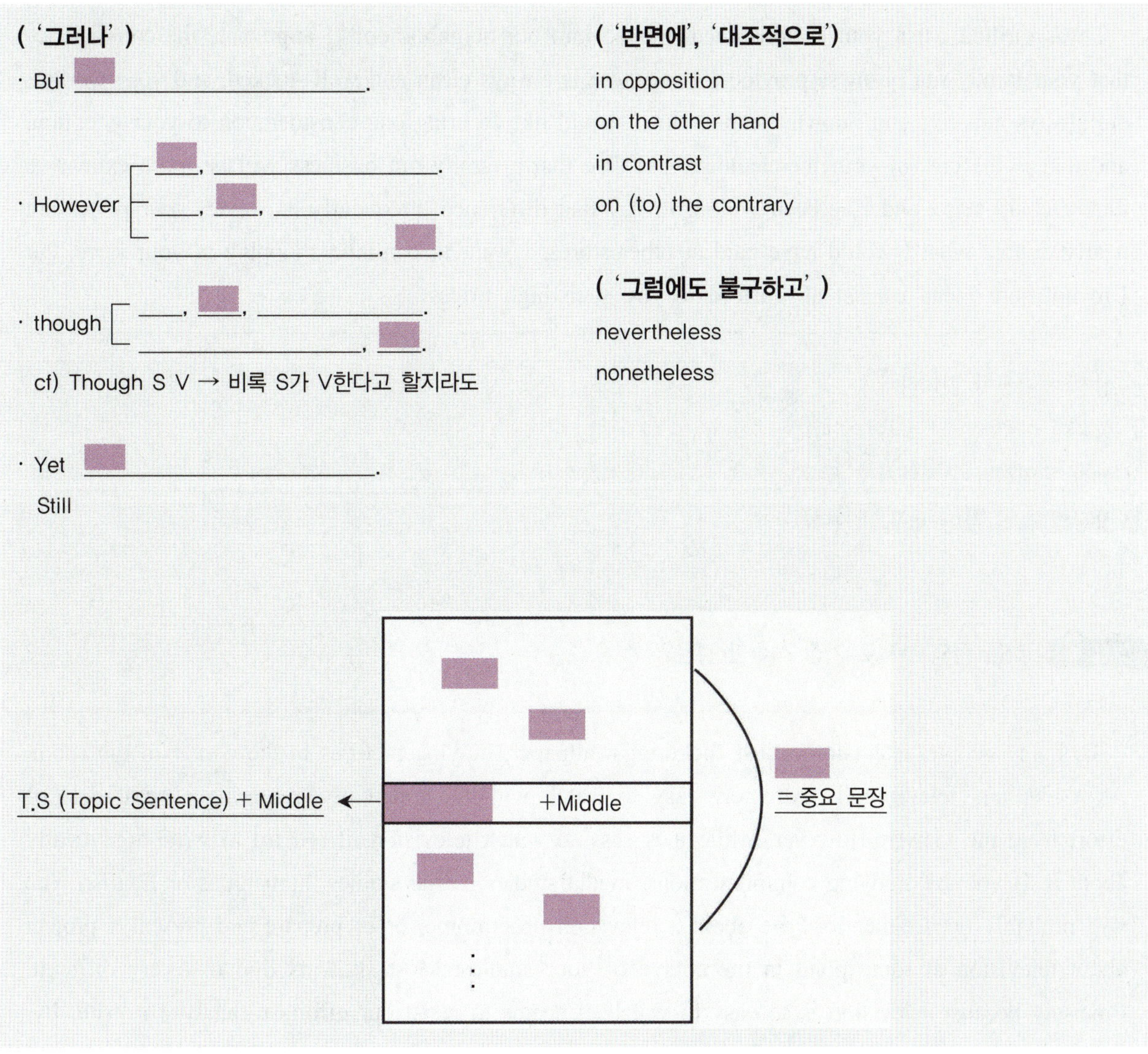

**예제 1**  다음 글의 요지로 가장 적절한 것은?

I was thrilled when your establishment moved into our neighborhood. I appreciate the convenience that your family-run business provides. Your store is always clean and well-stocked, and your workers are always attentive and knowledgeable. But I would like to bring one consideration to your attention, and that is the cost of your merchandise. I realize that a family-run business will be more expensive than a chain store, and I've been willing to pay that difference. Frequently, however, your prices are nearly double what I would have paid at other stores. I want to continue shopping at your store, but I'm not sure I can consistently afford to pay such high prices.

① 상점의 이용이 편리하다.
② 상품이 아주 잘 진열되어 있다.
③ 상점 운영시간이 지나치게 짧다.
④ 상점의 물건 값이 너무 비싸다.

**예제 2**  다음 글의 주제로 가장 적절한 것은?

To many people, television is just flickering wallpaper, moving pictures in the corner of the room. As a medium, television is extremely easy to watch without, apparently, requiring a great deal of effort from the viewer. However, while it is easy to watch television, it is hard to write analytically about it. If you are studying communications, media studies, social studies, humanities or English, you will probably need either to write about a television programme, or to prepare and present a project about television at some point in the course of your studies. Most students find this very difficult. Precisely because television is so easy to watch, it seems to resist our efforts to analyze it critically.

① 텔레비전 매체의 파급력
② 텔레비전 분석의 까다로움
③ 텔레비전의 기술적인 발전
④ 텔레비전 연구의 최근 동향

## STS 5 not과 but의 A B 접속사

(A가 아니라 B)

not A but B = B and not A
　　　　　= B, not A

(A뿐만 아니라 B)

not only A but (also) B = B as well as A
　　= just
　　= merely

(A라기보다는 B)

not so much A as B = not A so much as B

* Grammar : A, B '병렬'
* Reading : A < B*

### 예제 1  다음 글의 요지로 가장 적절한 것은?

Futurists are not prophets. They do not "predict" what will happen. They employ devices, ranging from extremely simple to highly sophisticated, to detect trends. However, their output is not a "fine" projection but an array of possibilities — a multiple series of alternatives, not a fixed singularity. Besides, futurists are not so much interested in predicting as in creating desirable futures; the stress is not on what it will be but what it can or should be. Futurists leap ahead to the future not so that they may stay in an escapist never-never land, but so that they can lure that future into the present and negotiate with it while the options are chosen rather than imposed. If there is indeed the prospect of future shock, then dealing with it now may transform future shock into something less intimidating.

① 미래학자는 올바른 미래의 방안을 선택하도록 이끈다.
② 미래학자는 미래에 대한 정확한 예측을 해내는 사람이다.
③ 미래학자는 우리가 미래에 갖춰야 할 행동양식을 연구한다.
④ 미래학자는 절대 미래 사건에 대해 가치 판단을 내리지 않는다.

## STS ⑥ 명령문

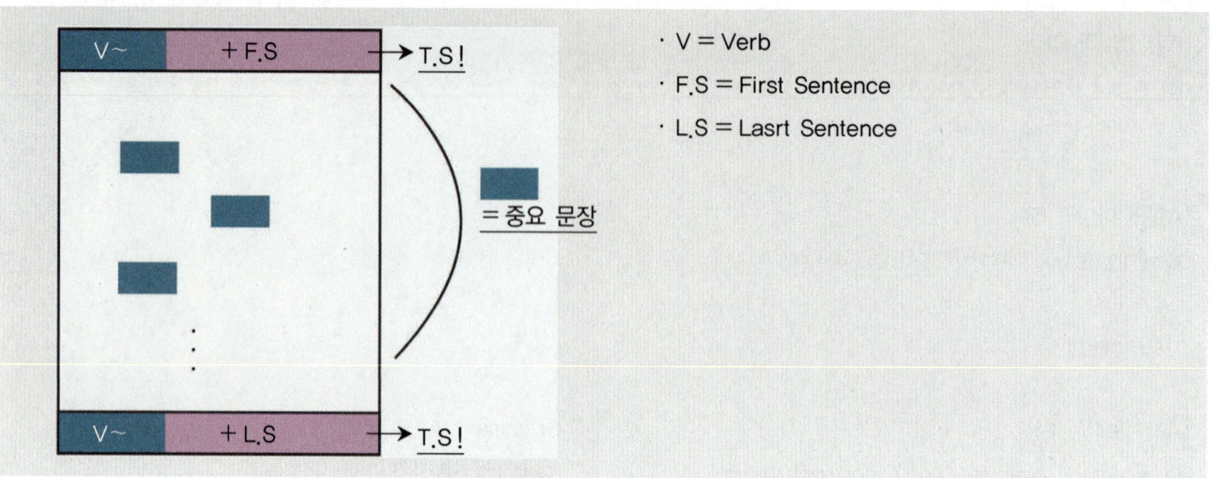


### 예제 1  다음 글의 제목으로 가장 적절한 것은?

Allow me to give you a little advice about writing fiction. First, make your characters believable. In real life, everyone is unique. If all your characters speak the same way and react to things in the same way, you'll lose your readers from the start. Once your readers believe in your characters, you must get them to care. Each reader must be able to identify with at least one character, to almost become that character in his or her mind. You can do this by developing characters with genuine human traits, both good and bad. Now it's time to weave your tale, to create a plot. Your readers are part of the story now; they are involved. One last thing is, your story must touch the readers' emotions. If you can make them laugh and cry along with your characters, you will be a successful writer.

① The Three Elements for a Storyline
② Investigation on Unique Human Traits
③ Identification with Characters of a Story
④ Some Useful Tips for Writing a Novel

## STS 7 양보절과 주절

* 양보절 → '비록 ~ 일지라도' 라고 해석

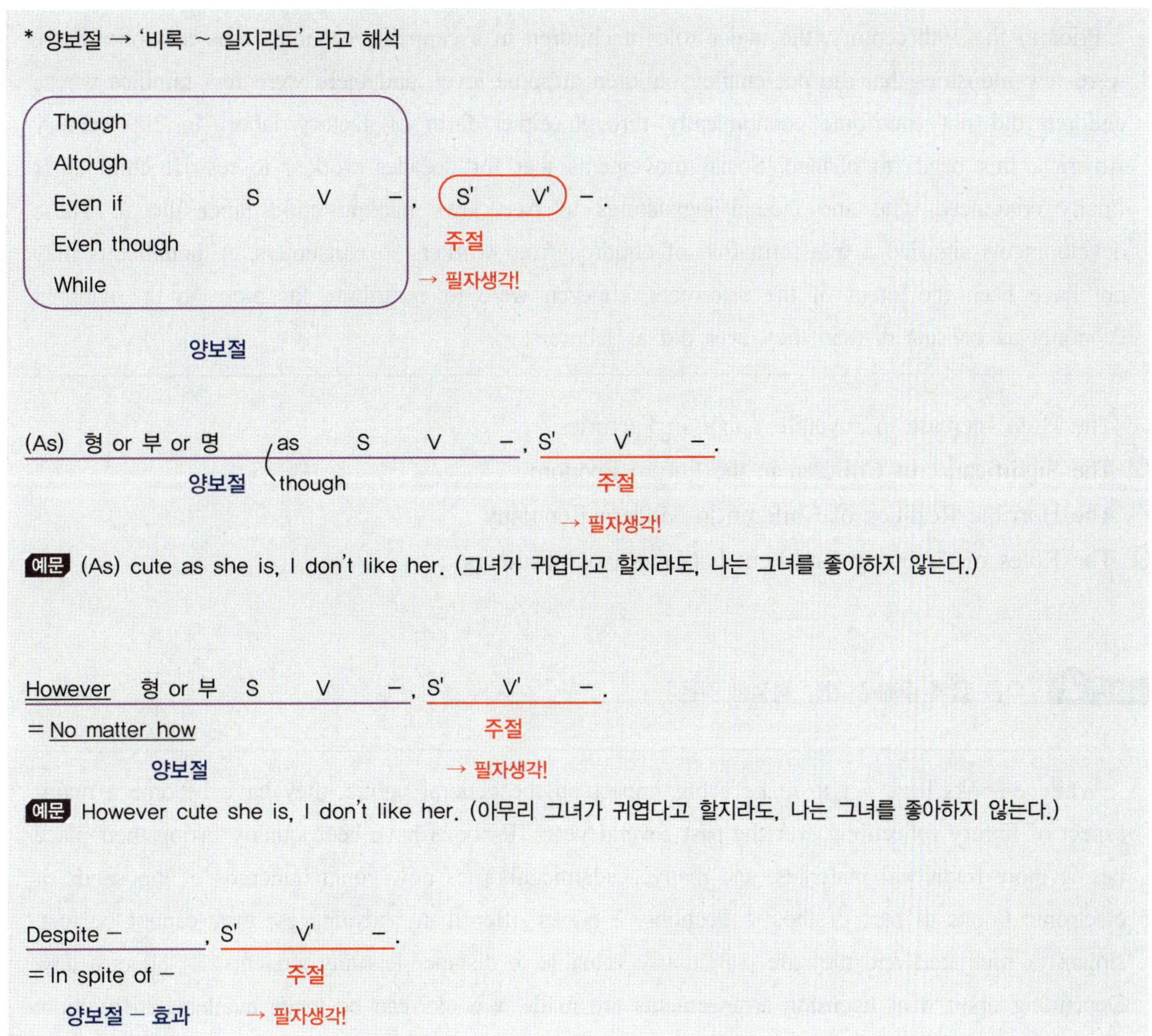


예문 (As) cute as she is, I don't like her. (그녀가 귀엽다고 할지라도, 나는 그녀를 좋아하지 않는다.)

예문 However cute she is, I don't like her. (아무리 그녀가 귀엽다고 할지라도, 나는 그녀를 좋아하지 않는다.)

## 예제 1  다음 글의 제목으로 가장 적절한 것은?

Prior to the 19th century, the major role of children in a capitalist economy was to work. There were few industries that did not employ children at some level, and there were few families whose children did not contribute economically through either farm or factory labor. In 20th-century America, this began to change. Social movements that for decades worked to restrict child labor finally convinced state and federal legislatures to pass laws making child labor illegal. These developments signaled a transformation of children from workers to consumers. Although this may not have been the intent of the reformers, children were to contribute far more to the national economy as consumers than they ever did as laborers.

① The High Increase in Juvenile Labor in Factories
② The Significance of Children in the Future Economy
③ The Horrible Realities of Children in Modern Economy
④ The Roles of American Children: Laborers or Consumers

## 예제 2  다음 글의 주제로 가장 적절한 것은?

While e-books have yet to make a big impact on the general public, they have become a major aspect of library collections over the past several years. E-books have been quietly taking their place beside more traditional materials, and many academic libraries now count hundreds of thousands of electronic books as part of their collections. E-books offer many advantages; they cannot be lost, stolen, or mutilated, and they are particularly valuable to distance-learning students, 24 hours a day. Depending upon what licensing arrangements are made, e-books can be made available to multiple users at once. Libraries that have suffered major physical disasters such as fires or floods can continue to offer large parts of their collection online. E-books may also offer a level of search-ability completely beyond what could be accomplished with more traditional printed text.

① 전자책의 종류
② 전자책의 역사
③ 전자책의 이점
④ 전자책의 검색 절차

## STS **8** 강조표현

### 1. It – that 강조구문

**① 모양**

|  | beV | 단어, 구, 절 강조내용 | that – . |
|---|---|---|---|
| It | is | 人 | – who |
|  | was | 物 | – which |
|  | has been | : | : |
|  | had |  |  |

**② 해석**

It　　beV　　강조내용②　　that　①– .

↳ –인 것은 바로 강조내용 이다.

**③ Reading Point : STS**

---

예제 **1** 다음 글의 제목으로 가장 적절한 것은?

As millions of men left to fight in World War I, women took over their jobs and kept national economies going. Many women worked in war industries, manufacturing weapons and supplies. Others joined women's branches of the armed forces. When food shortages threatened Britain, volunteers in the Women's Land Army went to the fields to grow their nation's food. Nurses shared the dangers of the men whose wounds they tended. At aid stations close to the front lines, nurses often worked around the clock. War work gave women a new sense of pride and confidence. They challenged the idea that women could not handle demanding and dangerous jobs. In many countries, including Britain, Germany, and the United States, it was women's support for winning the war that helped them finally win the right to vote.

① How the British Won World War I
② Improved Rights through Women's War Effort
③ Responsibilities of Women in Maintaining Society
④ Women as Victims of Long-standing Discrimination

## 2. 강조의 Only / 강조의 do / the very N

- 강조의 Only              '단지 −만', '꼭 −만'
- 강조의 do                do

                              does ⎫ V원형 : V 강조

                              did ⎭

- the very N            '바로 그 N' : N 강조

---

**예제 1**    다음 글의 제목으로 가장 적절한 것은?

> To some degree, biology is destiny when it comes to communication style. Studies of identical and fraternal twins suggest that traits including sociability, anger, and relaxation seem to be partially a function of our genetic makeup. Fortunately, biology isn't the only factor that shapes how we communicate: Communication is a set of skills that anyone can learn. As children grow, their ability to communicate effectively develops. For example, older children can produce more sophisticated persuasive attempts than can younger ones. Along with maturity, systematic education (such as the class in which you are now enrolled) can boost communicative competence. Even a modest amount of training can produce dramatic results. After only thirty minutes of instruction, one group of observers became significantly more effective in detecting deception in interviews.

① Communication Leading to Success in Life

② Communicative Competence Can Be Learned

③ Learning Requires Communicative Competence

④ Relaxation as A Major Part of Communication

**예제 2** 다음 글의 요지로 가장 적절한 것은?

Science is all about possibilities. We propose theories, conjectures, hypotheses, and explanations. We collect evidence and data, and we test the theories against this new evidence. If the data contradict our theory, then we change the theory. In this way science advances, and we gain greater and greater understanding. But there is always the possibility of new evidence arising which contradicts the existing theories. It's the very essence of science that its conclusions can change, that is, that its truths are not absolute. The intrinsic good sense of this is contained within the remark reportedly made by the distinguished economist John Maynard Keynes, responding to the criticism that he had changed his position on monetary policy during the 1930s Depression: "When the facts change, I change my mind. What do you do, sir?"

① 과학 이론은 새로운 증거에 의해 늘 변할 수 있다.

② 과학 이론에서 자료의 해석이 수집보다 더 강조된다.

③ 과학의 발전에 경제적 안정이 긍정적 영향을 미쳐 왔다.

④ 과학자들은 절대불변의 과학적 이론 확립을 위해 노력한다.

## 3. 최상급 / 비교급 강조 6가지

① 최상급 ┌ opinion STS
         └ fact

② 최상급 기본 모양  (the) –(e)st ┌ in 단수 N
                    most – ┤ of 복수 N
                           └ that have p.p

③ 최상급 해석  '가장 …한/하게'

④ 최상급 모양 X  ① 부정어 as … as A
   최상급 의미 O  ② 부정어 비교급 than A
                ③ A 비교급 than any other 단수 N
                ④ A 비교급 than all the other 복수 N

**예문** Beauty is the greatest recommendation in the world. 아름다움이 세상에서 가장 위대한 추천서이다.

= No recommendation is as great as beauty in the world. 세상에서 어떤 추천도 아름다움만큼 위대하지는 않다.

= No recommendation is greater than beauty in the world. 세상에서 어떤 추천도 아름다움보다 위대하지는 않다.

= Beauty is greater than any other recommendation. 아름다움이 어떤 다른 추천보다 더 위대하다.

= Beauty is greater than all the other recommendations. 아름다움이 모든 다른 추천보다 더 위대하다.

cf) The Sahara is the largest desert in the world. (fact) 사하라가 세상에서 가장 큰 사막이다.

+ 비교급 강조 6 ┌ opinion STS
              └ fact

   훨씬 더 ┌ –er
          └ more
          ↳ much, even, still, far, by far, a lot

Beauty is a far greater recommendation than any letter of introduction. (Aristotle)
아름다움이 어떤 소개장보다 훨씬 더 위대한 추천이다. (아리스토텔레스)

**예제 1** 다음 글의 주제로 가장 적절한 것은?

Suppose we need to measure the temperature in a vineyard. If we have only one temperature sensor for the whole plot of land, we must make sure it is accurate and working at all times; no messiness allowed. In contrast, if we have a sensor for every one of the hundreds of vines, we can use cheaper, less sophisticated sensors (as long as they do not introduce a systematic bias). Probably, at some points, a few sensors may report incorrect data, creating a less exact, or "messier," dataset than the one from a single precise sensor. Any particular reading may be incorrect, but the collection of many readings will provide a more comprehensive picture. Because this dataset consists of more data points, it offers far greater value that likely compensates for its messiness.

① forms of sensors appropriate for vineyards
② elements influencing the worth of the dataset
③ the advantage of acquiring a large set of data
④ the influences of technology on farming grape

**예제 2** 다음 글의 요지로 가장 적절한 것은?

It's striking to me that in all the heated debate about health care reform, one basic fact is rarely discussed, and that is the one thing that could dramatically bring down the costs of health care while improving the health of our people. Studies have shown that 50 to 70 percent of the nation's health care costs are preventable, and the single most effective step most people can take to improve their health is to eat a healthier diet. If we were to stop overeating, to stop eating unhealthy foods and to instead eat foods with higher nutrient densities and cancer protective properties, we could have a more affordable, sustainable, and effective health care system. And more importantly, we'd be less dependent on insurance companies and doctors, and more dependent on our own health-giving choices.

① 사람에 따라 일일 권장 섭취량은 다를 수 있다.
② 의료 혁신을 위해 다방면의 의견을 수용할 필요가 있다.
③ 식생활 개선을 통해 건강을 증진하고 의료비를 절감할 수 있다.
④ 현대에는 치료가 아닌 예방을 중시하는 의료 시스템이 더 효과적이다.

## STS ⑨ 1인칭의 활용

I think (생각한다) / believe (믿는다) / guarantee (보장한다) / encourage (권장한다) / wish (바란다) / hope(희망한다) / suggest (제안한다) / etc + that  S  V

In my opinion (내 의견으로는) / (As) to me (나에게 있어서) / (As) for me (나에 관한 한) / As far as I'm concerned (나에 관해서는) / etc + S  V

My belief (나의 신념은) / My advice (나의 충고는) / My opinion (나의 의견은) / My claim etc (나의 주장은) / is + that  S  V

### 예제 1  다음 글의 요지로 가장 적절한 것은?

I believe that it is a variety of responses that are most effective in dealing with the real social dilemmas. This is true of handling computerized information in this country. We need extensive information to manage rational and humane society, but what is needed is a ban by law on any computerized data banks that are so dangerous perse that they should not be allowed. Among other possible responses, we might convene hearings before legislatures and regulatory commissions so that government agencies may present their plans for computerized systems and demonstrate necessary safeguards before they are allowed to computerize sensitive files containing personal information. Within the computerized systems, we can reexamine existing rules, such as those which pertain to the confidential nature of data.

① 공익을 위해 어느 정도 개인의 신상 정보 공개는 용납될 수 있다.
② 처음부터 컴퓨터로 개인의 신상 정보를 다루는 것을 금지해야 한다.
③ 정부기관이 개인 신상 정보를 다루는 경우에는 사전 승인을 받도록 해야 한다.
④ 다양한 접근방법을 시도해 봄으로써 컴퓨터 처리된 개인 정보를 다뤄 볼 수 있다.

## STS ⑩ 필자의 판단 주입 어휘와 표현의 이용

### 1. 긍정적인 (+) / 부정적인 (−) 의 감정 어휘

① 긍정적인 (+) 감정, 주관 어휘

the best way (최고의 방법) / the real thing (실질적인 것은) / good (좋은) / right (올바른) / true (진실된) / truth (진실) / wonderful (아주 멋진) / logical (논리적인) / effective (효과적인) / value (가치), valuable (가치 있는), invaluable (매우 가치 있는) / etc

② 부정적인 (−) 감정, 주관 어휘

flaw (결점) / drawback (결점) / mistake (실수) / misunderstanding (오해) / wrong (잘못된) / illogical (비논리적인) / ineffective (비효과적인) / valueless (가치 없는) / etc

### 2. It's time that / to v

① 모양   It is ( high / about / 생략 가능 ) time ( that S should V원형 / S V 과거형 / to V )

② 해석   '−해야 할 ( 때이다.' / 시간 )

③ Reading Point   STS

### 3. 이성적 판단

It is essential(imperative, natural, reasonable) that A is B.

→ A가 B라는 것은 필수적(반드시 해야 하는, 당연한, 합리적인)이다.

It makes sense that A is B.

→ A가 B라는 것은 합리적이다.

(It is) No wonder that A is B.

→ A가 B라는 것은 놀라운 일이 아니다. (A가 B라는 것은 당연하다.)

It goes without saying that A is B.

= It is needless to say that A is B.

→ A가 B라는 것은 말할 것도 없이 분명한 사실이다.

### 4. 기타 감정

→ '중요 문장' 전 흥미 유발

surprise (놀라움) / surprising (놀라운) / astonishing (놀라운) / amazing (놀라운) / embarrassing (당황스러운) / perplexing (당황스러운) / puzzling (당황스러운) / etc

**예제 1** 다음 글의 주제로 가장 적절한 것은?

Our expectations are constructed through our value systems, upbringing, and past experiences and can be very different from those of others. These expectations can become major sources of frustration when not met by others' behavior, such as that of our tutees. The best thing to do is to try to enter tutoring without any expectations at all. This, of course, includes giving up expectations you may have of your future students and their personalities, their academic skills or progress, and their motivation and attitude toward you. All children are different. They have different backgrounds, different strengths, and different weaknesses. Some may be thrilled to be tutored; others may be suspicious. At the first meeting, a tutor's conception of a student should be a blank slate. Tutors must be prepared to accept and to work with any students to whom they are assigned.

① need for a tutor to accept a tutee as it is
② benefits of having tutees of diverse backgrounds
③ how to make children be responsible for their own learning
④ advantages of a group-based tutoring program for children

**예제 2** 다음 글에서 필자가 주장하는 바로 가장 적절한 것은?

All kinds of high-tech devices exist to test meat for microbial infestations like salmonella. The government is too cheap to invest in these, however, so federal food inspectors continue to inspect meat visually, as it rolls past on a conveyor belt. Micro-organisms are invisible and you can imagine how attentively a low-paid federal food inspector is going to be looking at each of 18,000 identical chickens sliding past him. By the government's own admission, as much as 20 percent of all chicken and 30 percent of turkey is contaminated. It is thought that as many as 10 million people may get sick each year from factory contaminated food, costing the economy about $2 billion in additional health care costs, lost productivity, and so on. Given all this, why doesn't the government turn to high-tech devices? It is high time that we should let the government be able to keep food safe for consumers by increasing its budget.

① 전염병을 예방하기 위해 가축 방역을 확대하자.
② 식품 안전 강화를 위해 더 많은 예산을 투입하자
③ 수입 육류에 대한 효율적 검역 시스템을 마련하자.
④ 식품 검사관의 열악한 근무 조건 개선책을 마련하자.

## STS ⑪ The + 비교급, the + 비교급

### 1. 모양

The + 비교급 ( S V ) ~, the + 비교급 ( S' V' ) ~.
　　　　　　생략 가능　　　　　　　　　　　　생략 가능

### 2. 해석

The + 비교급　S　V　~, the + 비교급　S'　V'　~.
　　　　　　　①　　　　　　　　　　　　　　②

→ ①할수록, ②하다.

### 3. Reading Point

* ┌ ①: **원인**
　└ ②: **결과**

* **STS**

---

예제 **1**　다음 글의 주제로 가장 적절한 것은?

It doesn't really matter whether we share a first name, a birthday, a home state, or a rare fingerprint pattern — similarity can help to create an in-group dynamic that brings people together. The more we can zero in on and accentuate the similarities we have with someone else, the more likely we are to get along with that person. This is especially useful in trying to connect with someone who seems very different from us. If the person is from a different cultural background or a different profession or industry, focus on the ways in which you are similar — music, sports, humor. You're more likely to create a connection.

① the chance of unexpected meetings
② the similarity-based relationship-building
③ the effect of hobbies on communication
④ the understanding of diversity of culture

**예제 2** 다음 글에서 필자가 주장하는 바로 가장 적절한 것은?

States that previously lowered the drinking age to 18, such as Massachusetts, Michigan, and Maine, experienced an increase in alcohol-related crashes among the 18 to 20 age group. Lowering drinking ages to 16, 17, or 18 like the MLDA (Minimum Legal Drinking Age) in some European countries is inappropriate for US standards because American teens generally start driving at earlier ages and drive more often than their European counterparts. American teens are thus much more likely to drive under the influence of alcohol if the drinking age is lowered in the US. Moreover, the earlier a person begins alcohol use, the greater the chances are of that person becoming an alcoholic later in life and suffering negative physical withdrawal symptoms.

① 청소년 대상 음주 문화 교육을 강화해야 한다.
② 알코올음료 광고의 시간대 제한이 도입되어야 한다.
③ 청소년들의 음주는 법률적으로 전면 금지되어야 한다.
④ 지금보다 음주 가능 최저 연령을 더 낮추어서는 안 된다.

# 장대영 영어
## Graphic 독해

# MDTS
# (글의 전개 방식)

# MDTS(글의 전개 방식)

## 2 | MDTS

MDTS | Methods of Developing Topic Sentence
〈전개 방식〉

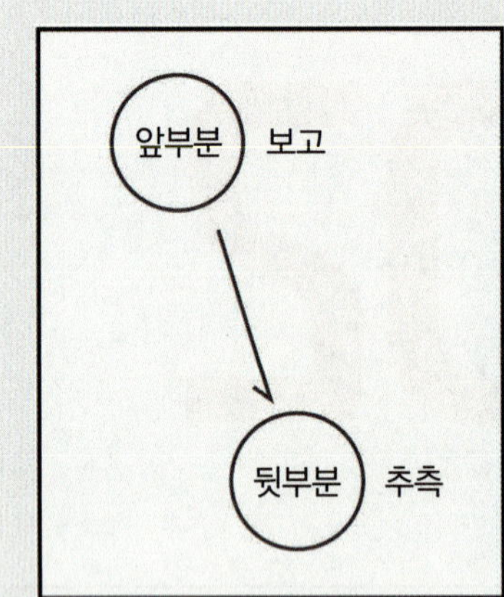


'시간 단축' 효과

## 1 연구 − 실험의 인용

### 1. 연구 − 실험

study (연구) / experiment (실험) / research (연구) / etc

→ 과정

→ 결과 (STS 12 연구 − 실험의 결과)

### 2. 실험자 − 피실험자

* 연구자 / 실험자
 − Experimenter
  Researcher
 − 실험자 이름 (人 이름)
  etc

* 피실험자
 − subject(s)
  participant(s)
  volunteer(s)
  group
  etc

## 3. 연구 과정

– A ask B / B be asked

A : 연구자 / 실험자    B : 피실험자

## 4. 연구 결과

ⓢ

Study (studies) (연구)
Experiment (experiments) (실험)
Research (researches) (연구)
Analysis (analyses) (분석)
Test (tests) (테스트, 검사)
Statistics (통계수치)
etc

ⓥ

find (found) (발견했다)
suggest (suggested) (제안했다)
show (showed) (보여줬다)
tell (told) (말했다)
indicate (indicated) (나타냈다. 보여줬다)
confirm (confirmed) (입증했다)
etc

According to ┌ study / experiment (연구 / 실험에 따르면) …
            └ researcher / experimenter (연구자 / 실험자에 따르면) …

---

**예제 1** 다음 글의 요지로 가장 적절한 것은?

Psychologists have frequently tested the notion that people's personalities cause them to exhibit consistently the same behavioral patterns in a variety of situations. In one study, for example, counselors working at a summer camp for teenage boys were asked to secretly note down the degree to which the boys displayed various forms of extroverted behavior, such as talking during mealtimes, seeking the limelight, and initiating conversations. The researchers then carefully analyzed the data by comparing the boys' level of extroversion on odd and even days. The 'personality causes behavior' theory predicts there would be a high level of consistency in the boys' actions, with the extroverted teenagers constantly chatting away and the introverted ones repeatedly hiding away in the corner. In fact, the results failed to show any evidence of such consistency. On one day, one of the boys would be full of beans and very chatty, while on the next day the very same boy was quiet and withdrawn.

① 사람은 상황에 따라서 다른 행동을 보일 수 있다.
② 사람의 특정한 행동은 성격으로부터 나온다.
③ 사람의 타고난 성격은 어떠한 상황에서도 변하지 않는다.
④ 사람의 성격으로부터 일관성 있는 행동이 나온다는 증거는 없다.

## 2  권위자

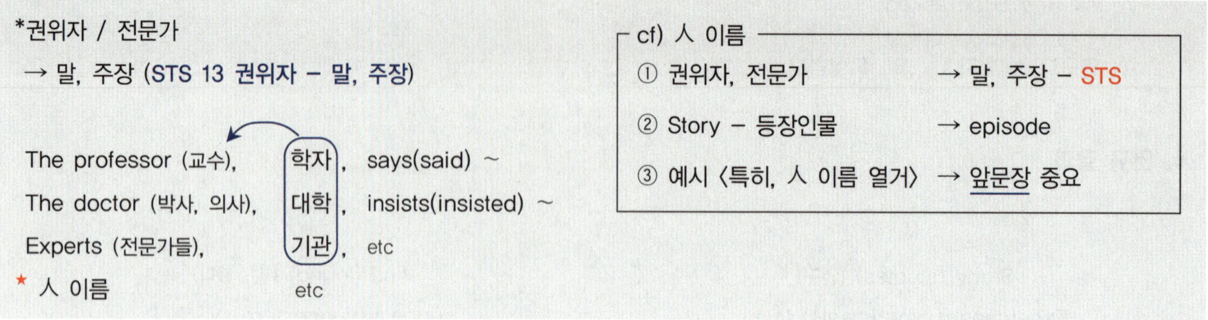

*권위자 / 전문가

→ 말, 주장 (STS 13 권위자 – 말, 주장)

The professor (교수),  학자,  says(said) ~

The doctor (박사, 의사),  대학,  insists(insisted) ~

Experts (전문가들),  기관,  etc

★ 人 이름  etc

cf) 人 이름

① 권위자, 전문가  → 말, 주장 – STS

② Story – 등장인물  → episode

③ 예시 〈특히, 人 이름 열거〉 → 앞문장 중요

---

**예제 1**  다음 글의 제목으로 가장 적절한 것은?

Some people believe that when they are alone they are lonely. However, if we accept our aloneness, we can give ourselves to our projects and our relationships out of our freedom instead of running to them out of our fear. In writing about solitude, Father William McNamara says that it is a misunderstanding to equate solitude with isolation. In his view, the opposite is true. When we enter into genuine solitude, we then have the ability to enter into the center of our being and connect in a meaningful way with others. Silence and solitude provide a means for coming to know ourselves better, for becoming centered, and for forming meaningful relationships. The Dalai Lama stresses that to make changes in our lives we need solitude, by which he means "a mental state free of distractions, not simply time alone in a quiet place."

① Solitude: What Must Be Overcome

② Being Alone: The Grave of a Relationship

③ Positive Aspects of Solitude

④ Solitude vs Isolation: Which is worse?

**예제 2** 다음 글의 빈칸 (A), (B)에 들어갈 말로 가장 적절한 것을 고르시오.

The people who do become top-level achievers are rarely child prodigies. That is certainly true in business; the early lives of the Welches, Ogilvies, and Rockefellers almost never hint at the success to come. Looking at more scientific research, this is one of the most notable findings in Benjamin Bloom's large study, which examined performers at the highest level — people who had achieved national or international recognition before age forty. _______(A)_______, all of the twenty-four pianists studied — each a finalist in at least one major international competition — had had lessons "forced upon them," in the words of the study, just the opposite of the kids who seemed driven to sit at the piano as toddlers. _______(B)_______, in no case did the parents of the future champion swimmers foresee their child's eventual achievements. Time and again the story is the same: Even by age eleven or twelve it would have been difficult to predict who the future exceptional performers would be.

|   | (A) | (B) |
|---|------|------|
| ① | For instance | Similarly |
| ② | For instance | Thus |
| ③ | However | Likewise |
| ④ | However | Thus |

**예제 3** 다음 글에 드러난 Boon Huat의 심경으로 가장 적절한 것은?

Boon Huat was outside the conference room waiting to be interviewed for the post of sales manager. His mind began to race as a hundred thoughts went through his mind at once. "What would they expect of me as a sales manager? Would they be kind, and would I be able to impress them, or make a fool of myself instead?" He kept his eyes fixed on the door, waiting for it to be opened any moment. Each time a telephone nearby rang, he was startled. His heart began beating faster and faster as he listened to his shallow and rapid breathing. His mouth felt dry. Quickly he rushed to the toilet. And looking into the mirror, he realized that he was sweating in the cold air-conditioned room. His hands trembled as he inspected his hair and adjusted his tie.

① nervous

② irritated

③ furious

④ sorrowful

## 3 의문문의 활용

**1. 첫 문장이 의문문**

**2. 중간 의문문***

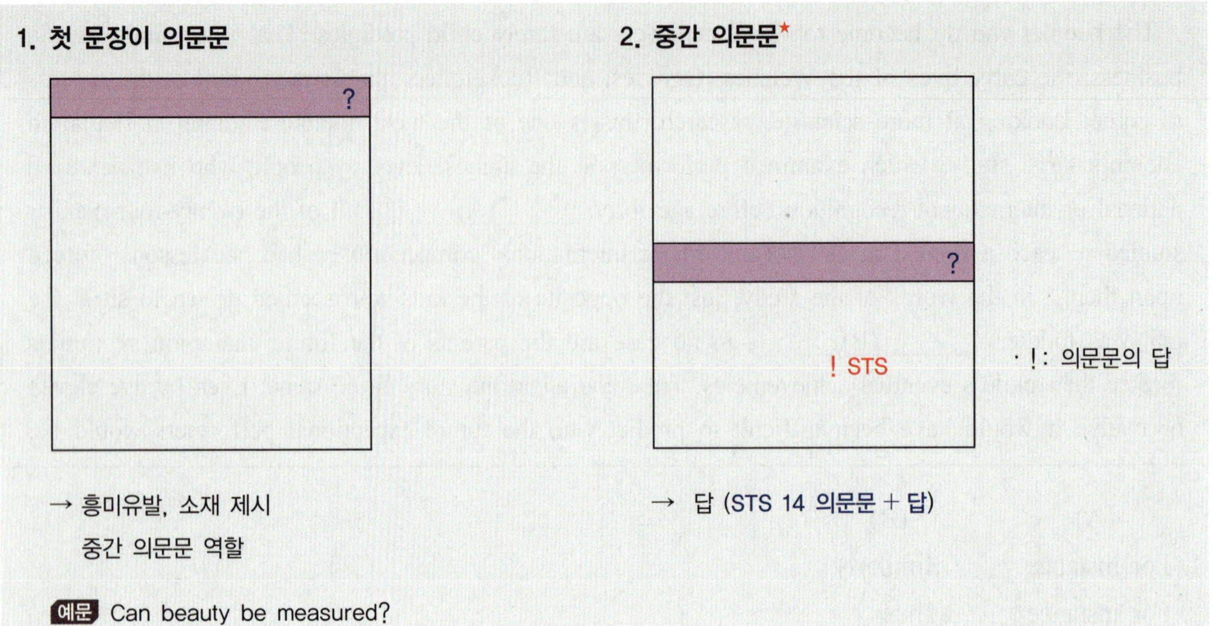


→ 흥미유발, 소재 제시
　　중간 의문문 역할

→ 답 (STS 14 의문문 + 답)

예문 Can beauty be measured?

### 예제 1 　다음 글의 요지로 가장 적절한 것은?

　　Arachnophobia, or fear of spiders, seems to be a universal human dread, especially in children. The biologist Tim Flannery asks, "Why do so many of us react so strongly, and with such primal fear, to spiders? The world is full of far more dangerous creatures that appear to barely worry most people." Flannery guesses that a Darwinian story connects human arachnophobia to our African prehistory. Homo sapiens emerged in Africa. Africa is the place where the human mind acquired many of its useful instincts. If humans evolved in an environment with poisonous spiders, a phobia could have been advantageous for human survival and could be expected to gain greater frequency in the larger human population. The six-eyed sand spider of western and southern Africa actually fits that guess very well. It is a crab-like spider that hides in the sand and leaps out to capture prey; its poison is extremely harmful to children. One can see how a fear of spiders would have been highly advantageous in this context.

① 인간은 생존을 위해 거미 공포증을 극복해 왔다.
② 거미는 전래동화 속에서 자주 등장하는 소재들 중 하나이다.
③ 치명적인 독을 가지고 있는 거미의 종류는 생각보다 많지 않다.
④ 거미에 대한 공포의 유래는 아프리카 선사시대에서 찾을 수 있다.

**예제 2** 다음 글의 내용을 한 문장으로 요약할 때 빈칸 (A)와 (B)에 들어갈 말로 가장 적절한 것은?

CHAPTER **02**

Often, you may have observed students reading a passage very slowly and vocalizing (i.e. reading every word aloud) and re-reading sentences they have already read earlier because they have not comprehended the passage. When tested for comprehension, they score very low. Why does it happen? Why do students score low on comprehension when they have read a passage repeatedly? This happens because in reading the passage very slowly and very carefully the students have concentrated so much on the individual words and created so many fixations that they have failed to get the overall meaning of the passage. It is like seeing a film slowly, frame by frame. Ask the people who read fast and they will testify that there is no need to read slowly. Reading slowly interferes with one's comprehension because it causes too many artificial breaks and fixations which only block the smooth intake of ideas.

Reading _____(A)_____ is a bad idea because it makes the readers get stuck on the _____(B)_____.

|     | (A) | (B) |
| --- | --- | --- |
| ① | quickly | plot |
| ② | slowly | point |
| ③ | slowly | details |
| ④ | fast | specifics |

## 3. 마지막 문장이 의문문

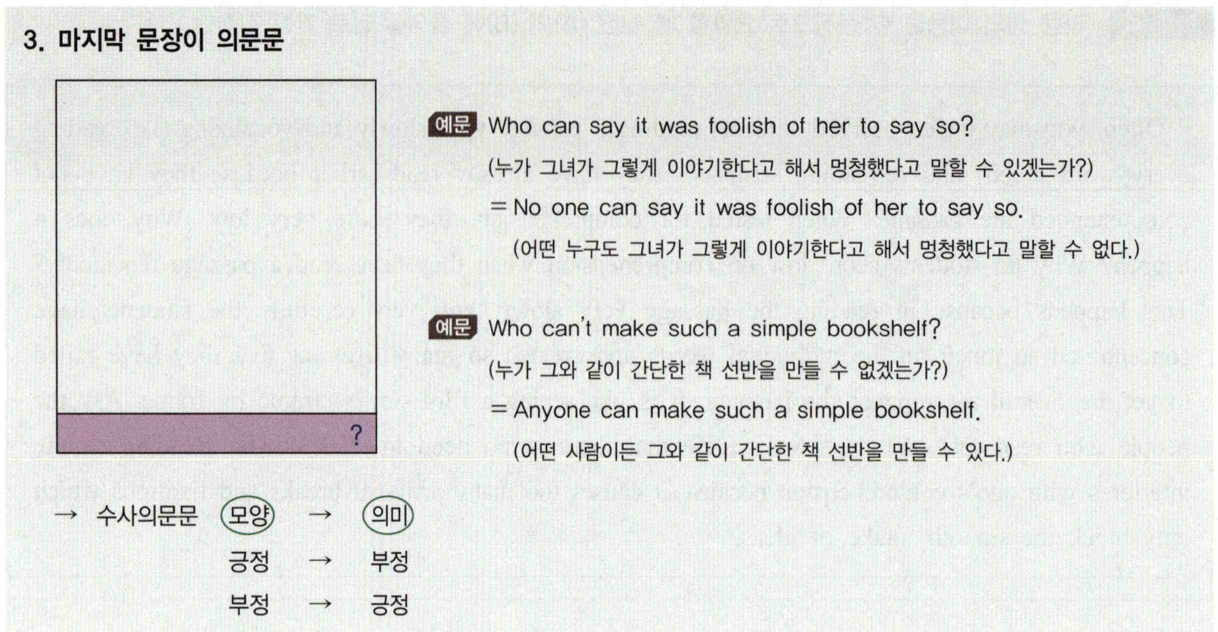


→ 수사의문문  모양  →  의미
　　　　　　긍정  →  부정
　　　　　　부정  →  긍정

예제 1  다음 글의 제목으로 가장 적절한 것은?

How can young people help to solve social problems, even though they don't have enough power and resources? Youngsters learn by digging in and finding out what the issue are all about. And by being informed, they can influence adults through direct action. In fact, given an opportunity, young people many times have brought their thinking about significant issues to the attention of public officials. Thanks to the actions of young people, historical sites have been saved, and several kinds of endangered species have been preserved. How can we solve social problems without such actions of young people?

① Need for Young People in Solving Social problems
② The Impact of Social Problems on Young People
③ Adult's Intervention in Young People's Problem
④ The Significance of Data Conservation in the Information Age

## ④ 통념비판의 원리

STS 15 통념에 대한 비판

*1st

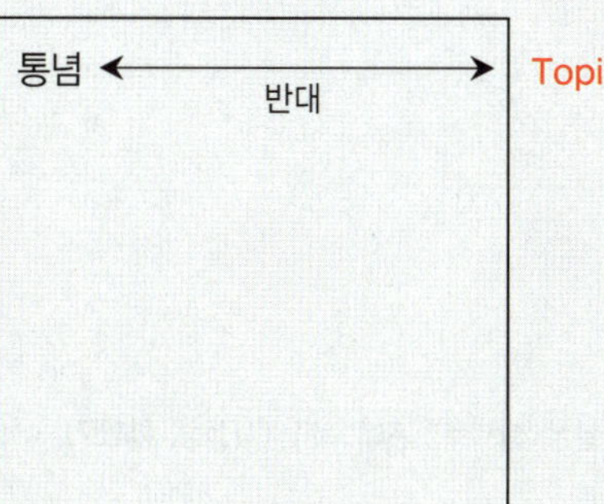


* 통념I : '통념'이라는 의미를 가진 단어가 직접 제시되는 경우

conventional   wisdom

common ⎰ idea
       ⎱ notion

myth

etc

*통념 Ⅱ : '통념'임을 보여주는 여러가지 문장의 모양틀

① 일반인 주어   We (우리는), They (그들은), One (어떤 사람이), Some people (몇몇 사람들이),
(Most) people((대부분의) 사람들이), etc

② 동사   say (말한다), believe (믿는다), think (생각한다), insist (주장한다), argue (주장한다),
look upon (간주한다), regard(간주한다), assume(가정한다), etc

③ 명사   saying (말), belief (신념), thought (생각), argument (주장), notion (관념), idea (생각), etc

④ 형용사/부사   common (흔한), widespread (널리 퍼진), prevalent (널리 퍼져 있는), frequently (자주, 흔히),
often (자주, 흔히), etc

문장 형식   a) S①       V②       that –
          b) It be  V② –p.p  that –
          c) 소유격① N③  is  that –
          d) It be  형④       that –

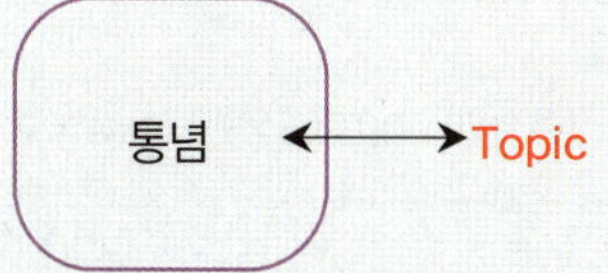


**예문**

a) Most people think that Won-young is more attractive than Karina.
(대부분의 사람들은 원영이 카리나보다 더 매력적이라고 생각한다.)

b) It is thought that Won-young is more attractive than Karina.
(원영이 카리나보다 더 매력적이라고 생각되어진다.)

c) Most people's thought is that Won-young is more attractive than Karina.
(대부분의 사람들의 생각은 원영이 카리나보다 더 매력적이라는 것이다.)

d) It is widespread that Won-young is more attractive than Karina.
(원영이 카리나보다 더 매력적이라는 것이 널리 퍼져있는 생각이다.)

* 2nd – 통념에 대한 비판이 등장

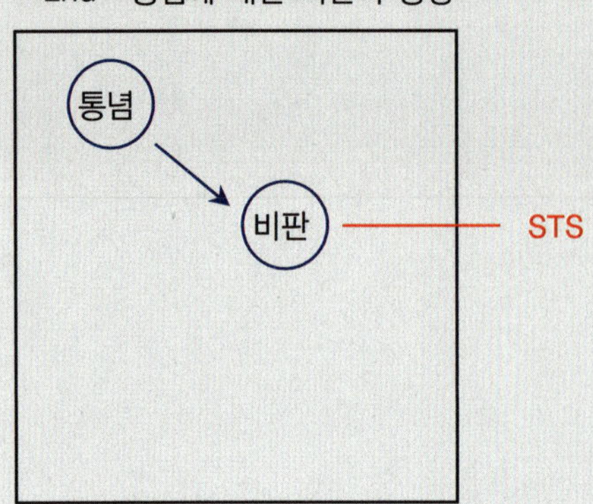


① 연결사　　　But (그러나), However (그러나), In fact (사실상, 실제로), In reality (사실상, 실제로), Actually (사실상, 실제로), etc

② 단어　　　　misconception (오해), misunderstanding (오해), etc

③ 문장 표현　　This (it) is not true.

(이것은 (그것은) 진실이 아니다.)

This (it) is not the case.

(이것은 (그것은) 사실이 아니다.)

This (it) is not so.

(이것은 (그것은) 그렇지가 않다.)

This (it) is an absurd opinion (idea).

(이것은 (그것은) 터무늬 없는 의견(생각)이다.)

They are wrong (mistaken).

(그들은 옳지 않다 (잘못되었다).)

④ 기타 표현　　untrue (진실이 아닌), false (거짓의), error (오류), biased (편향된), prejudiced (선입견에 찬),

inconsistent (일관성이 없는), etc

**예제 1** 다음 글의 주제로 가장 적절한 것은?

Many people believe that they will be free of their anger if they express it, and that their tears will release their pain. This belief derives from a nineteenth-century understanding of emotions, and it is no truer than the flat earth. It sees the brain as a steam kettle in which negative feelings build up pressure. But no psychologist has ever succeeded in proving the unburdening effects of the supposed safety valves of tears and anger. On the contrary, over forty years ago, controlled studies showed that fits of anger are more likely to intensify anger, and that tears can drive us still deeper into depression. Our heads do not resemble steam kettles, and our brains involve a much more complicated system than can be accounted for by images taken from nineteenth-century technology.

① 19세기 과학의 발전이 뇌 연구에 미친 영향
② 감정의 종류와 뇌 구조의 상관관계
③ 감정을 표현하는 것에 대한 사람들의 오해
④ 눈물과 분노를 담당하는 뇌의 영역

**예제 2** 다음 글의 제목으로 가장 적절한 것은?

Some people believe that when they are alone they are lonely. However, if we accept our aloneness, we can give ourselves to our projects and our relationships out of our freedom instead of running to them out of our fear. In writing about solitude, Father William McNamara says that it is a misunderstanding to equate solitude with isolation. In his view, the opposite is true. When we enter into genuine solitude, we then have the ability to enter into the center of our being and connect in a meaningful way with others. Silence and solitude provide a means for coming to know ourselves better, for becoming centered, and for forming meaningful relationships. The Dalai Lama stresses that to make changes in our lives we need solitude, by which he means "a mental state free of distractions, not simply time alone in a quiet place."

① Solitude: What Must Be Overcome
② Being Alone: The Grave of a Relationship
③ Positive Aspects of Solitude
④ Solitude vs Isolation: Which is worse?

## 5 문제점 발생 − 해결책 제시

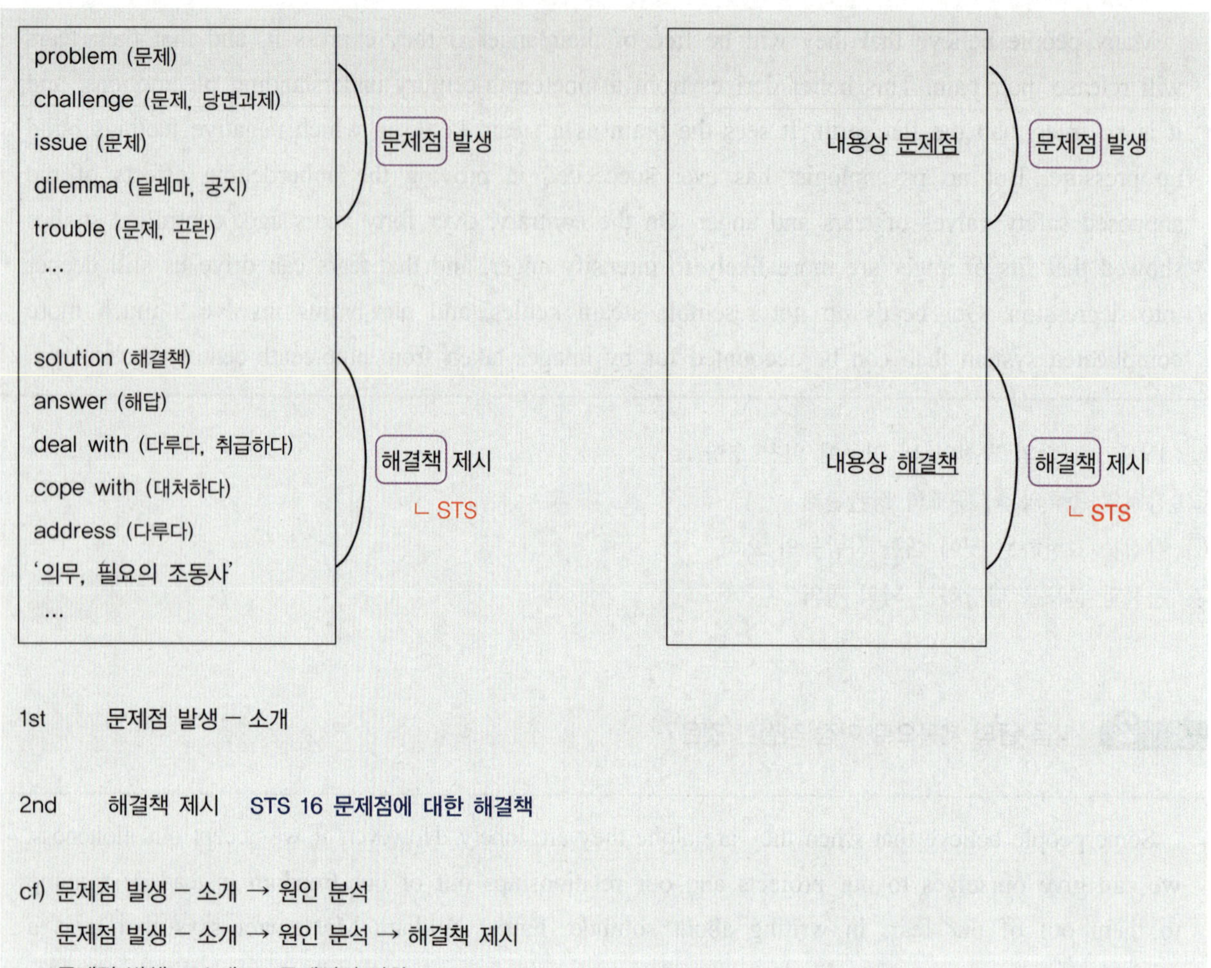


1st　　문제점 발생 − 소개

2nd　　해결책 제시　　STS 16 문제점에 대한 해결책

cf) 문제점 발생 − 소개 → 원인 분석
　　문제점 발생 − 소개 → 원인 분석 → 해결책 제시
　　문제점 발생 − 소개 → 문제점의 강화

**예제 1** 다음 글의 요지로 가장 적절한 것은?

Mass political opinion can be sort of like guessing the number of marbles in a glass jar. Most people's guesses will miss the mark, but the average guess of a large enough crowd is generally very accurate. The idea that the masses generally come up with good overall decisions is sometimes referred to as the "wisdom of crowds," and it really does work amazingly well for some things. The problem is that in politics we don't see the glass jar for ourselves — we view it through the lens of the media, and the media show us a distorted view of politics. Thus, we should be aware of such media biases in order to minimize the likelihood that they'll throw off our political judgment, even though there's no way to permanently "fix" them.

① 정치적 판단의 혼란을 최소화하려면 미디어의 편향을 의식해야 한다.
② 편향되지 않은 정보를 습득하기 위해서는 다양한 매체를 접해야 한다.
③ 정치적 견해는 소수보다 다수에서 더 정확할 수 있다.
④ 미디어의 발전으로 대중의 정치 참여가 확대되어 왔다.

**예제 2** 다음 글의 제목으로 가장 적절한 것은?

Most of the world does not have access to the education afforded to a small minority. For every Albert Einstein, Yo-Yo Ma, or Barack Obama who has the opportunity for education, there are uncountable others who never get the chance. This vast waste of talent translates directly into reduced economic output. In a world where economic ruin is often tied to collapse, societies are well advised to exploit all the human capital they have. The Internet opens the gates of education to anyone who can get her hands on a computer. This is not always a trivial task, but the mere feasibility redefines the playing field. A motivated teen anywhere on the planet can walk through the world's knowledge, from Wikipedia to the curricula of MIT's Open Course Ware.

① The Use of The Internet In A Variety of Fields
② The Internet Can Provide Equal Educational Opportunities
③ Internet: New Areas of Economic Activity
④ Internet: A luxury That Only Privileged People Can Enjoy

## 6 시간상의 대조

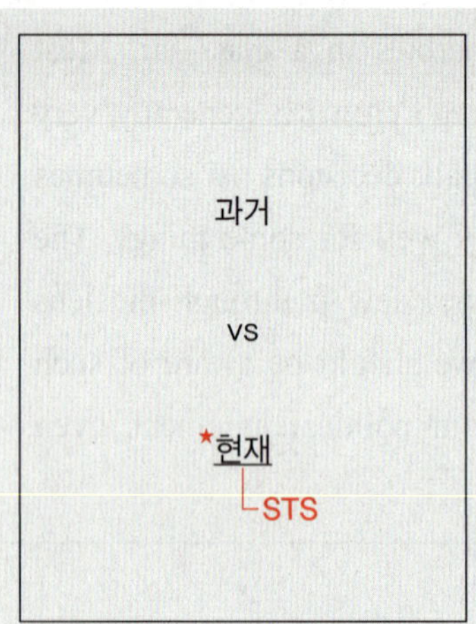

**1st 과거**　　　　　　　　　　vs　　**2nd 현재** {STS 17 시간상의 대조 (현재가 중요)}

| 1st 과거 | 2nd 현재 |
| --- | --- |
| – ago (–전에) | recently (최근에) |
| in (과거) 연도 ((과거 연도)에) | lately (최근에) |
| then (그때) | nowadays (요즈음에) |
| those days (그 당시에) | these days (요즈음에) |
| used to V원형 (~하곤 했다) / 동사–과거시제 | today (오늘날) / 동사–현재시제 |
| old (오래된) | new (새로운) |
| once (예전에) | now (지금) |
| traditional (전통적인) | etc |
| historically (역사적으로) | |
| etc | |

**예제 1** 다음 글의 제목으로 가장 적절한 것은?

In the 20th century social scientists undertook serious studies of the phenomenon of leadership. It has only been over the past thirty years that researchers have made a lot of progress in determining how people become effective leaders. We used to think that leaders were born and not made. Back in the old days, when strong social class barriers made it next to impossible for anyone to become a leader, we were trained to think that leadership was inherited. If your name wasn't Rockefeller, Firestone, Rothschild, or some other famous family name, you were not destined to become a leader. As class barriers crumbled and leaders arose from all parts of society, it became clear that leadership required more than being born into the right family. We begin to realize that everybody has the potential of becoming a leader, if they're given the chance.

① Leadership: Ability to Solve Social Problems
② Requirements For a Great Leader
③ Leaders: Are They Born or Made?
④ Why Is It Difficult To Study Leadership?

**예제 2** 다음 글의 주제로 가장 적절한 것은?

Within the societal cultures of the United States, subcultural differences once ignored by many managers now command significant attention and sensitivity. Historically, the U.S. workforce has consisted primarily of white males. Today, however, white males make up far less than 50 percent of business new hires in the United States, whereas women and African American, Hispanic, and Asian men account for increasingly large portions of the U.S. workforce. Moreover, in the last ten years the number of women and minorities assuming managerial positions in the U.S. workforce has grown by over 25 percent. It is becoming-and will continue to become-even more important for managers to know about and be ready to respond to the challenges deriving from individual differences in abilities, personalities, and motives. Knowledge about the workplace consequences of these differences can provide managers with help in this regard.

① problems resulting from cultural diversity in the United States
② the abolition of racism in employment in the United States
③ conflicts between minority and majority in the U.S. society
④ a change in the perception of the diversity in the U.S. workforce

# 7 예시

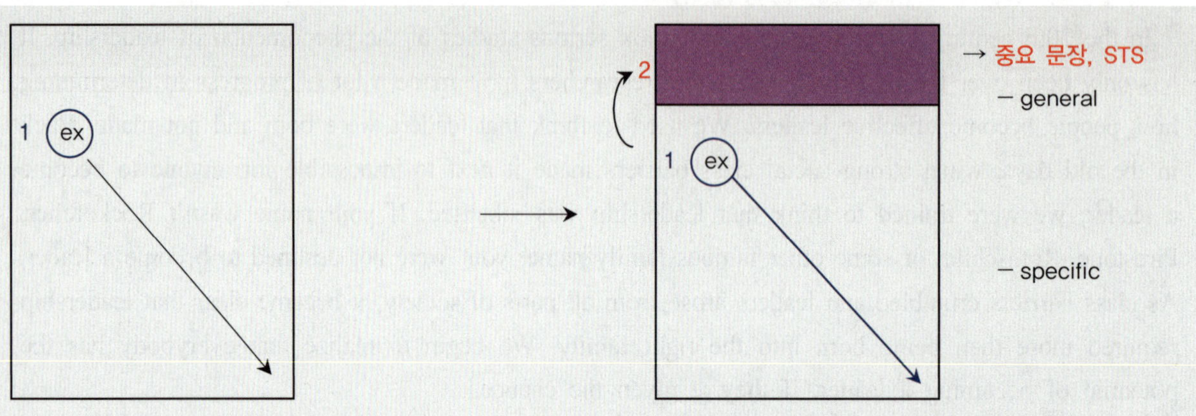


*예시 표현 (앞 문장 / 앞 부분)

① For example (예를 들어서) / For instance (예를 들어서) / etc

② Imagine (상상해 봅시다) / Suppose (가정해 봅시다) /

   Consider (고려해 봅시다) / Let's say (말해 봅시다) /etc

③ 고유 N

④ 人 이름

⑤ If S V / When S V

⑥ 수치 나열

⑦ a(n) + 사람

*예시표현 (문장 내 앞 부분)

such as ＝ like (~와 같은)

including (~을 포함하여)

**예문** There are writing tools such as pencil, ball-pen, fountain pen, and highlight pen.
연필, 볼펜, 만년필, 그리고 형광펜과 같은 필기도구가 있다.

**예제 1** 다음 글의 주제로 가장 적절한 것은?

There are many aspects of sustainability and, even if you decide you want to address all of them, the problem is that buildings are complex assemblies of different elements. There will always be a series of factors to balance. For example, if you put a building in a business park in the middle of nowhere, it will be possible to align it perfectly to make the most of the sun and to have windows that open because there will be very little noise. It will not, however, be possible for most users of the building to reach it by public transport or to walk or cycle there. Almost everyone will have to drive. Studies show that the overall carbon footprint of a super-green building in such a location will be greater than that of a less-than-ideal building in a city center well served by public transport.

① things to consider when building eco-friendly buildings
② factors to check when starting up a new business
③ the way to select a profitable location for business
④ advantages and drawbacks of going to work by public transportation

**예제 2** 다음 글의 주제로 가장 적절한 것은?

When people move from one country to another or from one area to another, their economic status may change. They will be introduced to new foods and new food customs. Although their original food customs may have been nutritionally adequate, their new environment may cause them to change their eating habits. For instance, if milk was a staple food in their diet before moving and is unusually expensive in the new environment, milk may be replaced by a cheaper, nutritionally inferior beverage such as soda, coffee, or tea. Candy, possibly a luxury in their former environment, may be inexpensive and popular in their new environment. As a result, a family might increase consumption of soda or candy and reduce purchases of more nutritious foods. Someone who is not familiar with the nutritive values of foods can easily make such mistakes in food selection.

① significance of a well-balanced diet
② negative effects of immigration on family budgets
③ influences of relocation on food habits
④ misunderstanding about the nutritional value of foods

**예제 3** 다음 글의 주제로 가장 적절한 것은?

Some distinctions between good and bad are hardwired into our biology. Infants enter the world ready to respond to pain as bad and to sweet (up to a point) as good. In many situations, however, the boundary between good and bad is a reference point that changes over time and depends on the immediate circumstances. Imagine that you are out in the country on a cold night, inadequately dressed for the torrential rain, your clothes soaked. A stinging cold wind completes your misery. As you wander around, you find a large rock that provides some shelter from the fury of the elements. The biologist Michel Cabanac would call the experience of that moment intensely pleasurable because it functions, as pleasure normally does, to indicate the direction of a biologically significant improvement of circumstances. The pleasant relief will not last very long, of course, and you will soon be shivering behind the rock again, driven by your renewed suffering to seek better shelter.

① variability in what is considered good and bad
② human's inborn instinct for gratification
③ biology as a instructor for our action
④ individual ability to distinguish cold from warmth

**예제 4** 다음 글의 주제로 가장 적절한 것은?

Suppose you wish to determine which brand of microwave popcorn leaves the fewest unpopped kernels. You will need a supply of various brands of microwave popcorn to test, and you will need a microwave oven. If you used different brands of microwave ovens with different brands of popcorn, the percentage of unpopped kernels could be caused by the different brands of popcorn or by the different brands of ovens. Under such circumstances, the experimenter would be unable to conclude confidently whether the popcorn or the oven caused the difference. To eliminate this problem, you must use the same microwave oven for every test. In order to reasonably conclude that the change in one variable was caused by the change in another specific variable, there must be no other variables in the experiment. By using the same microwave oven, you control the number of variables in the experiment.

① safety rules to be followed in an experiment
② benefits of using various experimental methods
③ impact of background knowledge on experiments
④ the need for controlling variables in experiments

CHAPTER 02

**예제 5** 다음 글의 주제로 가장 적절한 것은?

Radical developments in technology have revolutionized the way in which artists and entertainers tell their stories. From live-streamed transmissions from London's Royal Opera House and the New York Met to the innovative use of sound, film and projection in plays such as the National Theater's The Waves, technology is constantly opening up staged entertainment to new formats and audiences. The British producing company Artichoke are masters of harnessing technology to tell a story: In May 2006 they brought French company Royal de Luxe's The Sultan's Elephant to the streets of London, fascinating audiences young and old with a 42-ton mechanical elephant and a 6-meter-tall princess, who traveled on a London bus and disappeared in a rocket.

① reasons some performances are thought of as valuable
② growing popularity of diverse performing arts
③ effect of technology on artistic expression
④ using artistic formats in selling goods and services

**예제 6** 다음 글의 주제로 가장 적절한 것은?

As an advocate, mass media can promote the work of the nonprofit sector. Quite apart from sensational reports that amplify charity scandals, the media often does share on the positive aspects of the sector as well. The wide-ranging reach of nonprofit sector work has opened up new segments in the media industry. No longer confined to just the local news sections of the newspapers, there are magazines, such as Good and Ode to tell the stories of individuals, teams, and organizations that seek to do good in this world. There are also publications and websites that focus entirely on a growing nonprofit audience. Examples include The Chronicle of Philanthropy, Stanford Social Innovation Review, and Beyond Profit.

① 대중 매체가 비영리 부문의 사업의 폭을 넓혀주었다.
② 대중 매체의 선정적 보도는 비영리 부문의 긍정적인 측면을 가린다.
③ 다양한 분야의 보도가 미디어 산업의 진보를 가져왔다.
④ 비영리 부문을 홍보하는 대중 매체가 증가하고 있다.

**예제 7** 다음 글의 요지로 가장 적절한 것은?

In 1879 Thomas Edison announced that he would publicly display the electric lightbulb by December 31, even though all his experiments had, to that point, failed. He threw his knapsack over the brick wall — the numerous challenges that he still faced — and on the last day of that year, there was light. In 1962, when John F. Kennedy declared to the world that the United States was going to land a man on the moon by the end of the decade, some of the metals necessary for the journey had not yet been invented, and the technology required for completing the journey was not available. But he threw his and NASA's knapsack over the brick wall. Though making a verbal commitment, no matter how bold and how inspiring, does not ensure that we reach our destination, it does enhance the likelihood of success.

① 위대한 발명은 실현 불가능해 보이는 아이디어에서 비롯된다.
② 목표를 내세우고 이를 공표하는 것이 성공의 가능성을 높여준다.
③ 꿈을 이루려면 말만 하기보다 구체적인 행동을 해야 한다.
④ 여러 번의 실패와 끊임없는 재시도를 통해 과학의 발전이 이루어졌다.

## 8  Story/일화

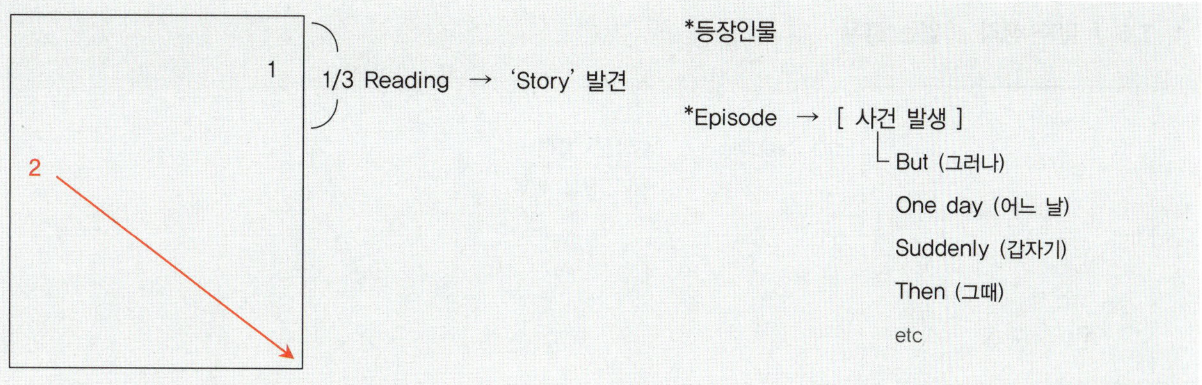



**예제 1**  다음 글의 제목으로 가장 적절한 것은?

It is said that a music student once approached Mozart and asked him for advice on what he should compose and how he should do it to create something really good. Mozart took a good look at him and said, "You are still young. I think you should start with composing a duet." This young man got upset and told Mozart that he too was still young, and that since he had composed more serious music than duets, why shouldn't he? Mozart replied, "That is true, but I did not go around asking people what to compose. I knew what to do." The point is that many have attempted to create great art, but only a very tiny percentage have become true masters.

① What Differentiates a Master from a Beginner
② Mozart's One and Only Mistake
③ Who laughs last: The Winner
④ Great Works Come From Endless Efforts

## 9 설명문

### 1. T.S / 필자 생각 – 없는 경우

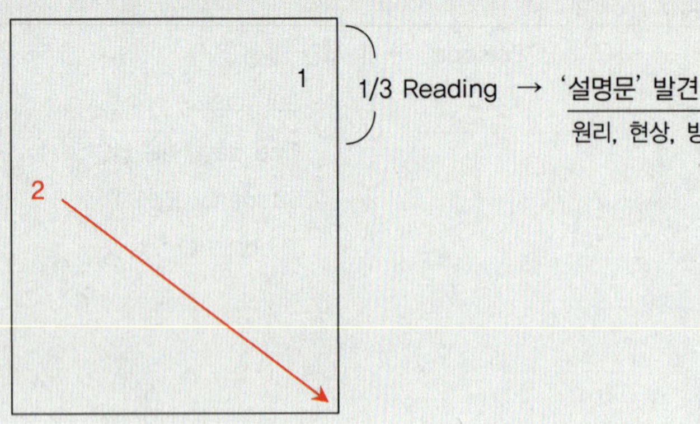


### 2. T.S / 필자 생각 – 있는 경우

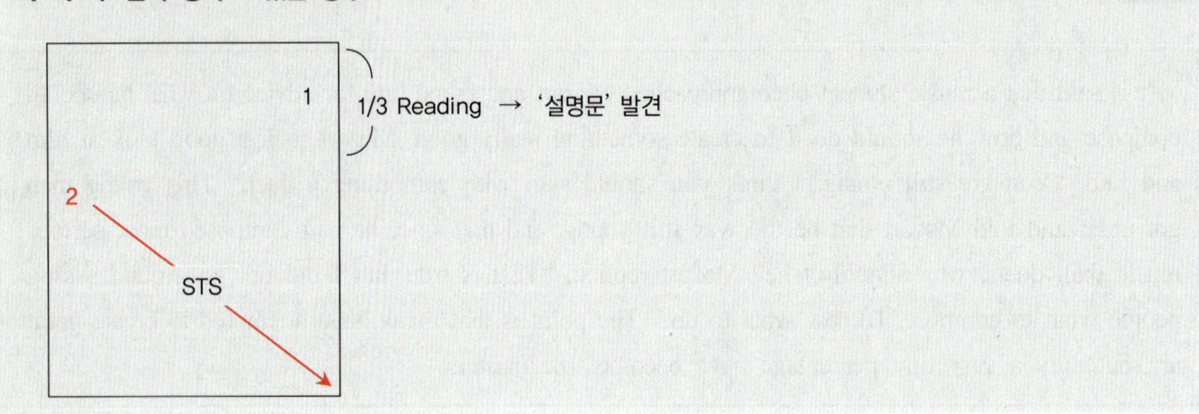

**예제 1** 다음 글의 주제로 가장 적절한 것은?

When scientists use a device called a calorimeter, the piece of food to be measured is placed inside the device, sealed, and then burned. The energy from the food heats the water surrounding the chamber. By weighing the amount of water heated, noting the increase in the water temperature, and multiplying the two, the energy capacity of the food can be measured. For example, if 10 liters of water surrounding the chamber is 20 degrees centigrade before combustion and then is measured at 25 degrees after combustion, the difference in temperature (5 degrees) is multiplied by the volume of water (10 liters) to arrive at the caloric value (50 calories of energy).

① the way to calculate the caloric value of food
② importance of water and temperature in food conservation
③ how to measure water content in a food
④ limitations of calorie measurements using a calorimeter

**예제 2** 다음 글의 요지로 가장 적절한 것은?

Unlike oil, we can't mine hydrogen gas from the Earth. The hydrogen that is present has all already "burned" — that is, combined with oxygen to make water ($H_2 O$), or with carbon to make sugars, starches, and hydrocarbons (including plant matter, wood, oil, and natural gas). To use hydrogen we have to separate the hydrogen from the other atoms. We can remove the hydrogen from water by running electric current through it — a process called electrolysis. But that process takes energy, and when we use the released hydrogen as fuel, we get back only 30% to 40% of the energy that we put in; the rest is wasted as heat. Beware of inventions that claim to use ordinary water as fuel; these usually obtain the hydrogen by using other energy to separate it from water, by electrolysis or use of another fuel such as a purified metal.

① 수소는 에너지 낭비 없이 연료로 사용할 수 있는 자원이다.
② 전기나 다른 연료를 이용하여 수소 연료를 얻는 것은 효율성이 떨어진다.
③ 대부분의 물질에 수소가 포함되어 있으므로 수소연료의 사용은 효율적이다.
④ 수소 연료의 효율성을 높이려면 수소 분리 과정의 개선이 필요하다.

## 10 열거

### 1. '열거'할 것을 시사하는 구체적인 표현이 있는 경우

− 주로 [ 두괄식 ]

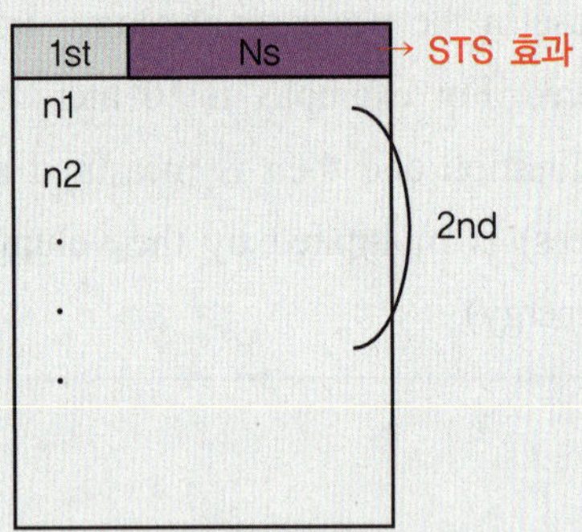


**1st 수적인 개념의 표현들 등장**          +          **2nd 구체적인 열거**

{STS 19 구체적인 열거의 앞 부분(문장)}

− many, a lot of, lots of, a number of, → 많은

several, → (몇)몇의, 여러 개의

various, a variety of, diverse, → 다양한          + Ns

different, → 다른, 여러 개의

etc

− two (둘), three (셋), four (넷), etc

− some (몇은), others (다른 사람들(것)은),

still others (또 다른 사람들(것)은)

− the first (첫 번째는), the second (두 번째는),

the third (세 번째는 … , the last (마지막은)

− one (첫째는), another (또 다른 것은), the next (그

다음은) … , the final (마지막은)

− also (또한),

in addition, additionally, moreover, what is

more, furthermore, besides (게다가, 더욱이)

etc

### 2. '열거'할 것을 시사하는 구체적인 표현이 없는 경우

− 주로 [ 미괄식 ]

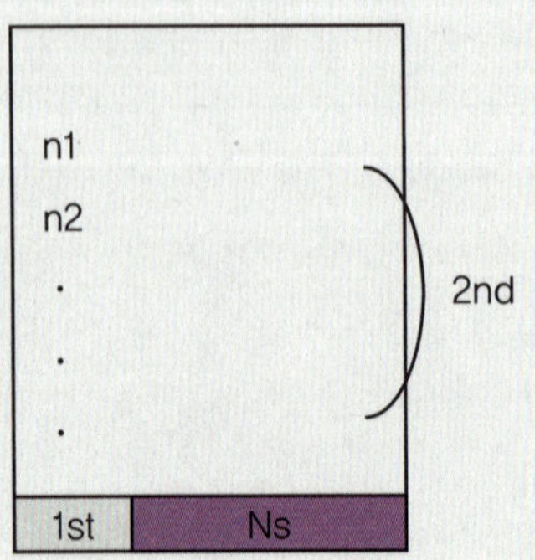


└ 필자가 앞에서 열거한 내용들을 정리

**예제 1** 다음 글의 주제로 가장 적절한 것은?

The public and donors expect charities to be "run by highly motivated but relatively modestly paid people." And charity workers have come to accept this. There are two reasons for this state of affairs. The first is that in meeting the goal of operating at minimum costs, staff costs also have to be kept low. The second is that charity workers are asked to be aligned, and show their alignment, with the charitable nature of the organization they are working for by taking a wage less than what they might have been offered elsewhere. The wage subsidy is thus a partial donation to the cause. Interestingly, this moral argument of contributing to the cause ignores the morality of paying a man less than he is worth; even if, at times, he is paid below-subsistence rates.

① the financial crisis of international charities
② the way to increase public donation
③ the reason charity workers are poorly paid
④ the influence of charity on society

**예제 2** 이 글의 제목으로 가장 적절한 것은?

Farming began about 12,000 years ago and it has developed very quickly in the last 300 years. There are no signs that the speed of development will slow down. Agriculture will continue to develop in several ways. First, farming will become even more efficient by using new types of technology. Many processes will be controlled by computers. Second, new ways of growing, storing, and selling crops will be developed which can be used by poor people as well as rich people. Third, agricultural products will be used in many different ways.

① The Development of Agriculture
② The Progress of Agriculture Technology
③ An Increase in Crop Yields
④ The Limitations of Agricultural Technology

## 11 나열식 구조

### 1. case 나열

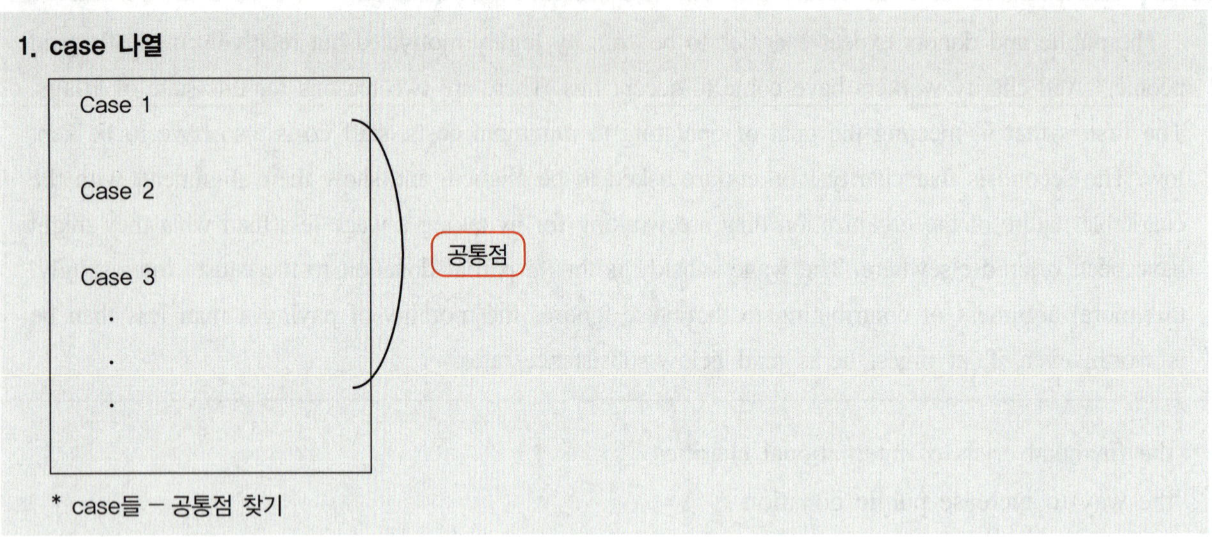


* case들 − 공통점 찾기

### 2. 모양 나열

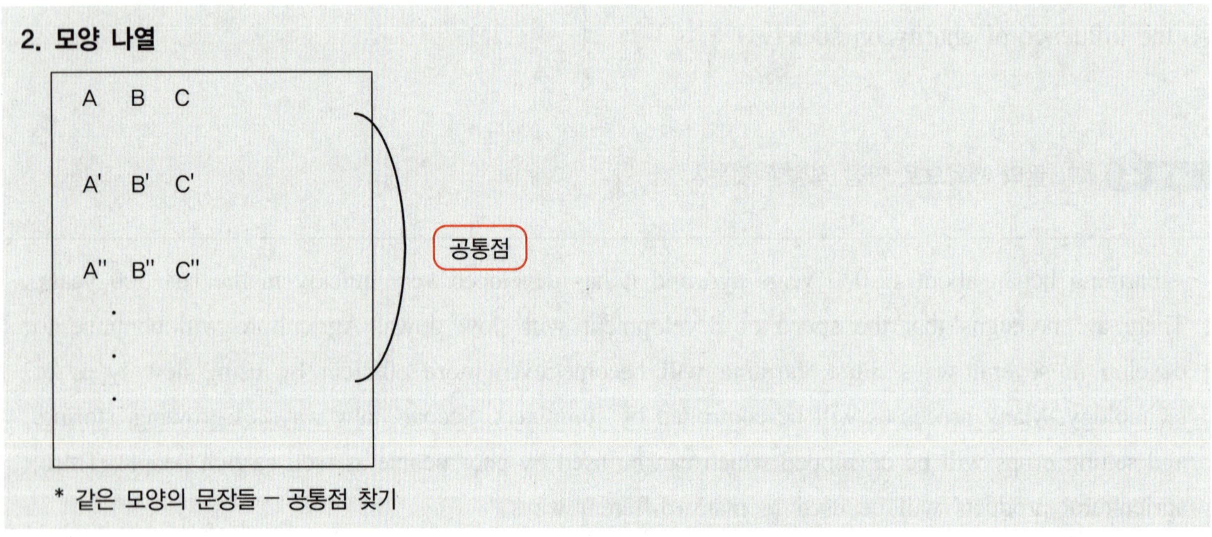


* 같은 모양의 문장들 − 공통점 찾기

**예제 1**  이 글의 제목으로 가장 적절한 것은?

Some people find that exercising when they have a mild cold makes them feel better. Illnesses vary in severity and people react differently to them, so listen to your body. If you have a minor problem, such as a cough or a tight muscle, and otherwise feel fine, it is probably acceptable to work out. Avoid exercise to the point of exhaustion. Avoid exercise if you have the flu, have a fever, have a body ache, feel extremely tired, have a breathing problem, or have swollen glands. Exercise does not cure illness. The old saying that "you can sweat out a cold" with exercise is untrue. When you recover from illness, do not start exercising at the same level as before. Give yourself a few days to build back to normal levels.

① Dangers of Living an Inactive Life
② How Does Your Body Respond To Illness?
③ Exercise: Medicine to Cure All Diseases
④ Exercising When Sick: A Good Move?

**예제 2**  다음 빈칸에 들어갈 말로 가장 적절한 것은?

Do you know people who have plenty of ideas but don't follow through? These people need collaborators to help them implement. What about artists who paint masterpieces that nobody sees? They need a collaborator to help them promote themselves. Then there are inventors who need help protecting their ideas, entrepreneurs who need help gaining capital, or composers who need help with lyrics. Working together allows for different points of view and sparks new ideas. It's not enough to be a lone innovator. Good ideas can be made into great ideas when we utilize each other's specialized expertise. In fact, venture capitalists say the most important quality they look for in businesses isn't the ideas but the ___________ . Look for partners who don't duplicate your skills but complement them.

① gifts
② teams
③ incentives
④ endeavors

**예제 3** 다음 글의 제목으로 가장 적절한 것은?

You may not always be aware of them, but you are continually making pictures in your mind. These pictures have a favourable effect if they are positive (and, in contrast, a harmful effect if they are negative). A writer said, "What the mind can conceive, the will can achieve." That's why top sportsmen and women use creative imagery and autosuggestion to help them win trophies and break world records; business executives use them to help make better sales presentations and gain promotion; leading doctors teach patients to relieve painful symptoms and even rid themselves of serious diseases, using these techniques; and psychotherapists help their clients overcome a wide range of emotional problems using them, including fears and panic attacks, eliminating unwanted habits, stress and lack of confidence.

① Making Desirable Conditions for Psychological Stability
② Powers of Positive Imagery for Better Achievement
③ Ways to Avoid a Negative Picture of Yourself
④ Mental Capacity for Creative Thinking

## 12  인과관계

- 원인(cause)과 결과(effect) 사이의 관계를 밝히는 전개 방식
- [최초 원인(cause)과 최종 결과(effect)] 상대적 중요

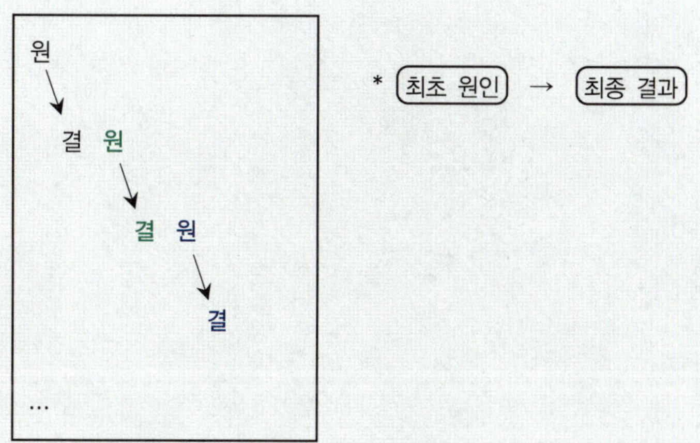


### 예제 1  다음 빈칸에 들어갈 말로 가장 적절한 것은?

The obvious role of sugar in ice cream is to sweeten the product. However, sugar also plays a role in determining the ___________________ of the frozen ice cream, because sugar causes the freezing temperature of the mixture to drop. In fact, a cup of sugar in a quart of the ice cream mixture will decrease the freezing point approximately 2°F. This means that the ice cream must be chilled below the normal freezing temperature of water if ice crystals are to form. The greater the content of sugar in an ice cream, the lower the freezing point. This delayed freezing temperature helps to keep the size of crystals in the ice cream very small because a reasonable amount of stirring can be done during the freezing process to help break up any ice crystal aggregates as they slowly form.

① textural characteristics
② nutritive value
③ expiration date
④ sweet flavor

# 장대영 영어
## Graphic 독해

# CLUES
## (문장 간의 연결 관계)

# CLUES(문장 간의 연결 관계)

## 1 | 3 CLUES

### 1  연결사

**대표 연결사 11**

| Not only | But also |
|---|---|
| 연결사 추론 < 독해 − 다른 유형 | |
| · 연결사 추론 | · 순서 배열<br>· 문장 삽입<br>· 문장 제거     · 빈칸<br>              · 독해 − 어휘 |

### 1. For example / For instance (예를 들어서)

속성

上 . 집합

For example

下 . 원소

### 2. However (그러나)

But (그러나) / Yet (그러나) / Still (그러나) / Conversely (반대로, 역으로) / In contrast (대조적으로) / By contrast (대조적으로) / On the other hand (반면에, 대조적으로) …

속성

A +   A −   A

However    반대

A −   A+   B

### 3. Likewise (마찬가지로) / Similarly (유사하게도)

In the same way (같은 방식으로, 유사하게도) / In like manner (마찬가지로) …

속성

A

Likewise   ≒

A'

## 4. Therefore (그러므로)

Thus (그러므로) / Hence (그러므로) / Consequently (결과적으로, 그러므로) / Accordingly (따라서, 그러므로) /
As a result (결과적으로, 그러므로) / For this reason (이러한 이유로, 그러므로) …

속성

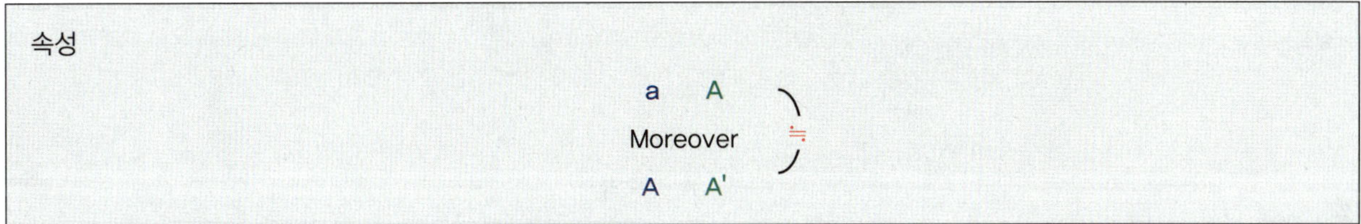


## 5. Furthermore / Besides / In addition / Moreover (게다가, 더욱이)

속성



## 6. Instead (대신에)

alternatively (그 대신에) / as an alternative (대안으로) …

속성

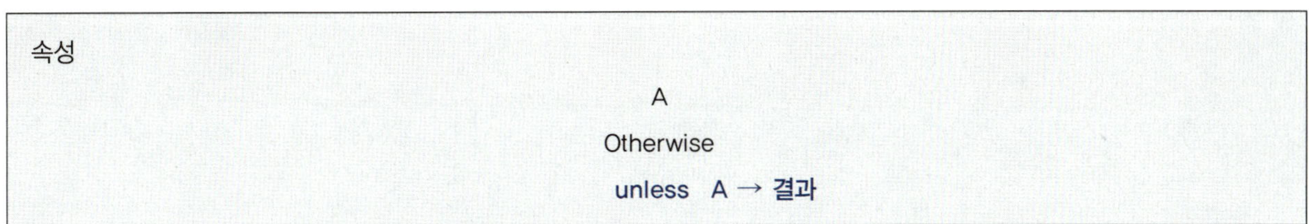


## 7. Otherwise (그렇지 않으면)

속성



## 8. Nevertheless / Nonetheless (그럼에도 불구하고)

속성

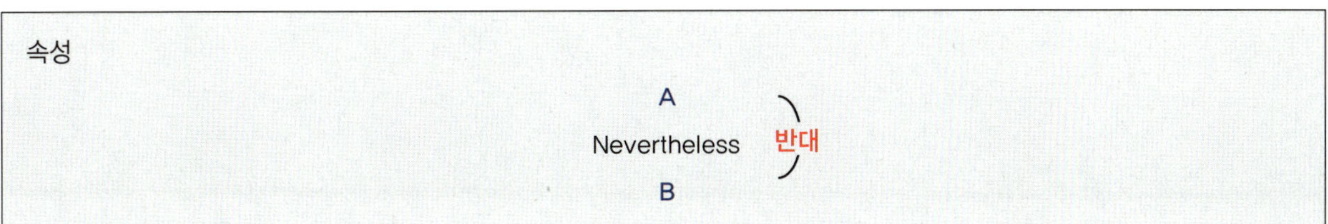

## 9. In other words / That is (to say) (즉, 다시 말해서)

Namely (즉, 다시말해서) / So to speak (말하자면, 다시 말해서) / As it were (즉, 다시 말해서) …

속성

A
In other words
A

## 10. In short (요약하자면) / In conclusion (결론적으로)

In brief (요약하자면) / to sum up (요약하자면) / to summarize (요약하자면) / ultimately (궁극적으로) / eventually (결국에) …

속성

A
In short
A – 요약

## 11. In fact

coping method → '제일 나중에'

속성
· For example
· But
· Moreover
'코에 걸면 코걸이, 귀에 걸면 귀걸이'

★ 연결사 추론

디와이 approaching

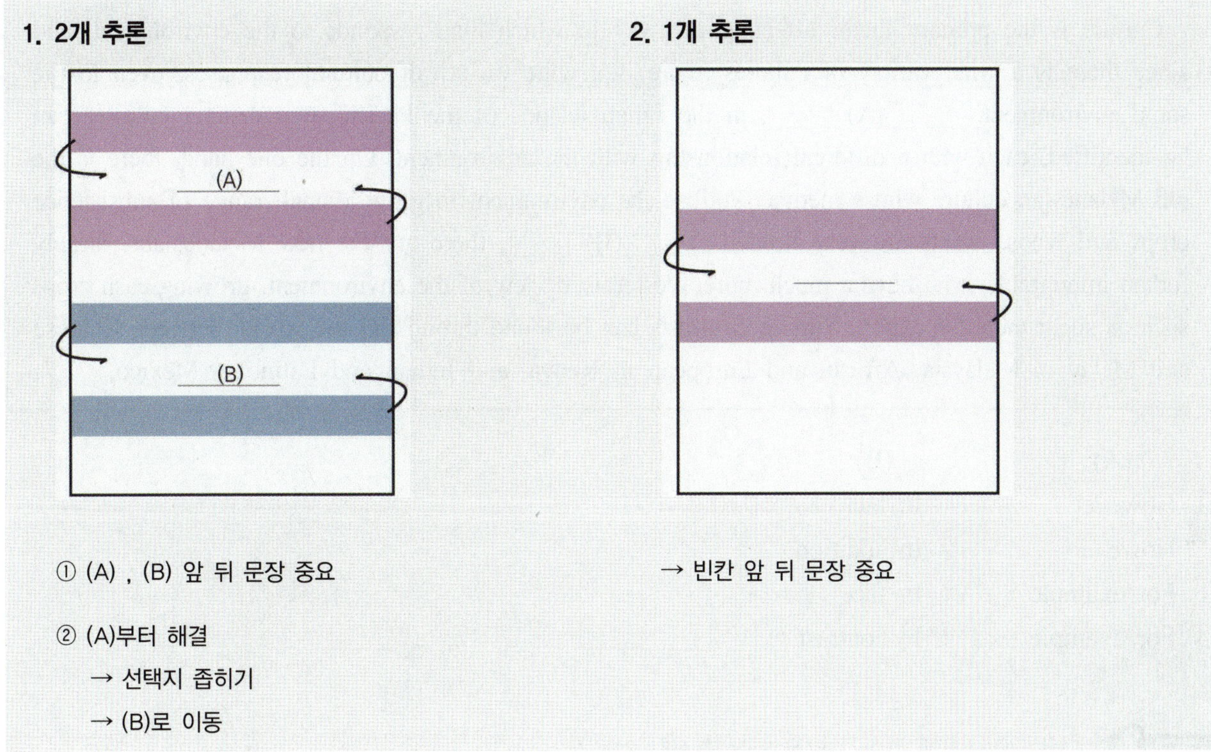



**1. 2개 추론**

① (A) , (B) 앞 뒤 문장 중요

② (A)부터 해결
  → 선택지 좁히기
  → (B)로 이동

**2. 1개 추론**

→ 빈칸 앞 뒤 문장 중요

**예제 1** 다음 (A), (B)에 들어갈 말로 가장 적절한 것은?

Culture is the primary factor affecting the way in which man responds to the environment, and since there is a wide variety of cultures, there is a wide variety of cultural responses, even to the same environment. _______(A)_______, in the Fijian Islands of the Pacific, two distinct cultures can be identified, each with a different relationship with the environment. On the one hand, there is the old Melanesian culture whose members utilise the environment to grow a small range of subsistence crops and whose wants are very limited. _______(B)_______, there are the new Melanesians, largely Indian immigrants, who have a much more Westernised view of the environment, growing cash crops such as sugar cane for export. Similar contrasts can be found throughout the world, between Chinese and Malay in Malaysia, African and European in Kenya, and Indian and Latino in Mexico.

|  | (A) | (B) |
|---|---|---|
| ① | However | In fact |
| ② | However | In addition |
| ③ | For example | In fact |
| ④ | For example | In contrast |

**예제 2** 다음 (A), (B)에 들어갈 말로 가장 적절한 것은?

Destination choice is an important attribute that significantly differentiates between inbound and outbound tourism. Typically mature age customers have more time at hand with greater disposable incomes. Therefore mature age customers would prefer to go on a real holiday and tend to be more inclined towards selecting an international destination. _______(A)_______, mature age customers may try alternative modes of travel such as cruises, trains etc., as time is not a factor that blocks them from selecting these options. However, younger customers have many limitations in comparison to mature age customers in terms of time, money, and career. _______(B)_______, outbound tourism is a preferred destination choice for younger customers only when it is linked to business or personal purposes. Also in comparison to mature age customers, younger customers would spend less time in a single destination and may tend to travel to a greater number of destinations in a year.

|  | (A) | (B) |
|---|---|---|
| ① | Similarly | Nevertheless |
| ② | Similarly | Therefore |
| ③ | In contrast | Moreover |
| ④ | For example | Therefore |

**예제 3** 다음 (A), (B)에 들어갈 말로 가장 적절한 것은?



Names are an important guide to the social significance of pets. Like pet food during the 1960s, pets themselves were frequently given dog-specific names such as Rex, Fido and Rover; or cat-specific names such as Kitty, Tibby or Sooty. _______(A)_______, in Australia, the UK and USA companion animals are now more likely to be given human names. In Britain, for example, the 1980s marked a turning point away from the use of 'traditional canine' names, especially Shep, Brandy, Whisky, Rex, Lassie and Rover. By 1995 the National Canine Defence League's survey found that the ten most popular dog names were all human. _______(B)_______, many of them, such as Ben, Lucy, Sam, Sophie and Charlie, were also currently among the most popular names given to babies. In 1996 the most common name given to a dog by Australians was Sam, whereas in the past Dog was the most common name.

| | (A) | (B) |
|---|---|---|
| ① | Therefore | In contrast |
| ② | However | Instead |
| ③ | Therefore | Moreover |
| ④ | However | Moreover |

**예제 4** 다음 (A), (B)에 들어갈 말로 가장 적절한 것은?

Even if the individual activities in which we engage in our life have the potential to make us feel satisfied, we can still feel unhappy or frustrated with the final result. The most delicious food in the world — be it chocolate, lasagna, or a hamburger — cannot be enjoyed if consumed in large quantities. _______(A)_______, we cannot enjoy activities if we have too much of them, no matter how potentially "delicious" they are. Quantity affects quality; there can be too much of a good thing. A wine connoisseur does not swallow the entire glass of wine in one gulp. _______(B)_______, to fully enjoy the richness of the drink, she smells, she tastes, she savors, and she takes her time. To become a life connoisseur, to enjoy the richness that life offers, we, too, need to take our time.

| | (A) | (B) |
|---|---|---|
| ① | Likewise | Instead |
| ② | Likewise | Moreover |
| ③ | Nevertheless | Instead |
| ④ | Nevertheless | Therefore |

**예제 5**  다음 (A), (B)에 들어갈 말로 가장 적절한 것은?

---

Shakespeare said, "Make use of time, let advantage not slip." This applies in every field of our activity today. There is a time and place for everything. No idleness and no laziness are allowed. You may know the true value of time: notice, seize, and enjoy every minute of it. Never put off until tomorrow what you can do today. If work is done now, it'll save a lot of labor later on. _______(A)_______, you notice that the button on your shirt is hanging loose. It would be better to sew it on tightly before you lose the button. This also applies to studying. If you keep studying daily and don't put it off to a later time, examination time would not be one of tension and worry. _______(B)_______ you would cram and try to learn too much at the last minute.

---

|  | (A) | (B) |
|---|---|---|
| ① | For example | Therefore |
| ② | For example | Otherwise |
| ③ | First of all | Otherwise |
| ④ | Nevertheless | Therefore |

**예제 6**  다음 (A), (B)에 들어갈 말로 가장 적절한 것은?

---

Thanks to the introduction of numerous politically correct words, we have become more sensitive in our speech. Instead of using 'disabled' or 'handicapped,' we use a more encouraging expression such as 'physically challenged.' _______(A)_______, 'stewardess' is now referred to as 'flight attendant' and 'garbage man' as 'sanitation officer.' It is undeniable that most politically correct terms are positive and encouraging. Some of them, however, are much too radical. For example, substituting 'gasoline transfer technician' for 'gas station attendant' is going much too far. Another extreme would be calling 'hunter' 'animal assassin.' There is nothing wrong with using indirect expressions and sensitive terms. _______(B)_______, we should not push such endeavors to the extreme, because as Leslie Fiedler puts it, 'The middle against both ends' is the best rule of thumb.

---

|  | (A) | (B) |
|---|---|---|
| ① | In spite of that | Similarly |
| ② | In spite of that | Conversely |
| ③ | For the same reason | Nevertheless |
| ④ | For the same reason | Therefore |

**예제 7** 다음 (A), (B)에 들어갈 말로 가장 적절한 것은?

Dave Dobbs, a sociologist, introduces the idea of two types of people, 'dandelions' and 'orchids.' Dandelions can thrive anywhere, despite their environment. ________(A)________, orchids are more sensitive and require a stable environment to survive. They are likely to be affected by mood disorders and psychological disease. The astonishing part of Dobbs' report is that given the right care, or environment, the orchids do not just do OK, but far surpass the dandelions in performance. ________(B)________, given the right training, orchids may in fact be destined for greatness. This finding redefines conditions we typically may have classified as undesirable. Depression and generalized anxiety disorder are no longer conditions to dread, because given the right training, people with these conditions may in fact be the true 'movers and shakers' in the world.

|  | (A) | (B) |
|---|---|---|
| ① | However | In other words |
| ② | However | On the contrary |
| ③ | Similarly | In conclusion |
| ④ | Similarly | In other words |

**예제 8** 다음 (A), (B)에 들어갈 말로 가장 적절한 것은?

Most people are slightly nervous about flying. According to several recent reports, "economy-class syndrome" has captured as much public attention as concerns about high levels of cosmic radiation and the questionable quality of the air we breathe in cabins. ________(A)________, it is believed that the cramped sitting leads some passengers to develop the blood clots, causing sharp pain and swelling in the lower leg. Then, more seriously, part of the clot may travel through bloodstream to the lungs. The airlines, ________(B)________, maintain there is no conclusive evidence so far that suggests the cramped aircraft cabin might be more dangerous than sitting still on a crowded train, bus, or car. They say it's basically a matter of self-care.

|  | (A) | (B) |
|---|---|---|
| ① | In fact | therefore |
| ② | In fact | however |
| ③ | In contrast | besides |
| ④ | On the other hand | therefore |

## ❷ 중요 표현 정리

### 1. 결론 / 요약

| | | |
|---|---|---|
| · in conclusion | · in the end | · as a result |
| · to conclude | · in the long run | · consequently |
| ∟결론적으로 | ∟결국에, 마침내 | · in consequence |
| | | · accordingly |
| · in short | · therefore | ∟따라서, 결과적으로 |
| · in brief | · so | |
| · to be brief | · thus | · thereby |
| · in sum | · hence | ∟그것에 의하여 |
| · to sum up | ∟그래서, 그러므로 | |
| · to summarize | | |
| · in a word | | |
| ∟요약하자면 | | |

### 2. 재진술 [즉, 다시 말해서]

| | | |
|---|---|---|
| · namely | · that is | · as it were |
| · in other words | · that is to say | · so to speak |

**예문** He became, **as it were**, a man without a country.

즉, 그는 나라 없는 사람이 되었다.

**예문** The dog is, **so to speak**, a member of the family.

말하자면, 그 강아지는 가족의 일원이다.

### 3. 원인 [ ～ 때문에]

| * 접속사 + S V | * 전치사 + ~~S V~~ |
|---|---|
| · Because | · because of |
| · As | · due to |
| · Since | · owing to |
| · Now that | · on account of |
| · ,for | · thanks to |

**예문** **Now that** my big work project was done, I can go riding freely.

나의 가장 큰 일과 관련된 프로젝트가 끝났기 때문에, 나는 자유롭게 라이딩을 갈 수 있다.

**예문** I couldn't sleep last night, **for** I was so afraid.

나는 너무 두려웠기 때문에, 어젯밤에 잠을 잘 수가 없었다.

## 4. 강조 [무엇보다도 / 우선 / 특히]

| | | |
|---|---|---|
| · above all | · in the first place | · primarily |
| · first of all | · to begin with | · in particular |

## 5. 대조 [반면에]

| | |
|---|---|
| · while | · *while  1 – 동안에 |
| · whereas |          2 – 반면에 |
| |          3 – 일지라도 |

예문 I need someone to look after my puppies **while** I'm on vacation.

내가 휴가를 가있는 동안 나의 강아지들을 돌봐 줄 누군가가 필요하다.

예문 Spring and fall are short seasons, **while** summer and winter are long.

봄과 가을은 짧은 계절인 반면에 여름과 겨울은 길다.

예문 I married you **while** I didn't love you.

나는 너를 사랑했다고 할지라도 너와 결혼했다.

## 6. 역접 [그러나]

| | * '그러나'의 위치 |
|---|---|
| · But | ■________ . |
| · however | ■,________ . / ________, ■, ________ . / ________, ■. |
| · though | ________, ■, ________ . / ________, ■. |
| · Yet / Still | ■ ________. |

예문 However, the tundra is actually home to many living things.

그러나, 툰드라는 실제로 많은 살아 있는 것들의 고향과 같은 곳이다.

예문 Long-term loans, however, didn't rise as much.

그러나, 장기 대출은 그만큼 오르지 않았다.

cf) A law is a law, **however** undesirable it may be.

그것이 아무리 바람직하지 않다고 할지라도, 법은 법이다.

예문 The difference, **though**, is sheer numbers.

그러나, 그 차이점은 순전히 수이다 (수에 불과하다.)

예문 I do not understand you, **though**.

그러나, 나는 너를 이해하지 못한다.

## 7. 대조 [그와는 반대로 / 반면에 / 대조적으로]

| | | |
|---|---|---|
| · on the other hand | · conversely | · contrary to |
| · on the opposite | · on the contrary | · in contrast |
| · on the reverse | | |

## 8. 비슷하게 / 유사하게

- similarly
- likewise
- in the same way
- in like manner
- by the same token

## 9. 그럼에도 불구하고 / ~임에도 불구하고

- nevertheless
- nonetheless
- still
- notwithstanding
- with all
- for all
- despite
- in spite of

**예문** Nevertheless, I do believe I shall purchase it.

그럼에도 불구하고, 나는 그것을 구매할 것이고 믿고 있다.

**예문** Notwithstanding some major financial problems, the school has had a successful year.

몇 가지 중요한 재정적인 문제가 있음에도 불구하고, 그 학교는 성공적인 한 해를 거두었다.

**예문** For all its clarity of style, the book is not easy reading.

문체의 명확함에도 불구하고, 그 책은 읽기에 쉽지 않다.

**예문** Despite the recession, demand is growing.

경기침체에도 불구하고, 수요가 커지고 있다.

## 10. ~일지라도

- though
- although
- even though
- even if

**예문** Even though she had a criminal record, the shop owner hired her.

그녀가 전과가 있다고 할지라도, 그 가게 주인은 그녀를 고용했다.

## 11. 화제전환 [그런데 / 어쨌든]

- by the way
- anyhow
- anyway
- at any rate
- in any case

**예문** At any rate, the next meeting will be on Tuesday.

어쨌든, 다음번 회의는 화요일에 있을 것이다.

## 12. 예를 들어서

- for example
- for instance
- as an example
- as an illustration
- to illustrate
- such as (=like)
- including

**예문** I need to buy some writing supplies **including** pencils, erasers and highlighters.

나는 연필, 지우개 그리고 형광펜을 포함한 약간의 필기도구를 구매할 필요가 있다.

## 13. 게다가 / 더욱이 / 또한 / 이외에도

- besides
- also
- as well
- in addition
- in addition to
- on top of
- additionally
- moreover
- furthermore
- what is more
- all the more
- still more

**예문** I don't really want to go. **Besides**, it's too late now.

나는 사실 가고 싶지 않다. 게다가, 지금은 너무 늦었다.

**예문** And then we needed a system of satellites **as well**.

그리고 그때 우리는 또한 위성 시스템이 필요했다.

**예문** **In addition**, exercise can help you sleep better at night.

게다가, 운동은 밤에 잠을 더 잘 잘 수 있도록 너를 도와줄 수 있다.

**예문** **In addition to** modern cities, Mexico has many ancient ruins.

현대적인 도시 이외에도, 멕시코는 많은 고대 유적지를 가지고 있다.

## 14. 조건

- if (~한다면)
- unless (~하지 않는다면)
- in case (~인 경우에)
- otherwise (그렇지 않으면)
- provided (~한다면)

**예문** **Unless** you're answering my questions, I'll be disappointed.

네가 나의 질문에 답하지 않는다면, 나는 실망할 것이다.

**예문** **Provided** that you have the money in your account, you can withdraw up to $100 a day.

당신의 계좌에 돈을 가지고 있다면, 당신은 하루에 100달러까지 인출할 수 있습니다.

**예문** You'd better take the keys **in case** I'm out.

내가 외출한 경우를 대비하여, 너는 열쇠를 가져가는 것이 좋겠다.

## 15. ~에 관하여

| | | |
|---|---|---|
| · about | · regarding | · with respect to |
| · on | · when it comes to | · as for |
| · as to | · with regard to | |
| · concerning | | |

cf) · as far as A be concerned (A에 관해서)

**예문** The two groups were similar with respect to income and status.

그 두 집단은 소득과 지위에 관해서는 비슷했다.

**예문** As for this quarter's result, we have reached the ceiling.

이번 분기의 결과에 관하여 (말하자면), 우리는 한계점에 도달했다.

**예문** As far as memory is concerned, I'm by far the best.

기억력에 관해서는, 내가 단연코 최고이다.

## 16. ~에 관계없이

| | |
|---|---|
| · regardless of | · irrespective of |

**예문** Order whatever you want regardless of expense.

비용과 관계없이 네가 원하는 것은 무엇이든지 주문해라.

**예문** Needs are irrespective of race, nationality or religion.

욕구는 인종, 국적 또는 종교와 관계없이 존재한다.

## 17. ~를 제외하고 / 이외에도

| | | |
|---|---|---|
| · apart from | · aside from | · other than |
| · except | · but | |

**예문** I've finished apart from the last question.

나는 마지막 질문을 제외하고 다 끝마쳤다.

**예문** Aside from their house in London, they also have a villa in Spain.

런던에 있는 그들의 집 이외에도, 그들은 또한 스페인에 빌라를 가지고 있다.

## 18. 사실상 / 실제로

| | | |
|---|---|---|
| · in fact | · actually | · as a matter of fact |

**예문** As a matter of fact, I can feel full by watching cooking show.

사실은, 나는 요리 프로그램을 보면서 배부름을 느낄 수 있다.

## 19. 기타

| | | |
|---|---|---|
| · once  ① 예전에<br>　　　② 한 번<br>　　　③ 일단 ~하면<br>· at least (적어도)<br>· at most (기껏해야) | · at the same time (동시에)<br>　= simultaneously<br>· indeed (정말로, 실제로) | · on the whole (전체적으로)<br>· fortunately (다행히도)<br>· so long as (~하는 한) |

**예문** No way so long as I'm alive!

　　　내가 살아있는 한 절대 안 돼!

---

· instead (대신에)　　　　　　　· instead of (~대신에)

**예문** He didn't reply. Instead, he turned on his heel and left the room.

　　　그는 대답하지 않았다. 대신에, 그는 휙 돌아서서 방을 나가버렸다.

**예문** Instead of complaining all the time, do something about it.

　　　항상 불평하는 대신에, 그것에 대한 행동을 해라.

---

· by means of (~에 의해)　　　· by all means (항상, 반드시)　　　· by no means (절대로 ~아닌)

**예문** The piano was lifted by means of a crane.

　　　그 피아노는 크레인으로 들어 올려졌다.

**예문** By all means, go with DY.

　　　항상, 디와이와 함께해라.

**예문** She is by no means an inexperienced teacher.

　　　그녀는 절대로 경험이 없는 교사가 아니다.

---

· to make matters worse<br>　(설상가상으로) | · as if (마치 ~처럼)<br>· as though (마치 ~처럼) | · since (① ~때문에, ② ~이래로)

**예문** Don't talk about me as if I'm not standing right here!

　　　내가 바로 여기에 서있지 않은 것처럼 나에 대해서 말 하지마.

**예문** She has been worrying ever since the letter arrived.

　　　그 편지가 도착한 이후로 그녀는 걱정하고 있다.

**예문** Since we live in the computer era, you should get used to personal computers.

　　　우리는 컴퓨터 시대에 살고 있기 때문에, 너는 개인용 컴퓨터에 익숙해져야 한다.

## ③ 지시사

### 1. 대명사

┗ 앞 명사    (대명사는 앞에 명사를 뒤에서 받는 말로 순서, 삽입, 제거 유형에서 유용하게 쓰인다.)

### 2. the + N

┗ 앞  N 등장  ( a(n) N )    * N: Noun(명사)

N 내용    (앞에 나온 명사나 그 명사에 해당하는 내용을 뒤에서 받는 형태로 순서, 삽입, 제거 유형에서 유용하게 쓰인다.)

### 3. this + N    / that + N
### these + Ns / those + Ns

┗ 앞  N 등장    * this + N – 이 명사 / these Ns – 이 명사들

N 내용    * that + N – 저 명사 / those Ns – 저 명사들

(앞에 나온 명사나 그 명사에 해당하는 내용을 뒤에서 받는 형태로 순서, 삽입, 제거 유형에서 유용하게 쓰인다.)

### 4. Such + a(n) + N / Such + Ns

┗ 앞  N 등장    * Such + N – 그와 같은 명사 / such Ns – 그와 같은 명사들

N 내용    (앞에 나온 명사나 그 명사에 해당하는 내용을 뒤에서 받는 형태로 순서, 삽입, 제거 유형에서 유용하게 쓰인다.)

**예문** There is an apple on the table. 테이블 위에 사과가 하나 있다.

[          ] is the thing that anybody can buy in the market. [      ]는 시장에서 누구나 살 수 있는 것이다.

① It (그것은)　　　　　　② The apple (그 사과는)

③ This / That apple (이/저 사과는)　　　　④ Such an apple (그와 같은 사과는)

| +α 1 | +α 2 | +α 3 | +α 4 |
|---|---|---|---|
| another + N | there | the same | the former |
| other + Ns | then | | the latter |

· another + N (또 다른 N)　· there (거기에서)　· the same (똑같은 것)　· the former (전자)

· other + Ns (다른 N들)　· then (그때)　　　　　　　　　　　· the latter (후자)

### 5. 앞 V → 뒤 N

**예문** He believed that she had lied during the critical period.　→　His belief is wrong.

그는 그녀가 그 결정적인 기간 동안에 거짓말 했다고 믿었다.　　　그의 믿음은 잘못된 것이다.

**예제 1** 글의 흐름으로 보아, 주어진 문장이 들어가기에 가장 적절한 곳은?

> This cooperation can only be secured by allowing every level of employee to suggest ideas, express their views, and share their experiences.

To a large extent, the success of an organization requires an atmosphere in which there is a free flow of information — upward, downward, and horizontally. At the workplace, the primary goal is getting things done. ( ① ) For this, instructions, guidelines, supervision, monitoring, and periodic reporting are usually considered enough. ( ② ) But if the company wishes to achieve more than the set task, a real involvement of all employees, from the highest to the lowest levels, is required. ( ③ ) Such a system of communication can only be established within the organization by the manager. ( ④ ) In fact, the manager functions as the point of intersection for all communication channels. One of the most important concerns of the manager is to organize and ensure an effective information system across the organization.

**예제 2** 주어진 글 다음에 이어질 글의 순서로 가장 적절한 것은?

Someone hands you a piece of paper bearing a fine grid — as in a school exercise book. The person tells you that he is thinking of just one of the small squares.

(A) If the answer is 'no' then the box must be in B — there is nowhere else it could be. So you now forget about A and proceed to divide B in half, lettering each half as before.

(B) He wants you to locate that square by asking questions which will only get a 'yes' or 'no' answer. So you divide the sheet in half with a line and call one half A and the other half B. You ask: 'Is the desired box in A?'

(C) Again you ask the question. In the end you must come to the chosen box. The point about this simple strategy is that at every moment the desired box must lie in A or not A (which is B). There is nowhere else. Nor can the box lie in both A and B.

① (C) − (B) − (A)  ② (B) − (A) − (C)

③ (B) − (C) − (A)  ④ (C) − (A) − (B)

# 장대영 영어
## Graphic 독해

# 04

# Types
## (유형별 접근법)

# TYPES(유형별 접근법)

## 1 TYPES

### 1 주제/제목/요지/주장

#### 1. 주/제/요/주 Basic Mind

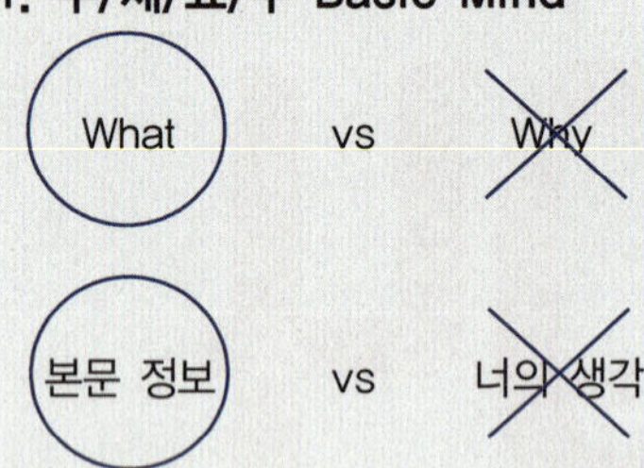


#### 2. 주/제/요/주 Reading Skills

① STS

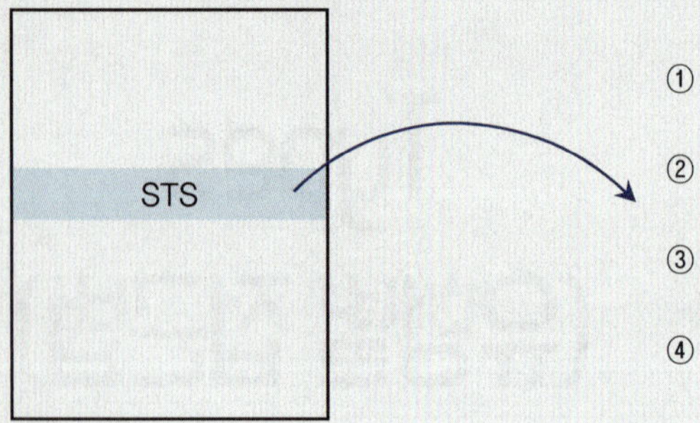


**STS**

STS 1 의무/필요

STS 2 '중요한' 의미를 가진

STS 3 결론/요약

STS 4 역접

STS 5 not과 but의 A, B 접속사

STS 6 명령문

STS 7 양보절과 주절

STS 8 강조 표현

STS 9 1인칭의 활용

STS 10 필자의 판단/감정

STS 11 The＋비, the＋비

STS 12 연구/실험 − 결과

STS 13 권위자 − 말 주장

STS 14 의문문? + 답변!

STS 15 통념+비판

STS 16 문제점 + 해결책

STS 17 시간상의 대조 − 현재

STS 18 예시/비유 − 윗 문장

STS 19 열거 − 윗 문장

② F·S + L·S

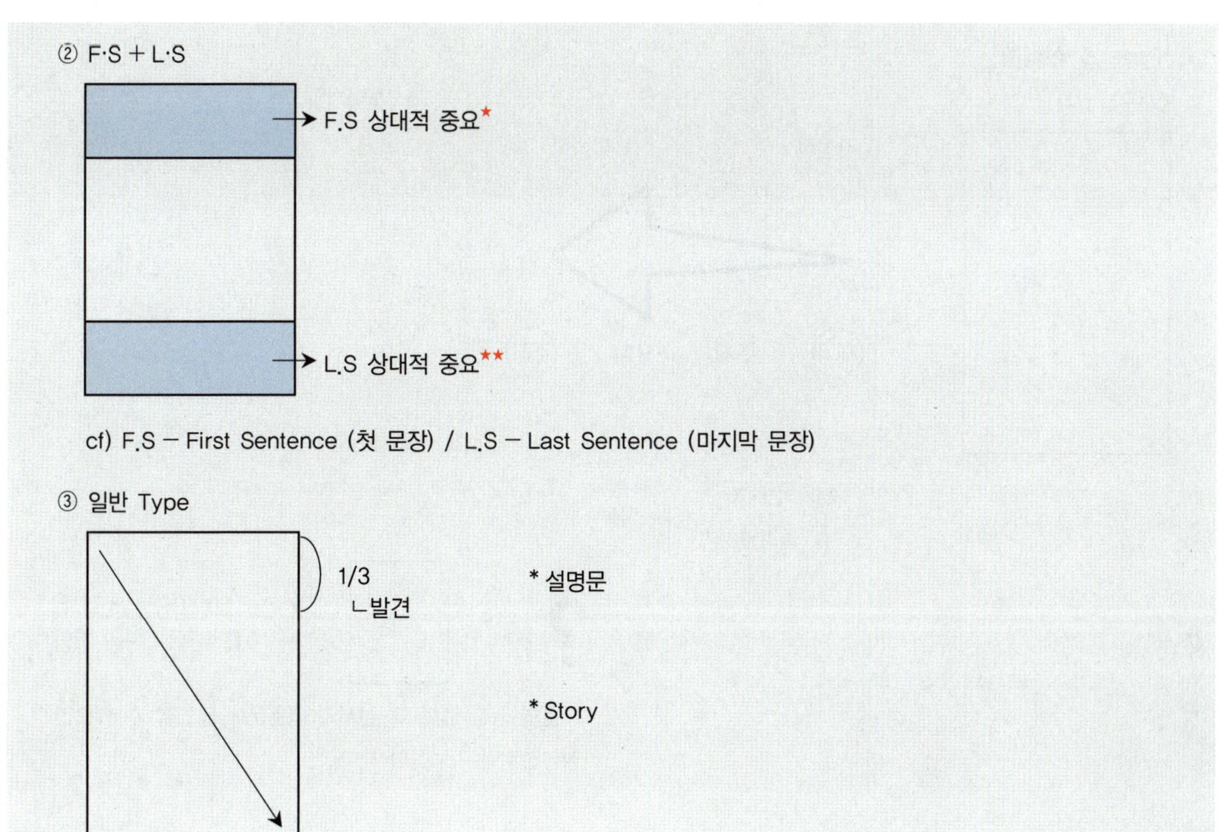


cf) F.S − First Sentence (첫 문장) / L.S − Last Sentence (마지막 문장)

③ 일반 Type

1/3
ㄴ발견

* 설명문

* Story

## 3. Type & 선택지

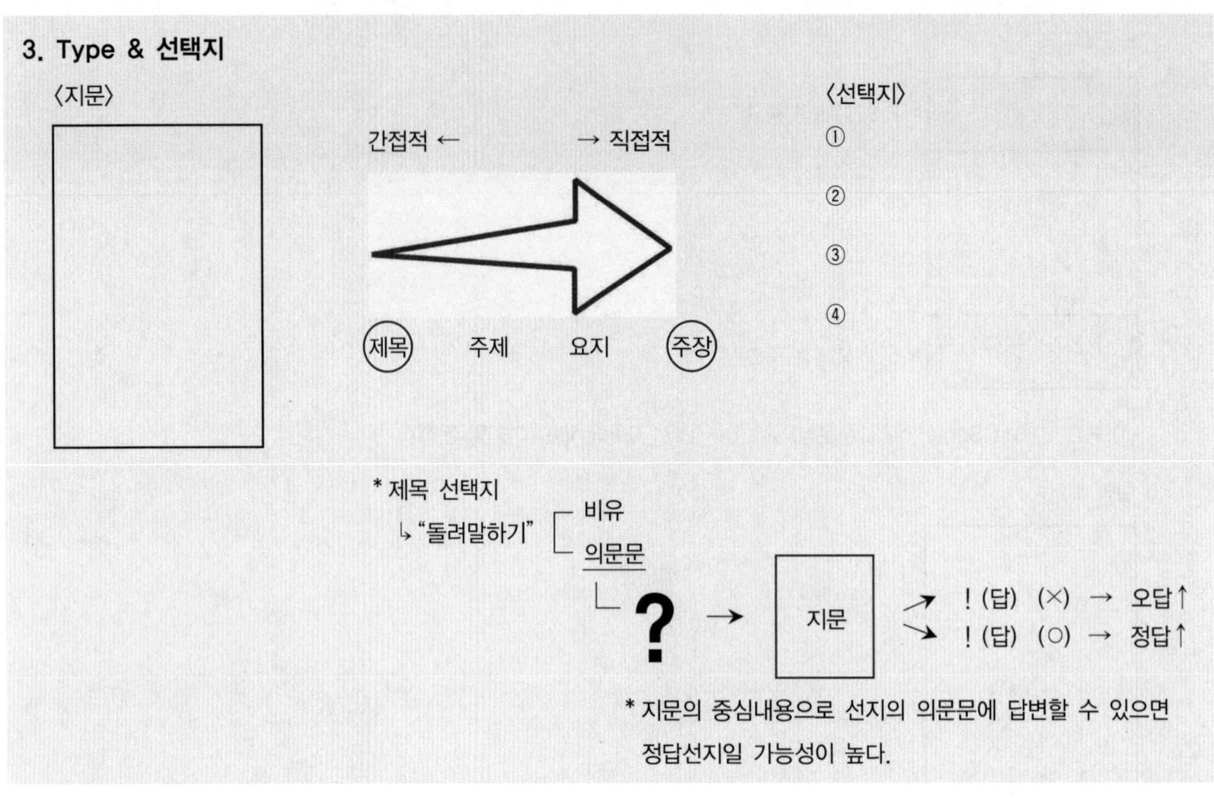


## 4. 오답 PXC+T

— 출제자가 주제/제목/요지/주장/빈칸추론 선택지 오답을 만드는 원리

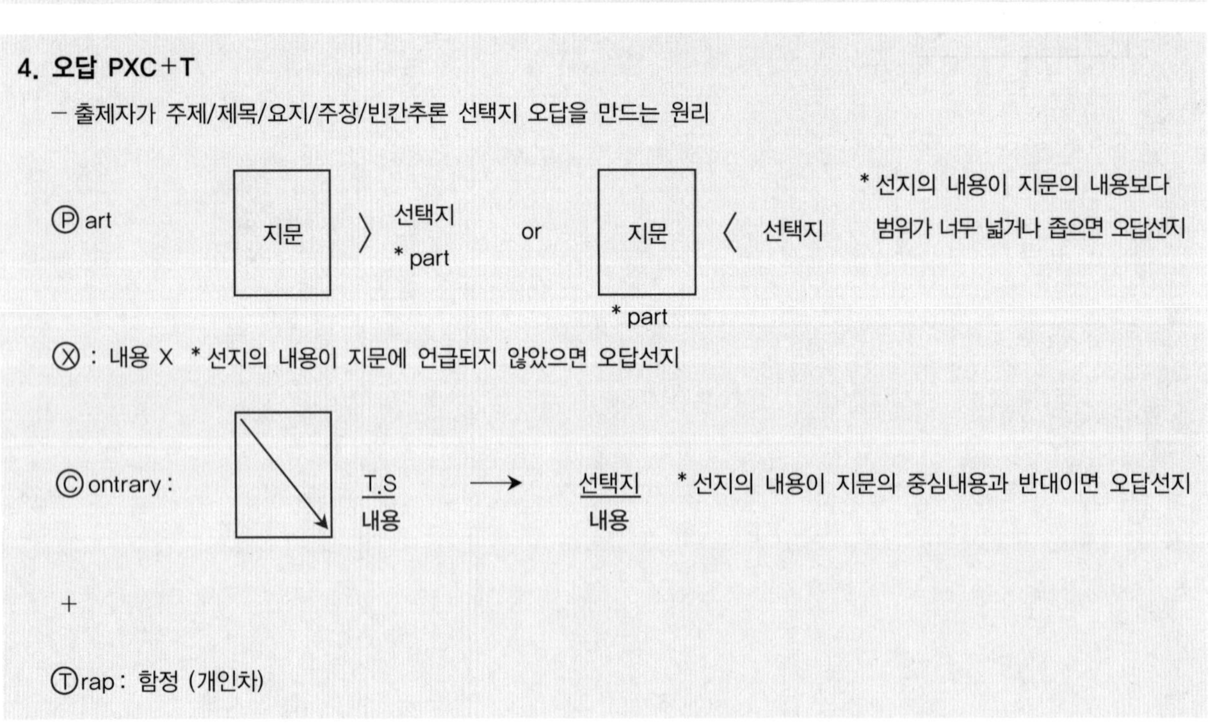

## 1-2  주제/제목/요지/주장 Application

**예제 1**  다음 글의 요지로 가장 적절한 것은?

What most parents do is stop sharing books as soon as a child can read alone. That makes reading a solitary happening, with no chance to talk about a book or discuss what it is saying. Read aloud together. Read alone yourself, then say, "Have you read this book? I really liked it." Once you begin to be book-sharers you will have no end of delight in sharing. Our son brought us a copy of Brian Jacques' Redwall and said, "I think you'll like this. It's a good book." We respect each other's opinions because we have read aloud together and talked about books. That son is in college now and recently visited us. He left a book behind, saying, "I'd like you to read this. It tells you some of my thinking about relationships." Sharing a book makes for a delightful companionship. It is sharing yourself.

① 부모는 자녀와 함께 독서를 할 때 그들의 이해를 돕기 위해 설명을 해주어야 한다.
② 부모와 자녀가 함께 책 읽기를 하면 행복한 동반자 관계를 형성할 수 있게 된다.
③ 아이들에게는 부모가 없이 혼자 힘으로 자발적인 독서를 할 수 있는 환경이 필요하다.
④ 부모는 자녀에게 책을 읽어 줄 때 그들의 눈높이에 맞는 적정 수준의 책을 선택해야 한다.

**예제 2**  다음 글의 요지로 가장 적절한 것은?

Having a business card is an obvious, but very important, everyday method to get your name, your artwork, and your message out. It's also an easy way for people to access your name at some later date. Amazingly enough, though, most artists don't use them. It's surprising but true that many fine artists are inept at designing anything with type and small graphic elements, especially for themselves. Maybe you think business cards are too businesslike. Try thinking of them as calling cards or, with your artwork on them, as art cards — little gifts you give away. Business cards are too important to your success to avoid. Imagine if you, with your business cards, and another artist, without business cards, meet a dealer or collector at the same time. Which one of you is more likely to be contacted later? It won't matter who's the better artist.

① 명함 디자인이 더 특이할수록 그 판매량이 증가하게 된다.
② 인맥 관리를 위해서 받은 명함을 잘 분류해서 관리하는 것이 좋다.
③ 명함 디자인에는 반드시 필요한 내용만 간단명료하게 적어 넣어야 한다.
④ 명함의 사용은 미술가의 성공에 있어서도 매우 중요한 필수 요소이다.

**예제 3** 다음 글에서 필자가 주장하는 바로 가장 적절한 것은?

---

    Active, energetic, rambunctious boys are not bad boys and should not be made to feel so. Boys are naturally active. They have energy to burn. That's why they need avenues where they can be active, burn up that energy, and test their strength. Boys need exercise. It is not a luxury, it is a necessity. Video games don't provide exercise. And neither do television or computers. All boys need to romp and learn that even in rambunctious play, there are rules and order. Through sports and exercise, they learn to control their muscles, control their bodies, and even control their emotions and their minds. As a boy grows older, he can transfer these skills he learns into other areas of his life. He can never learn to control his energy if he is not allowed to experience the fullness of its power.

---

① 부모는 자녀가 원하는 것을 파악해 이를 충족시켜 주어야 한다.
② 부모는 어린 자녀들이 지나친 경쟁에 빠지지 않게 해야 한다.
③ 남자아이들에게는 충분한 운동의 기회가 제공되어야 한다.
④ 아동 비만 예방을 위해서 체육 수업을 확대해야 한다.

**예제 4** 다음 글에서 필자가 주장하는 바로 가장 적절한 것은?

---

    Suppose that you and I are discussing the current president of the United States. I feel that he is the best president we have ever had. You totally disagree and feel that he is the worst one we have ever had. In the discussion that follows, you ask, "Why do you think he is the most important or best president?" I then give you a list of reasons, as well as some of the important things that he has done. Rather than trying to explain how I'm wrong or thinking up arguments about what I've said, you should try to listen to me and try to understand my position. In other words, the listener should try to hear and understand where the other person is coming from, and not prepare arguments or retaliations. The individual who is really listening tends not to interrupt and give her own point of view, but rather will ask additional questions in order to clarify and understand the other person's position.

---

① 상대방의 의견을 무조건 반박하기보단 경청하고 이해해야 한다.
② 주장을 제시할 때 해당 논점을 벗어나는 주장인지 주의해야 한다.
③ 상대방이 반박할 수 있는 여지를 남기는 표현의 사용은 지양해야 한다.
④ 상대방에게 자신의 주장을 간단명료하고 모호하지 않게 전달해야 한다.

**예제 5**  다음 글의 주제로 가장 적절한 것은?

The massive tombs and ceremonial structures built from huge stones in the Neolithic period are known as megalithic architecture, from the Greek words for "large" (megas) and "stone" (lithos). Archaeologists disagree about the nature of the societies that created them. Some believe megalithic monuments reflect complex, stratified societies in which powerful religious or political leaders dictated their design and commanded the large workforce necessary to accomplish these ambitious engineering projects. Other interpreters argue that these massive undertakings are clear evidence for cooperative collaboration within and among social groups, coalescing around a common project that fueled social cohesion without the controlling power of a ruling elite. Many megalithic structures are associated with death, and recent interpretations stress the fundamental role of death and burial as public theatrical performances in which individual and group identity, cohesion, and disputes were played out.

① megalithic architecture as emblematic reflection of the natural scenery
② various ideas about the nature of societies that built megalithic architecture
③ the importance of megalithic memorials in archaeological investigation
④ the defining requirements of civilization in the Neolithic Era

**예제 6**  다음 글의 주제로 가장 적절한 것은?

The domestication of animals occurred some 10,000 years ago and represented a milestone for the history of human civilization. The origin and sequence of domestication is a hotly debated topic among anthropologists and historians. Richard Bulliet, professor of history at Columbia University, argues that animals were probably first kept in captivity for use in sacrificial rites. This practice allowed ancient civilizations to observe which species were tame enough for use as work animals. Animals, notably cattle, provided labor and locomotion when they were harnessed to plows, sledges, and wagons beginning in about 4000 BC. Thus, animal agriculture was indispensable to accelerating the development of crop agriculture. The flesh and hides of sacrificial animals were routinely consumed by those in the royal house or the priesthood. Eventually, the habit of having the animals under human control at all times provided a constant and consistent food supply ready at hand. It also thereby created the leisure time necessary to societal progress.

① different forms of sacrificial rites in diverse cultures
② significance of animal's labor in production of food
③ origin and usefulness of the domestication of animals
④ limitations on the further growth of crop agriculture

Recent measurements using radiometers on satellites suggest that solar energy, which is an input to our climate system, can vary considerably. Changes of the order of 0.1% of the total solar energy reaching the Earth have already been measured, within a period of less than 20 months. This kind of change could be linked to sunspot activity, which has a periodicity of 11 years. Sunspots are magnetic storms giving (or showing) cooler regions on the Sun's surface. Thus a sunspot maximum corresponds to a minimum of received solar energy. According to measurements during the period 1976 to 1980, the Sun's surface cooled by about 6°C corresponding to an increase in the number and the size of sunspots. These changes may alter the Earth's climate since, according to numerical climate models, a 0.5% change in solar output could be enough to change the climate. In addition, a decrease in solar energy of the order of 1% could lead to a decrease in the Earth's average temperature by 1.0°C.

① potential effects of solar output variations on global climate change
② common factors of the global greenhouse effect in modern society
③ general definition of the Earth's mean temperature
④ great accuracy of measurements derived from satellite



The innovativeness of cities is related directly to the quality of human talent. China's coastal cities have been quicker off the mark because they have been more successful in nurturing quality, retaining the most talented knowledge workers, and attracting the cream of the knowledge workers from other parts of the country. The coastal cities are also more open and accessible to outsiders and have integrated with global knowledge networks. For smaller inland cities to become innovative smart cities, they will need to specialize and pull in some of the best brains in their fields of specialization from across the country. Any serious attempt to become an innovative city built on the quality of talent, which after all is the life blood of innovation, will have to combine urban design and renewal with a focus on developing a few core areas of world-class expertise.

① Risky Chances for China's Coastal City to Grow
② Innovation: An Element of Organizational Sustainability
③ What Can We Do to Motivate Knowledge Workers?
④ What Makes a City More Innovative?

**예제 9** 다음 글의 제목으로 가장 적절한 것은?

U.S. manufacturing companies discovered the bright side of decision problems when they were forced by law to eliminate environmentally harmful materials from their operating processes. At first, the companies saw only the negatives — disruptions, higher costs, more paperwork. But then some of them began to see opportunities. Instead of viewing the problem in its narrow and obvious form — How can we get rid of the harmful materials? — they redefined it more broadly: How can we produce our product in the best and most efficient way? As a result, they made breakthroughs in their operations that have actually enabled them to have lower production costs without toxic materials than with them. By changing a problem into an opportunity, they gained an important advantage over their less savvy competitors.

① Reframe a Problem: Turn Crisis into Opportunity
② Making a Problem Clear Before Seeking a Solution
③ Cost Efficiency: A Significant Factor in Decision-making
④ Green Technology: Is it Truly Beneficial?

**예제 10** 다음 글의 제목으로 가장 적절한 것은?

Minorities tend not to have much power or status and may even be dismissed as troublemakers, extremists or simply 'weirdos'. How, then, do they ever have any influence over the majority? The social psychologist Serge Moscovici claims that the answer lies in their behavioural style, i.e. the way the minority gets its point across. The crucial factor in the success of the suffragette movement was that its proponents were consistent in their views, and this created a considerable degree of social influence. Minorities that are active and organised, who advocate and defend their position consistently, can create social conflict, doubt and uncertainty among members of the majority, and ultimately this may lead to social change. Such change has often occurred because a minority has converted others to its point of view. Without the influence of minorities, we would have no innovation, no social change. Many of what we now regard as 'major' social movements (e.g. Christianity, trade unionism or feminism) were originally due to the influence of an outspoken minority.

① Why Consistency Matters in Public Relations
② How Does the Minority Bring Change to Society?
③ Minority Rights: the Secret of Conflict Prevention
④ What Encourages People to Accept Common Rules?

## 2 빈칸

### 〈빈칸 Basic Mind〉

PREMISE (전제조건)

* 빈칸 문장 → (내용상) 중요 문장

* 지문의 첫 부분 (특히 첫 문장)의 어려움 → 2번째 문장으로 넘어가기

### 1. 풀기 전 빈칸 위치

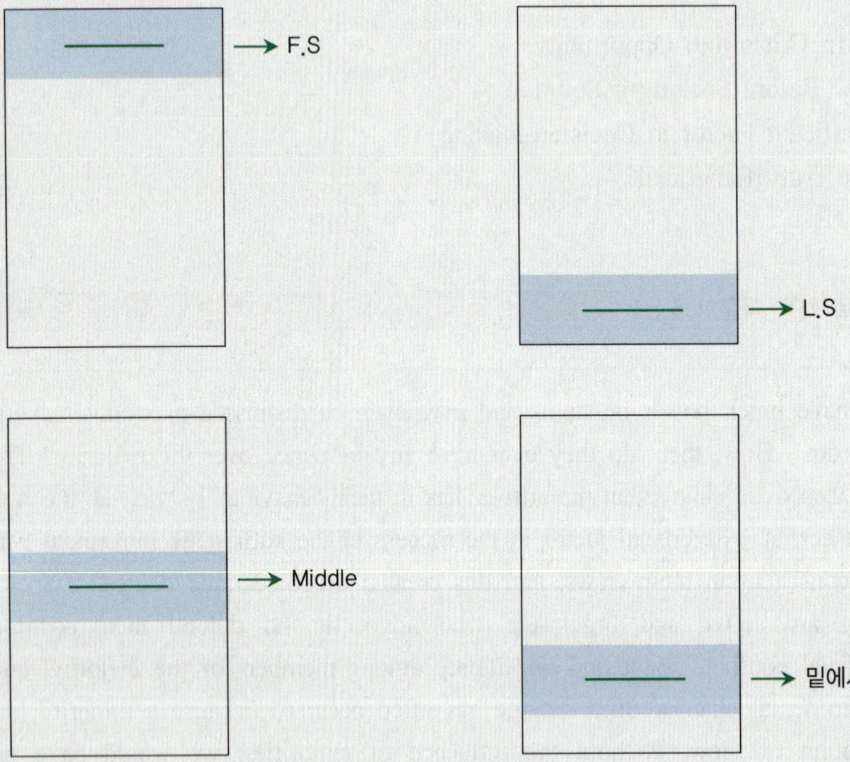

→ F.S

→ L.S

→ Middle

→ 밑에서 2번째 문장

cf) F.S — First Sentence (첫 문장) / L.S — Last Sentence (마지막 문장)

## 2. 풀면서 Discovering [Reading Skills]

① Types

ⓐ STS

cf) T.S − Topic Sentence (주제문)



**예제 1** 다음 빈칸에 들어갈 말로 가장 적절한 것은?

The opposite of talking is knowing when to stop. Speakers often have a problem with that. They're afraid that stopping might look like they forgot or lost what to say next. It's difficult to realize that as eloquent as well-chosen words are, ＿＿＿＿＿＿ is equally, and often more, eloquent. Eloquent not because it gives the audience a chance to stop and think but because it compels them to do so. When you're hot on the trail of delivering a message, the audience is busy absorbing it, and you're both moving at quite a pace. It is therefore invaluable for them to be given a pause in which to consider what you have just said. Not only for relief from the one-way charge but to be able to think on their own instead of running with you.

① silence

② refusal

③ sound

④ action

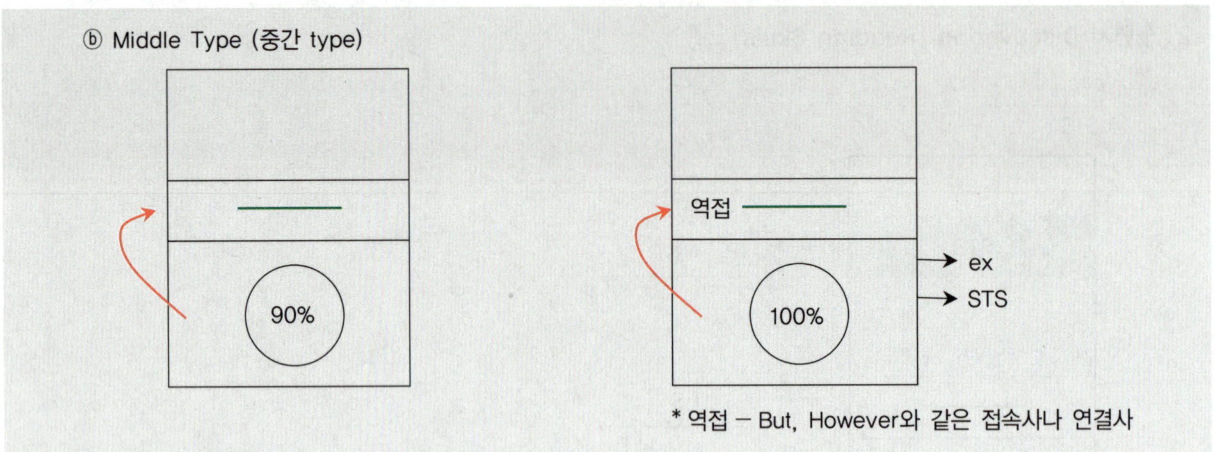



## 예제 2  다음 빈칸에 들어갈 말로 가장 적절한 것은?

We often forget that the main purpose of criticizing is not to be negative but to be constructive: to fix something. But general criticism is destructive. It doesn't lead anyone to know how to fix things; it just makes people feel bad. We all have different verbal and visual styles and conceive different ways to say the same thing. But, unless you can explain ________________, you haven't started fixing anything. To help the criticized person know how to fix what you object to, define exactly what went wrong and why it is unsatisfactory. Most people are generally so sensitive to criticism that they'll say, "Yes, I understand," when they actually don't, just to get the criticism to end. Specific examples for improvement as well as specific descriptions of exactly what you mean are a must.

① typically
② respectfully
③ specifically
④ originally

© – 1 General (Story)

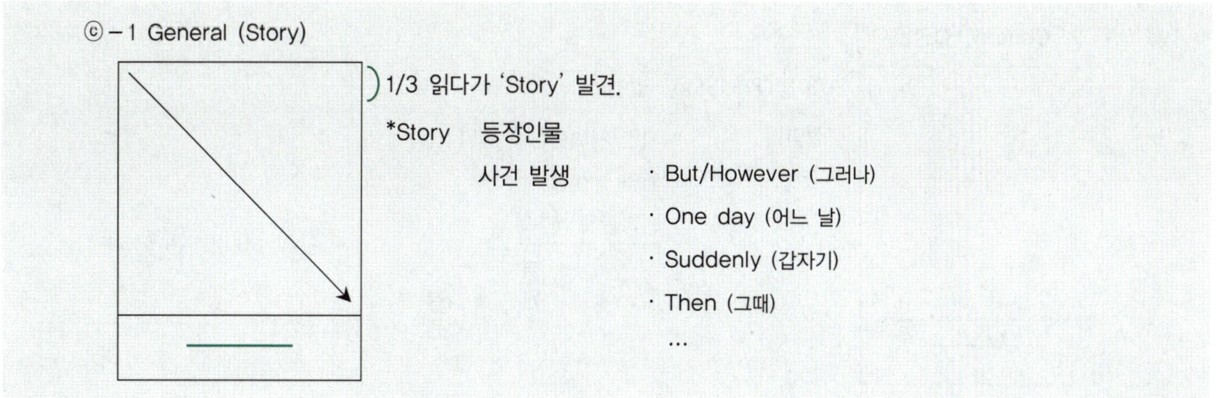



**예제 3**  다음 빈칸에 들어갈 말로 가장 적절한 것은?

A small business owner could never afford to offer his employees healthcare benefits. It was not typically a problem because most of the employees accessed healthcare through their working spouses. However, tragedy struck one year when two of his most productive employees were stricken with life-threatening illnesses. One had a heart attack, and the other had lung cancer. They each, obviously, had to miss work. With productivity gone and the business hurting, he chose to give the employees the only portion of their salary he could afford. The business operated at a loss that year, but when the two individuals overcame their life-threatening illnesses, he found that their new-found loyalty reaped a new set of rewards as they told their stories of a business owner who ___________________________.

① cares about much more than a profit

② be able to maximize productivity

③ doesn't take care of employee benefits

④ responds sensitively to the voices of the employees

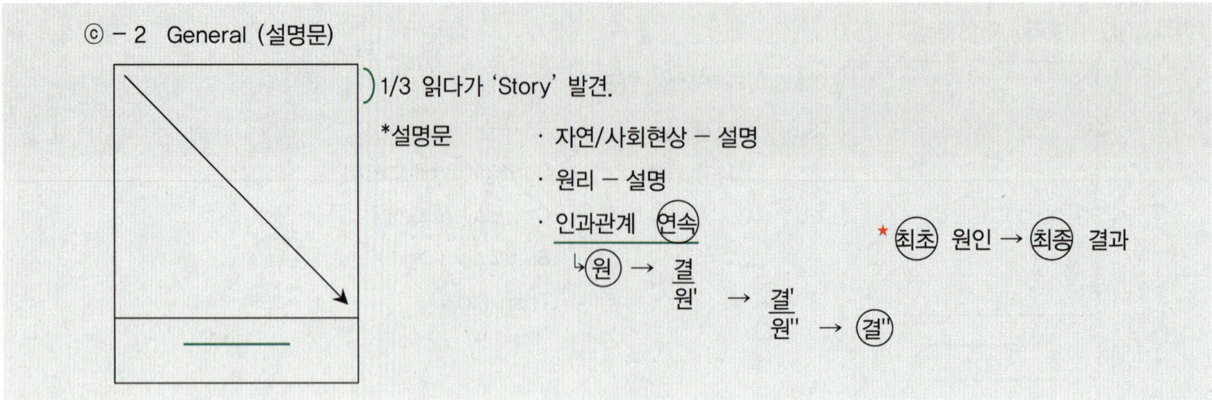


## 예제 4  다음 빈칸에 들어갈 말로 가장 적절한 것은?

A new study suggests that children who often get serious ear infections are twice as likely to ________________________ than kids with healthier ears. To explain the findings, lead researcher Linda Bartoshuk from the University of Florida says repeated ear infections might permanently damage a nerve called the chorda tympani. This nerve starts at the front of the tongue, where it pick up taste sensations. From there, where it delivers messages about what the tongue just tasted. When the nerve is damaged, she says, people become extra sensitive to the feel or texture of fatty foods, such as butter, which tend to be creamy and slippery. The food doesn't taste different, but feeling fatty sensations more than usual. That drives them to eat even more fatty foods.

① get nervous easily
② be mentally challenged
③ become obese later in life
④ damage their sense of taste

## 2. 활용

① For example

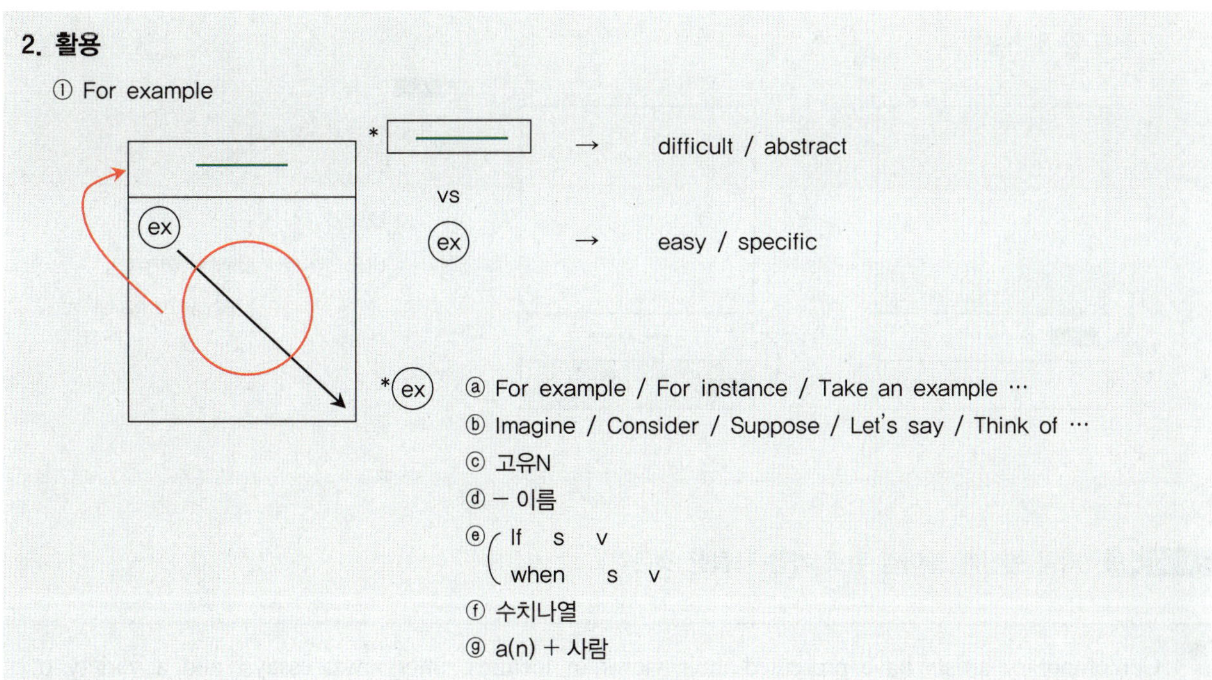


**예제 1** 다음 빈칸에 들어갈 말로 가장 적절한 것은?

In the classical notion of pleasure and pain, an organism strives to maintain equilibrium with its environment. Pain occurs as it deviates from equilibrium and pleasure occurs as it returns. For instance, when cold threatens body temperature, it registers as unpleasantness that can become intense pain if carried to an extreme. Conversely, we feel immediate pleasure in warming up from being cold. Pleasure results not from the warmth in itself, but from the approach to ideal body temperature. Too much warmth can also upset equilibrium, and a different kind of discomfort or outright pain will set in. So pleasures are not absolute but rather are ___________________________________ . The same taste or feeling or sight or sound that is pleasurable in one context can become painful in another.

① permanent in the overall scheme of things

② often relative to the individual's feelings

③ generally dependent upon different stimuli

④ always relative to an equilibrium point

② 빈칸 앞 뒷 부분

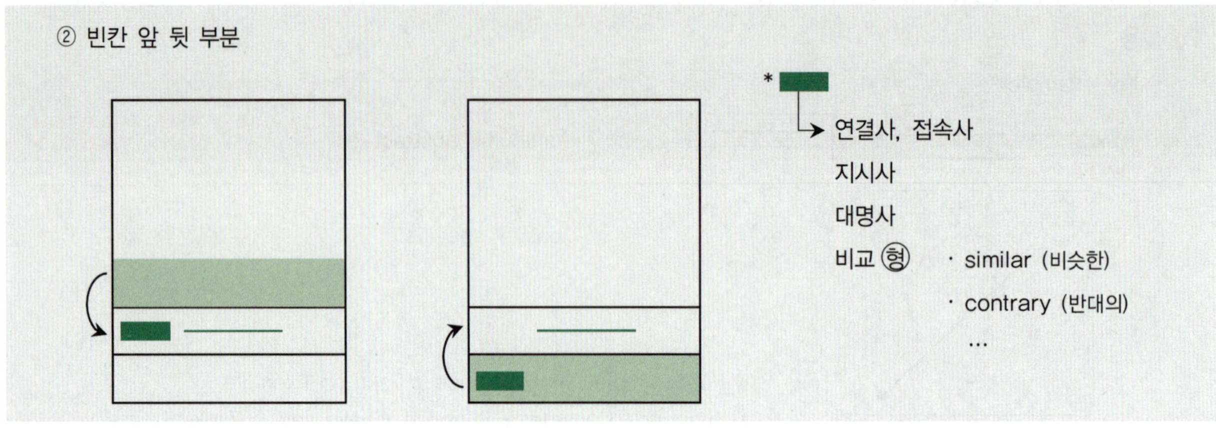


**예제 2**  다음 빈칸에 들어갈 말로 가장 적절한 것은?

Contemporary artists have presented their views in lectures, interviews, essays, and a variety of novel formats. E-mails, text and voice messages, and other virtual public forums have all but replaced letters and journals. Many artists have sophisticated websites with blogs, chats and, nowdays, some social media accounts. These new possibilities allow the audience, not just specialists, to be informed and to engage in meaningful dialogues, with these exciting electronic platforms. Unlike tangible documents, e-mails and other electronic textual, visual, and audio materials may be, and often are deleted. Every when they are saved, digital media's endurance over time is still unknown. This raises important questions about ________________________ .

① whether a change in the way artists express their views is desirable
② how many contemporary art records might be available in the future
③ what will make it easier to express emotions in the future
④ how artists express their views using social network services

**예제 3**   다음 빈칸에 들어갈 말로 가장 적절한 것은?

The ability to detect danger in the posture of others has been studied by neuroscientist Beatrice Gelder. Her research has demonstrated that the brain of an observer reacts more powerfully to the body language of a person in a posture indicating fear than it does even to a fearful facial expression. Looks of fear can paralyze or, at least, evoke our own potent fear-based reactions. Yet as powerful as facial expressions are in conveying danger, a person's uptight posture and furtive movements make us even more uncomfortable. Wouldn't you, too, be startled by the sudden recoiling of the hiker in front of a coiled snake? This type of ______________ behavior occurs throughout the animal world. If, for example, one bird in a flock on the ground suddenly takes off, all the other birds will follow immediately after, they do not need to know why.

① calculative

② redundant

③ imitative

④ scaring

**예제 4**   다음 빈칸에 들어갈 말로 가장 적절한 것은?

There is no doubt that mountainous areas with low valleys among them tend to have higher species richness than surrounding areas of flat land. This is partly because there are more different environments, each with its own characteristic set of species. For one thing there are different climate zones on a mountain, but only one climate in a flat lowland area. For example, in the Santa Catalina Mountains of Arizona, many different plant species occur in the same mountains but at distinct altitudes, each species at its own climatic optimum. A similar ______________ of species composition with elevation is found in the Siskiyou Mountains of Oregon, and in fact on almost any set of high mountains, simply because there is a wide range of climates there. Even on a very local scale, a varied landscape can have micro climatic differences adding to species richness.

① diversity

② activity

③ competition

④ extinction

**예제 5**  다음 빈칸에 들어갈 말로 가장 적절한 것은?

---

Pet food used to be about selecting a small, medium, or large bag of whatever your local feed of grocery store stocked. Today, choosing pet food from among the hundreds of varieties in the $17 billion United States market can be a complicated task. Beef, duck, vegetables, and salmon are part of today's pet diets. Once created to profit from human food manufacturing waste, the pet food industry now makes products with human-grade ingredients that sell well because people want something better for their beloved animal companions. The number of people purchasing pet food with human-grade ingredients is on increase. As a result, pets truly do increase the burden on agriculture, because _______________________________.

---

① it is difficult for farmers to choose crops for them

② there is no standard for classifying animals' edible food

③ there is a limit to the amount of crops farmers can harvest

④ they are no longer eating the "leftover" products

③ 빈칸 앞 뒤 부정어

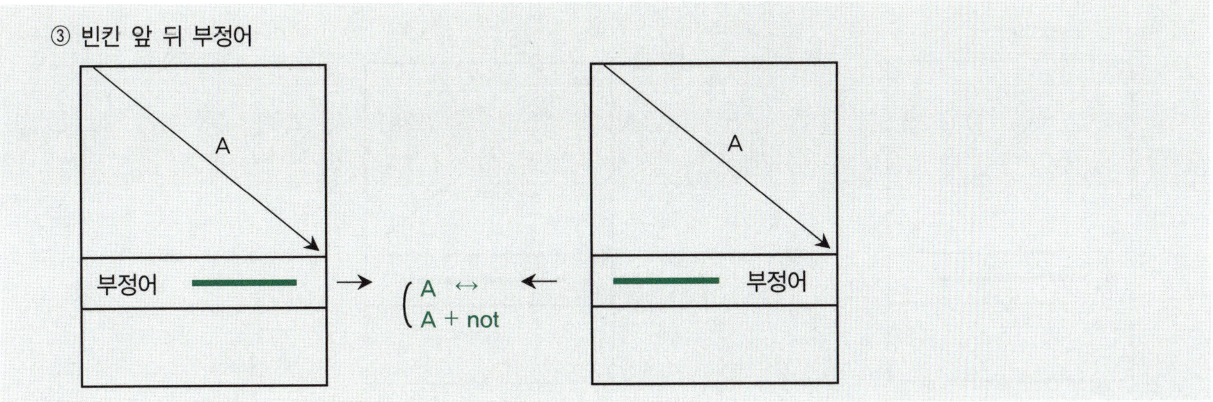



**예제 6** 다음 빈칸에 들어갈 말로 가장 적절한 것은?

Modern psychological theory states that the process of understanding is a matter of construction, not reproduction, which means that the process of understanding takes the form of the interpretation of data coming from the outside and generated by our mind. For example, the perception of a moving object as a car is based on an interpretation of incoming data within the framework of our knowledge of the world. While the interpretation of simple objects is usually an uncontrolled process, the interpretation of more complex phenomena, such as interpersonal situations, usually requires active attention and thought. Psychological studies indicate that it is knowledge possessed by the individual that determines which stimuli become the focus of that individual's attention, what significance he or she assigns to these stimuli, and how they are combined into a larger whole. This subjective world, interpreted in a particular way, is for us the "objective" world; we cannot know any world other than ___________________.

① the reality placed upon us through social conventions
② the one we know as a result of our own interpretations
③ the world of images not filtered by our perceptual frame
④ the external world independent of our own interpretations

④ + / − pattern

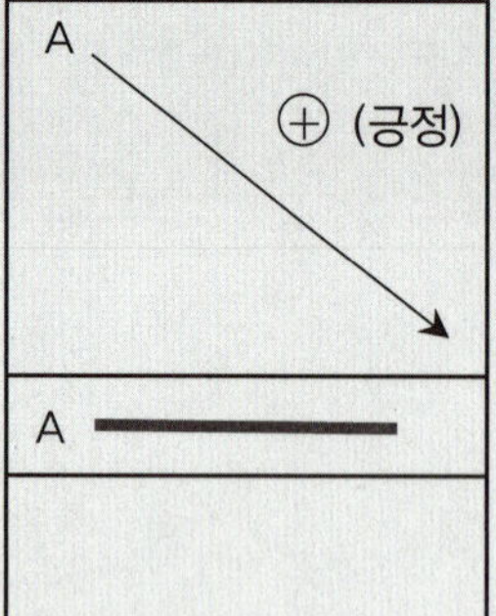

① = (중립)

② − (부정)

③ − (부정)

④ + (긍정)

지문의 내용이 A라는 소재에 대하여 '⊕(긍정)'의 내용이 나오면 A라는 소재로 시작하는 빈칸 문장의 빈칸에 '⊕(긍정)'의 내용을 담고 있는 선지가 정답 선지이다.

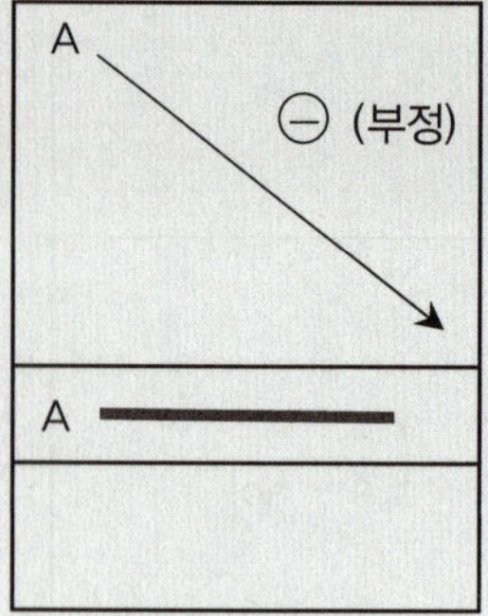

① − (부정)

② + (긍정)

③ = (중립)

④ + (긍정)

지문의 내용이 A라는 소재에 대하여 '⊖(부정)'의 내용이 나오면 A라는 소재로 시작하는 빈칸 문장의 빈칸에 '⊖(부정)'의 내용을 담고 있는 선지가 정답 선지이다.

## 예제 7  다음 빈칸에 들어갈 말로 가장 적절한 것은?

To say that we need to curb anger and our negative thoughts and emotions does not mean that we should deny our feelings. There is an important distinction to be made between denial and restraint. The latter constitutes a deliberate and voluntarily adopted discipline based on an appreciation of the benefits of doing so. This is very different from the case of someone who suppresses emotions such as anger out of a feeling that they need to present a facade of self-control, or out of fear of what others may think. Such behaviour is like closing a wound which is still infected. We are not talking about rule-following. Where denial and suppression occur, there comes the danger that in doing so the individual ___________ anger and resentment. The trouble here is that at some future point they may find they cannot contain these feelings any longer.

① fades out

② copes with

③ stores up

④ soothes

⑤ 인과관계 (＋선후관계)

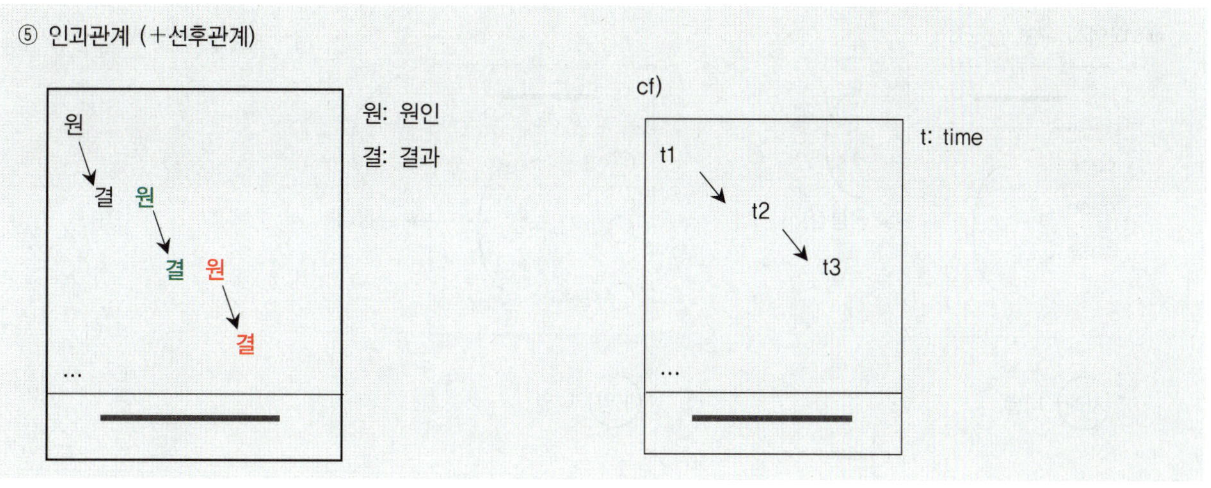





**예제 8** 다음 빈칸에 들어갈 말로 가장 적절한 것은?

Recent evidence suggests that the common ancestor of Neanderthals and modern people, living about 400,000 years ago, may have already been using pretty sophisticated language. If language is based on genes and is the key to cultural evolution, and Neanderthals had language, then why did the Neanderthal toolkit show so little cultural change? Moreover, genes would undoubtedly have changed during the human revolution after 200,000 years ago, but more in response to new habits than as causes of them. At an earlier date, cooking selected mutations for smaller guts and mouths, rather than vice versa. At a later date, milk drinking selected for mutations for retaining lactose digestion into adulthood in people of western European and East African descent. ________________________________. The appeal to a genetic change driving evolution gets gene-culture co-evolution backwards: it is a top-down explanation for a bottom-up process.

① Genetic evolution is the mother of new habits
② The linguistic shovel paves the way for a cultural road
③ The cultural horse comes before the genetic cart
④ When the cultural cat is away, the genetic mice will play

⑥ 나열식 구조

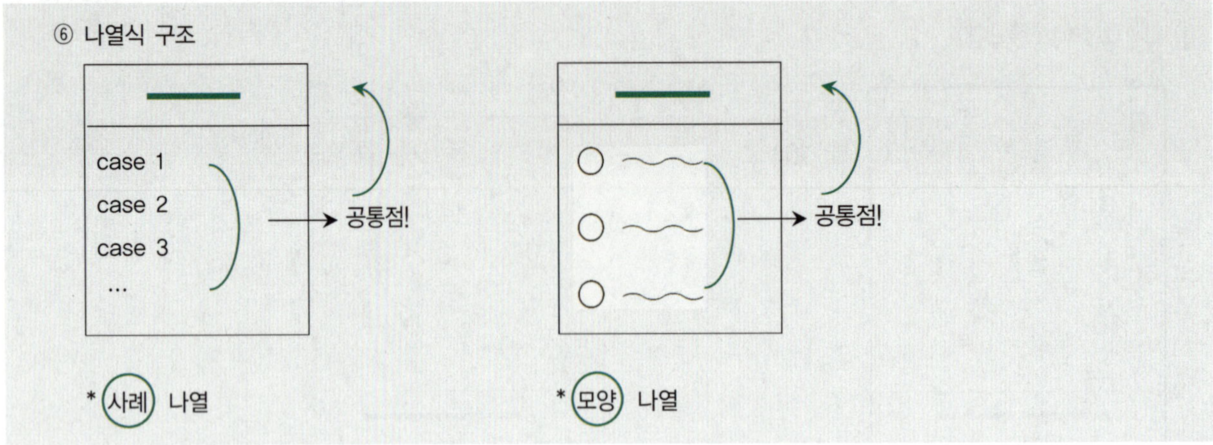


**예제 9** **다음 빈칸에 들어갈 말로 가장 적절한 것은?**

Human are predisposed to ________________________________ . We have all seen the shape of the Big Dipper among the stars  at night, even though the only thing we have really seen are seven points of light. Humans infer meanings not only with visual perceptions but other information as well. Errors in logic are committed by drawing conclusions from  a few facts when no such conclusion is warranted by the available evidence. Retailers know this when they announce low prices on a few very visible items, leading to the inference that overall prices are lower at that store. If one person wins the lottery with a ticket purchased at the local mini-mart, that becomes the lucky location to purchase tickets.

① see whole patterns from partial or random evidence

② prefer simple answers that can be readily comprehended

③ understand the new by a closer study of the world

④ assume that two events which occur together must be related

## + 선택지 Filtering

### 1. 오답 PXC+T

− 출제자가 주제/제목/요지/주장/빈칸추론 선택지 오답을 만드는 원리

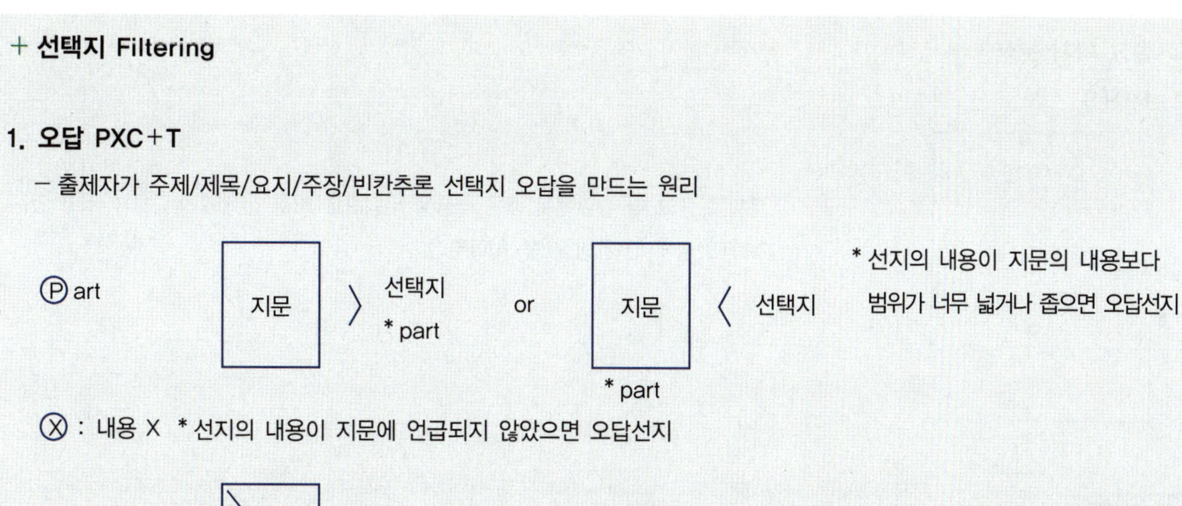


### 2.

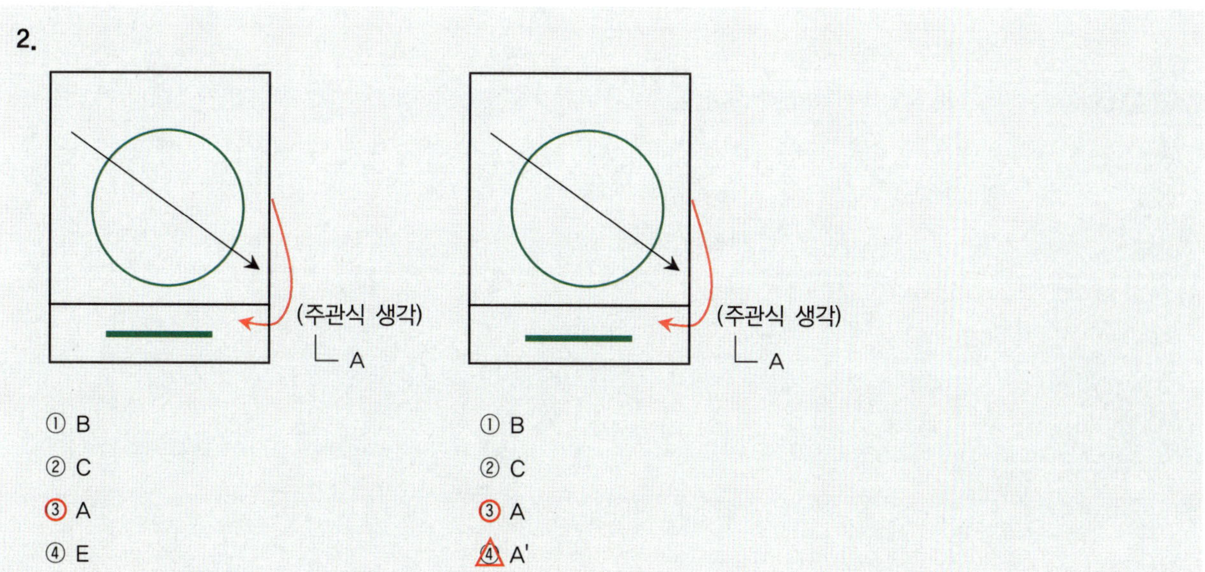

## + 풀고 나서 분석

### 1. MDTS

문제를 풀고 나서 앞에서 배운 내용을 바탕으로 지문 전체에 영향을 미치고 있는 'MDTS(글의 전개 방식)'를 찾아본다.

### 2. $S_2VH$

Vocabulary (어휘)

Structure ((문장)구조)

Heart (마음 – 의미파악)

Selection (선택지)

└ V + S + H + S = $S_2VH$

지문에서 Vocabulary – 몰랐던 어휘 정리

Strucutre – 문장 구조 파악

Heart – 내용 이해

Selection – 선지 분석

이 4가지 '$S_2VH$'를 정리한다.

## 3  순서 배열

### 1. 순서 배열 Basic Mind

CLUES
- 연결사 □
- 지시사 △
- 기타 / paraphrasing ○
  (표현 바꾸기)

### 2. 순서 배열 Approach [Reading Skills]

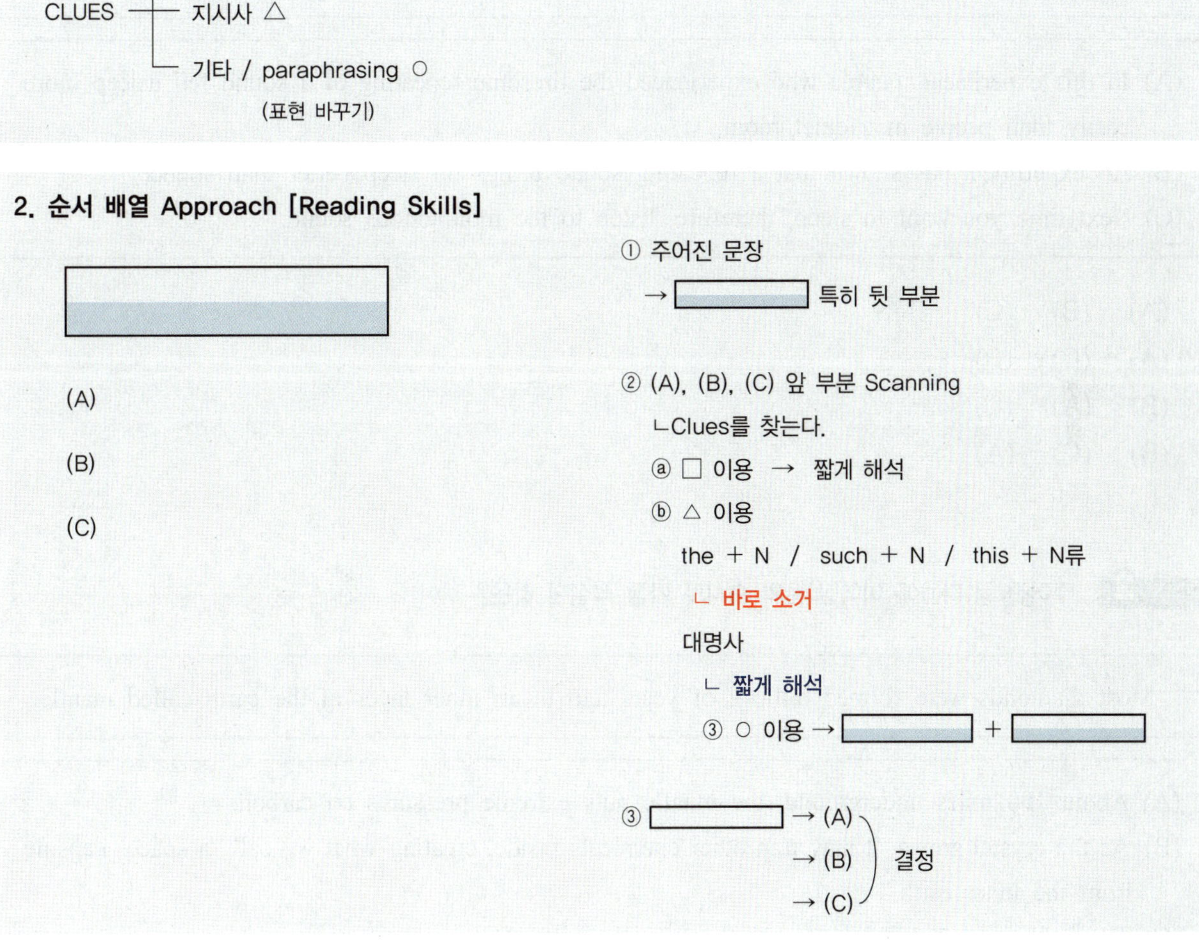

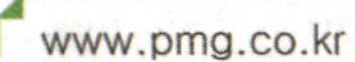

## ③-1  순서 배열 Warming Up!

**예제 1**  주어진 글 다음에 이어질 글의 순서로 가장 적절한 것은?

> If you were trying to fall asleep, would a quiet room be the best place to go?

(A) In this experiment, people who experienced the tiresome repeating of a sound fell asleep more easily than people in a quiet room.
(B) An experiment has shown that a repeating sound brings on sleep better than silence.
(C) Next time you want to sleep, therefore, listen to the monotonous sound.

① (A) − (B) − (C)
② (A) − (C) − (B)
③ (B) − (A) − (C)
④ (B) − (C) − (A)

**예제 2**  주어진 글 다음에 이어질 글의 순서로 가장 적절한 것은?

> Most diamonds were formed billions of years ago in an inner layer of the earth called mantle.

(A) About 100 miles underground, the mantle puts extreme pressures on carbon.
(B) As the crystal grows, it may trap other chemicals inside, creating what we call "a space capsule from the inner earth."
(C) These forces turn black carbon into clear diamond crystal.

① (A) − (B) − (C)
② (A) − (C) − (B)
③ (B) − (C) − (A)
④ (C) − (A) − (B)

**예제 3** 주어진 글 다음에 이어질 글의 순서로 가장 적절한 것은?

Footwear has a history which goes back thousands of years, and it has long been an article of necessity.

(A) The earliest footwear was undoubtedly born of the necessity to provide some protection when moving over rough ground in varying weather conditions. In ancient times, as today, the basic type of shoes worn depended on the climate.

(B) Shoes have not always served such a purely functional purpose, however, and the requirements of fashion have dictated some curious designs, not all of which made walking easy.

(C) For instance, in warmer areas the sandal was, and still is, the most popular form of footwear, whereas the modern moccasin derives from the original shoes adopted in cold climates by races such as Eskimos and Siberians.

① (A) − (B) − (C)
② (A) − (C) − (B)
③ (B) − (C) − (A)
④ (C) − (A) − (B)

## ③ -2  순서 배열 Application

**예제 1**  주어진 글 다음에 이어질 글의 순서로 가장 적절한 것은?

Most consumer magazines depend on subscriptions and advertising. Subscriptions account for almost 90 percent of total magazine circulation. Single-copy, or newsstand, sales account for the rest.

(A) For example, the Columbia Journalism Review is marketed toward professional journalists and its few advertisements are news organizations, book publishers, and others. A few magazines, like Consumer Reports, work toward objectivity and therefore contain no advertising.

(B) However, single-copy sales are important: they bring in more revenue per magazine, because subscription prices are typically at least 50 percent less than the price of buying single issues.

(C) Further, potential readers explore a new magazine by buying a single issue; all those insert cards with subscription offers are included in magazines to encourage you to subscribe. Some magazines are distributed only by subscription.

Professional or trade magazines are specialized magazines and are often published by professional associations. They usually feature highly targeted advertising.

① (B) − (A) − (C)
② (B) − (C) − (A)
③ (C) − (A) − (B)
④ (C) − (B) − (A)

**예제 2** 주어진 글 다음에 이어질 글의 순서로 가장 적절한 것은?

It takes time to develop and launch products. Consequently, many companies know 6—12 months ahead of time that they will be launching a new product.

(A) This marketing technique is called demand creation. It involves creating a buzz about a new potentially revolutionary nutrient or training technique through publishing articles and/or books that stimulate the reader' interest. Once this is done, a new product is launched.

(B) In order to create interest in the product, companies will often launch pre-market advertising campaigns. In the nutrition industry, articles are often written discussing a new nutrient under investigation.

(C) Over a series of issues, you begin to see more articles discussing this new nutrient and potential to enhance training and/or performance. Then, after 4-6 months, a new product is coincidentally launched that contains the ingredient that has been discussed in previous issues. Books and supplement reviews have also been used as vehicles to promote the sale of fitness and nutrition products.

① (B) − (A) − (C)
② (B) − (C) − (A)
③ (C) − (A) − (B)
④ (C) − (B) − (A)

## 예제 3 주어진 글 다음에 이어질 글의 순서로 가장 적절한 것은?

Psychologists Dember and Earl suggested that the motivation for exploration had its roots in a curiosity drive.

(A) This is very important for understanding why people will often return to explore things that they explored before or do things they have done before. In our daily lives, for example, we might decide to listen to a piece of music that we have listened to many times.

(B) They suggested that curiosity is stimulated by novelty and argued that novelty is in the eye of the beholder. We could have seen something many times before, but as the result of having new skills or competence, we discover new or different aspects of that object.

(C) By returning to that music with a new or fresh perspective, perhaps as a result of listening to other music, we find something new and interesting. One reason that people can play a card game such as bridge over and over is that no matter how many times you have played the game, it will be different in some way.

① (B) − (A) − (C)
② (B) − (C) − (A)
③ (C) − (A) − (B)
④ (C) − (B) − (A)

**예제 4** 주어진 글 다음에 이어질 글의 순서로 가장 적절한 것은?

The ancient Greeks sought to improve memory through brain training methods such as memory palaces and the method of loci. At the same time, they and the Egyptians became experts at externalizing information, inventing the modern library, a grand storehouse for externalized knowledge.

(A) We don't know why these simultaneous explosions of intellectual activity occurred when they did (perhaps daily human experience had hit a certain level of complexity). But the human need to organize our lives, our environment, even our thoughts, remains strong.

(B) Dogs have been known to collect their toys and put them in baskets; ants carry off dead members of the colony to burial grounds; certain birds and rodents create barriers around their nests in order to more easily detect invaders.

(C) This need isn't simply learned; it is a biological imperative — animals organize their environments instinctively. Most mammals are biologically programmed to put their digestive waste away from where they eat and sleep.

① (A) − (B) − (C)
② (A) − (C) − (B)
③ (B) − (A) − (C)
④ (B) − (C) − (A)

# 4 문장 삽입

## 1. 문장 삽입 Basic Mind

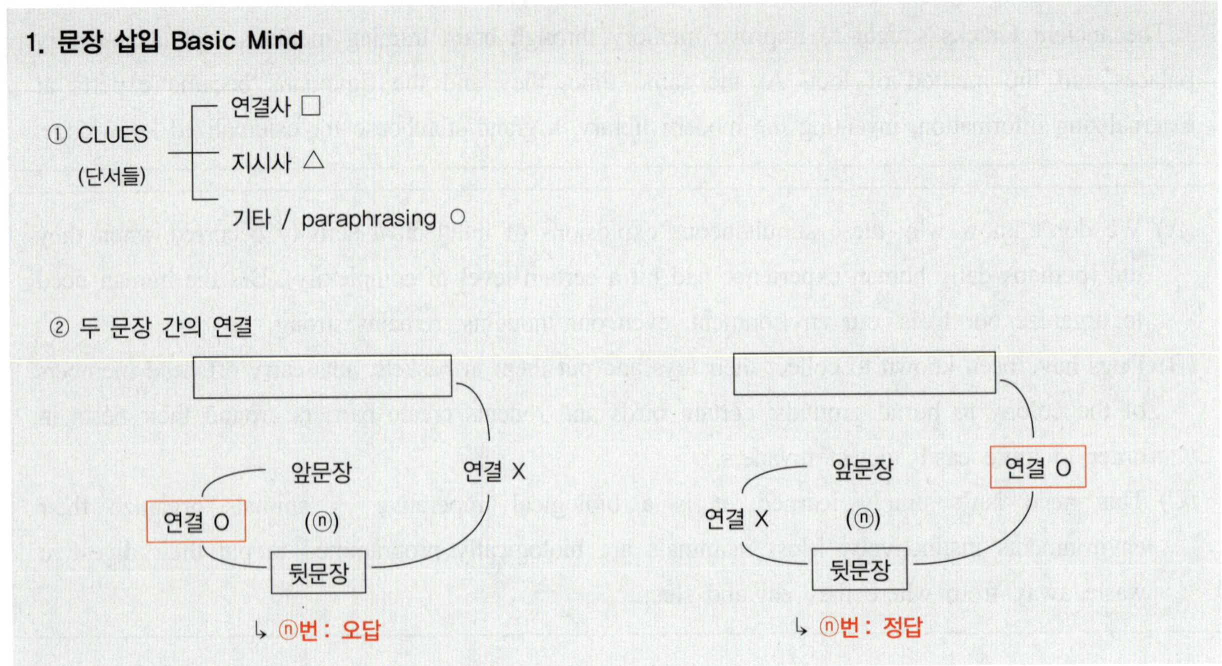


## 2. 문장 삽입 Approach [Reading Skills]

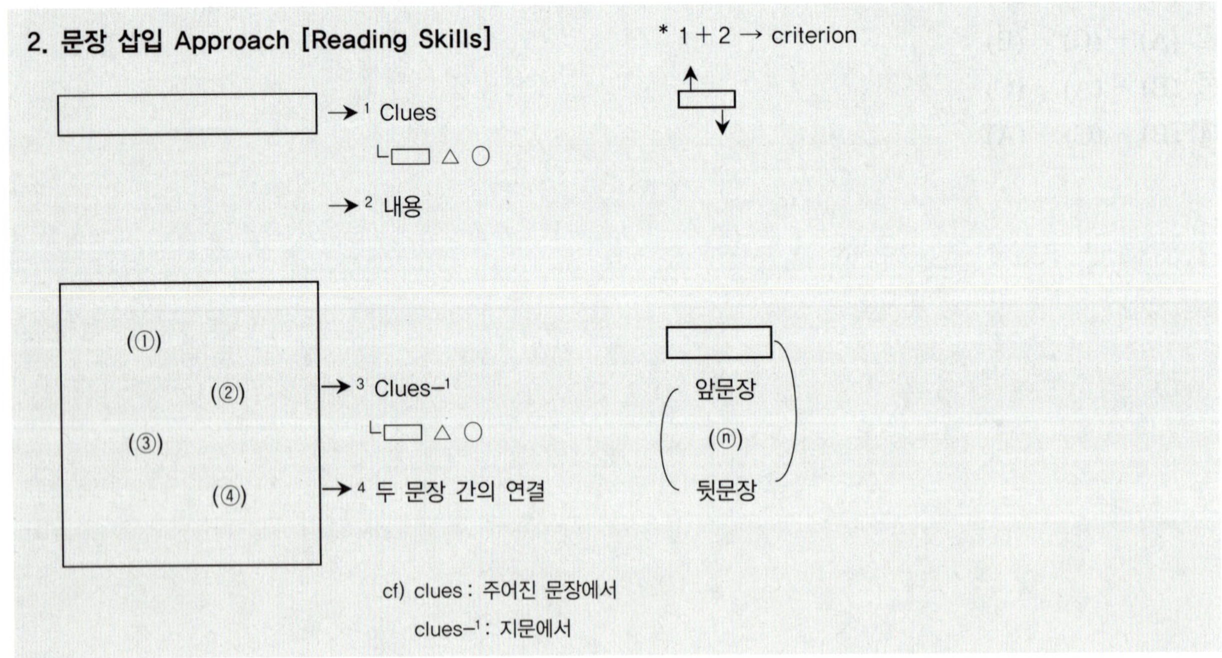

## 4 -1  문장 삽입 Warming Up!

**예제 1**  글의 흐름으로 보아, 주어진 글이 들어가기에 가장 적절한 곳은?

The army gave up on camels, but not everyone did.

Camels are often called ships of the desert. They can carry heavy loads for many days without drinking water. ( ① ) Their broad feet don't sink in the sand and long eyelashes protect their eyes during sandstorms. ( ② ) In 1856, the U.S. Army imported camels for desert duty. ( ③ ) American solders never learned to manage the stubborn animals, though. ( ④ ) Today, over a century later, an American farmer raises fine racing camels in Arizona.

**예제 2**  글의 흐름으로 보아, 주어진 글이 들어가기에 가장 적절한 곳은?

However, sometimes our facial expressions do not match our words.

We often express our feelings by doing things like smiling or frowning. ( ① ) Sometimes we use facial expressions to add information to something we are saying. ( ② ) Think about your classmate. ( ③ ) As she raised her eyebrows, she probably said, "Oh, what a surprise to see you here!" Both her face and words expressed her feeling. ( ④ ) If someone says to you, "I'm fine," but he is looking down and frowning, how do you think he really feels? You can easily know he is trying to hide his feeling.

**예제 3**  글의 흐름으로 보아, 주어진 글이 들어가기에 가장 적절한 곳은?

From there they were taken to Arizona and were reassembled by workers in the Arizona desert.

In the early 1960s, London Bridge was in trouble. Cars, trucks, and buses were too heavy for it, and the bridge was sinking into the Thames river. ( ① ) London city officials wanted to build a new bridge, and a businessman named Robert McCulloch decided to buy the old bridge and move it to Arizona. ( ② ) Workers disassembled the bridge in 1968, numbering the bricks, and sent them to Los Angeles. ( ③ ) The bridge was finally completed in 1971. ( ④ ) However, McCulloch knew he needed more than a famous bridge to attract people to Lake Havasu City, so he created an English village with typical English shops and restaurants. Today, London Bridge is one of Arizona's biggest attractions.

## **4**-2　문장 삽입 Application

**예제 1**　글의 흐름으로 보아, 주어진 글이 들어가기에 적절한 곳은?

Experiments show that rats display an immediate liking for salt the first time they experience a salt deficiency.

Both humans and rats have evolved taste preferences for sweet foods, which provide rich sources of calories. A study of food preferences among the Hadza hunter-gatherers of Tanzania found that honey was the most highly preferred food item, an item that has the highest caloric value. Human newborn infants also show a strong preference for sweet liquids. ( ① ) Both humans and rats dislike bitter and sour foods, which tend to contain toxins. ( ② ) They also adaptively adjust their eating behavior in response to deficits in water, calories, and salt. ( ③ ) They likewise increase their intake of sweets and water when their energy and fluids become depleted. ( ④ ) These appear to be specific evolved mechanisms, designed to deal with the adaptive problem of food selection, and coordinate consumption patterns with physical needs.

**예제 2**　글의 흐름으로 보아, 주어진 글이 들어가기에 적절한 곳은?

But the examination of the accuracy of information obtained in this manner is not a simple matter.

The one area in which the Internet could be considered an aid to thinking is the rapid acquisition of new information. But this is more fictional than real. ( ① ) Yes, the simple act of typing a few words into a search engine will virtually instantaneously produce links related to the topic at hand. ( ② ) What one often gets is no more than abstract summaries of lengthy articles. ( ③ ) As a consequence, I suspect that the number of downloads of any given scientific paper has little relevance to the number of times the entire article has been read from beginning to end. ( ④ ) My advice is that if you want to do some serious thinking, then you' better disconnect the Internet, phone, and television set and try spending twenty-four hours in absolute solitude.

**예제 3**  글의 흐름으로 보아, 주어진 글이 들어가기에 적절한 곳은?

Human beings discovered this art thousands of years ago, and they have invented several devices to make it easier and faster.

In fiber processing the word 'spinning' means two quite different things. One is the formation of individual fibers by squeezing a liquid through one or more small openings in a nozzle called a spinneret and letting it harden. ( ① ) Spiders and silkworms have been spinning fibers in this way for millions of years, but chemists and engineers learned the procedure from them only about a century ago. ( ② ) In the other kind of spinning — sometimes called throwing to prevent confusion with the first kind — two or more fibers are twisted together to form a thread. ( ③ ) The ancient distaff and spindle are examples that were replaced by the spinning wheel in the Middle Ages. ( ④ ) Later came the spinning jenny, the water frame, and Crompton' mule - spinning machines that became symbols of the Industrial Revolution.

**예제 4**  글의 흐름으로 보아, 주어진 글이 들어가기에 적절한 곳은?

Even so, research confirms the finding that nonverbal cues are more credible than verbal cues, especially when verbal and nonverbal cues conflict.

Researchers have reported various nonverbal features of sarcasm. Most disagree as to whether nonverbal cues are essential to the perception of sarcasm or the emotion that prompts it. ( ① ) Also, nonverbal cues are better indicators of speaker intent. ( ② ) As the nature of sarcasm implies a contradiction between intent and message, nonverbal cues may "leak" and reveal the speaker's true mood as they do in deception. ( ③ ) Ostensibly, sarcasm is the opposite of deception in that a sarcastic speaker typically intends the receiver to recognize the sarcastic intent; whereas, in deception the speaker typically intends that the receiver not recognize the deceptive intent. ( ④ ) Thus, when communicators are attempting to determine if a speaker is sarcastic, they compare the verbal and nonverbal message and if the two are in opposition, communicators may conclude that the speaker is being sarcastic.

## 5 문장 제거

### 1. 문장제거 Basic Mind

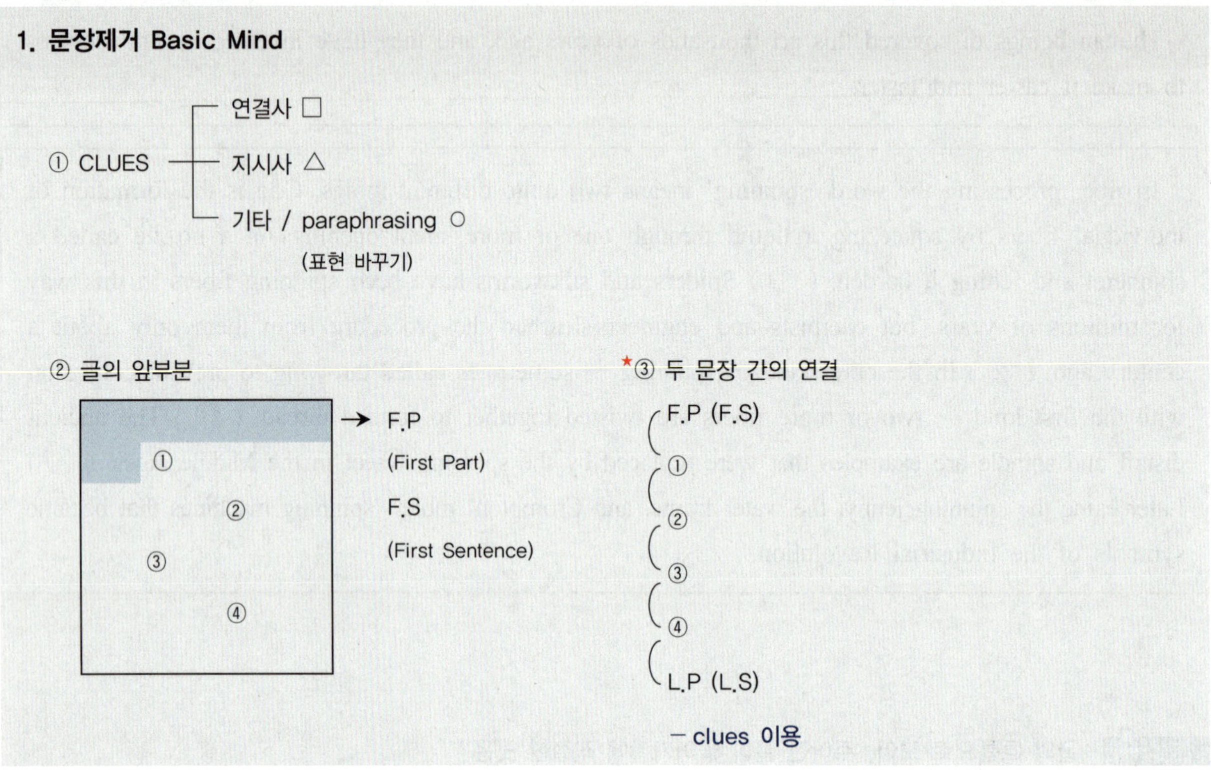

① CLUES ─┬─ 연결사 □
         ├─ 지시사 △
         └─ 기타 / paraphrasing ○
            (표현 바꾸기)

② 글의 앞부분

→ F.P
(First Part)
F.S
(First Sentence)

*③ 두 문장 간의 연결

F.P (F.S)
①
②
③
④
L.P (L.S)

─ clues 이용

### 2. 문장제거 Approch [ Reading Skills]

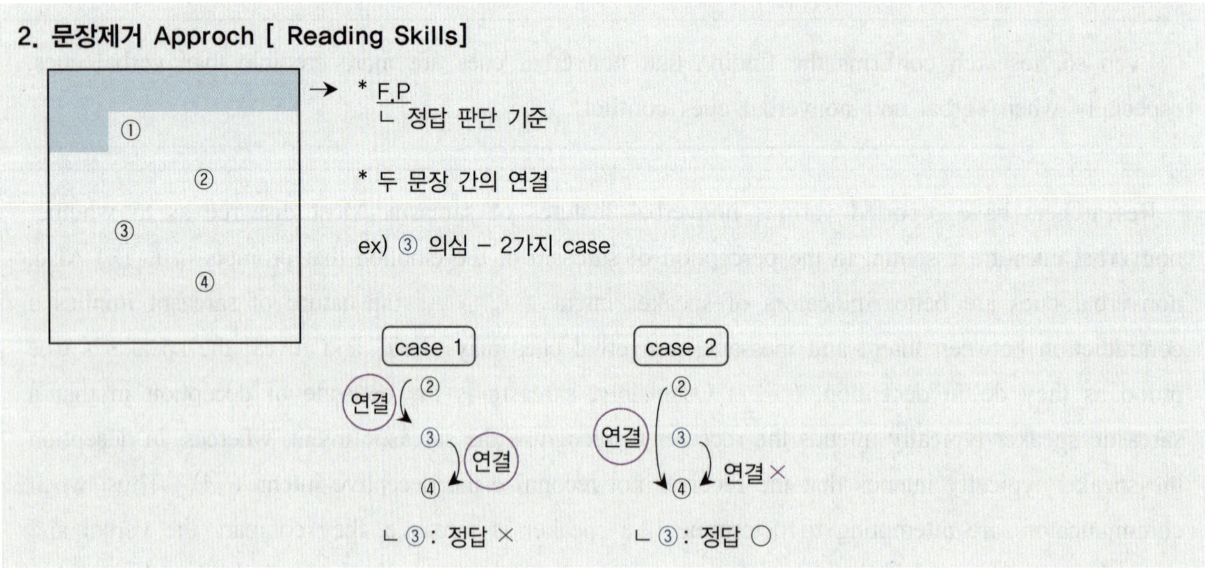

→ * F.P
   └ 정답 판단 기준

* 두 문장 간의 연결

ex) ③ 의심 ─ 2가지 case

case 1
연결 ②
     ③ 연결
       ④
└ ③ : 정답 ×

case 2
연결 ②
     ③
     ④ 연결 ×
└ ③ : 정답 ○

## **5** -1  문장 제거 Warming Up!

**예제 1**  다음 글에서 전체 흐름과 관계없는 문장을 고르시오.

A snowflake forms inside a winter storm cloud when a microscopic piece of dust is trapped inside a tiny drop of water. ① This happens in the atmosphere 10 kilometers above the earth. ② In Alaska, billions of snowflakes fall every winter. ③ The water freezes around the dust, and as this flake is blown by the wind, it collects more drops of water. ④ These drops freeze too. The snowflake becomes heavy enough to fall to the earth.



**예제 2**  다음 글에서 전체 흐름과 관계없는 문장을 고르시오.

The domestic yak is so useful to the inhabitants of Tibet. ① From this animal, the Tibetans get milk and butter. ② They use its hair to make cloth, mats, and tent covering. ③ The flesh of the domestic yak is also useful, as it is often dried or roasted and used as food. ④ The yak is found at heights of 500 meters above sea level. The yak's skin is made into saddles and boots.

**예제 3**  다음 글에서 전체 흐름과 관계없는 문장을 고르시오.

The rainforests are full of plants and animals that need each other and help each other. For example, the ant plants has tunnels in its stems which are just right for ants to live in. ① The ants put bits of dead insects inside some of the tunnels, and then the  ant plant uses them for food. ② The ants also look after a caterpillars which lives inside the ant plant and eats its leaves. ③ Because of this, the ants come out of the ground and attack the caterpillar. ④ In return, the caterpillar makes a special honey mixture which the ants eat. In this way, these three all live together in harmony.

## 5 -2  문장 제거 Application

**예제 1**  다음 글에서 전체 흐름과 관계없는 문장은?

Of the many forest plants that can cause poisoning, wild mushrooms may be among the most dangerous. ① This is because people sometimes confuse the poisonous and edible varieties, or they eat mushrooms without making a positive identification of the variety. ② Many people enjoy hunting wild species of mushrooms in the spring season, because they are excellent edible mushrooms and are highly prized. ③ Farming edible mushrooms at a reasonable cost is an important part to increase profit. ④ However, some wild mushrooms are dangerous, leading people to lose their lives due to mushroom poisoning. To be safe, a person must be able to identify edible mushrooms before eating any wild one.

**예제 2**  다음 글에서 전체 흐름과 관계없는 문장은?

Since the concept of a teddy bear is very obviously not a genetically inherited trait, we can be confident that we are looking at a cultural trait. However, it is a cultural trait that seems to be under the guidance of another, genuinely biological trait: the cues that attract us to babies (high foreheads and small faces). ① Cute, baby-like features are inherently appealing, producing a nurturing response in most humans. ② Indeed, using baby-like images of teddy bear for commercial purposes was faced with severe criticism from animal rights activists. ③ Teddy bears that had a more baby-like appearance — however slight this may have been initially — were thus more popular with customers. ④ Teddy bear manufacturers obviously noticed which bears were selling best and so made more of these and fewer of the less popular models, to maximize their profits. In this way, the selection pressure built up by the customers resulted in the evolution of a more baby-like bear by the manufacturers.

**예제 3** 다음 글에서 전체 흐름과 관계없는 문장은?

Most often, you will find or meet people who introduce themselves in terms of their work or by what they spend time on. These people introduce themselves as a salesman or an executive. ① There is nothing criminal in doing this, but psychologically, we become what we believe. ② People who follow this practice tend to lose their individuality and begin to live with the notion that they are recognized by the job they do. ③ However, jobs may not be permanent, and you may lose your job for countless reasons, some of which you may not even be responsible for. ④ In addition, identifying what we can do in the workplace is not enough to enhance the quality of our professional career. In such a case, these people suffer from an inevitable social and mental trauma, leading to emotional stress and a feeling that all of a sudden they have been disassociated from what once was their identity.

**예제 4** 다음 글에서 전체 흐름과 관계없는 문장은?

Most of the animal-training practices considered good and normal in our world do not take the animals' viewpoint into account. ① Animals should have the right to participate, and to have a say, in their training. ② The true goal of training should be to get animals to do something because they want and choose to, not because we force them to. ③ No matter what anyone says, we must believe that our animals can do whatever task they've set for themselves. ④ Instead, people typically get so involved in doing a program or getting a result-like winning a title in a dog show-or they worry so much about getting hurt, that they fail to listen to what their animals have to say. That's when I get calls about the dogs who are refusing to go in the show ring or the horses who are acting crazy.

# 장대영 영어
## Graphic 독해

1 복합지문
2 글의 목적
3 내용 일치, 불일치

# 실용문

# 실용문

## 1 복합지문

영어 출제기조 변화에 따른 1차, 2차 샘플 문항과 2025년 국가직 시험을 기준으로 봤을 때, 복합지문 (1지문 2문항)은 크게 두 가지 형태로 출제되고 있다.

### 01 제목과 내용 일치, 불일치 문항과의 조합

1. 이 경우 제목 문제는 세부 정보가 나오기 전 앞부분을 보고 답을 선지에서 찾을 수 있는 형태의 문제가 출제된다.
2. 내용 일치, 불일치 문제는 기존의 공무원 내용 일치, 불일치 문제와 다르게 선지가 한글선지이고, 지문과 선지의 배열이 순방향이라서 덜 어렵다.
   cf) 순방향 배열 – 지문의 앞 내용이 선지의 ① ②번에 배치 / 지문의 중간 내용이 선지의 ② ③번에 배치 / 지문의 뒷 내용이 선지의 ③ ④번에 배치되는 형태를 말한다.

### 02 글의 목적과 밑줄 친 단어의 유의어 고르기 문항과의 조합

1. 글의 목적 문제는 앞에서 배운 STS를 이용하거나, 필자의 주관(특히, 1인칭 표현)이 실린 문장을 찾으면 선지에서 답을 쉽게 고를 수 있다.
2. 밑줄 친 유의어 고르기는 기존의 공무원 어휘 문제에 나온 유의어 고르기보다 더 쉬운 단어로 구성되기 때문에 기본 어휘를 숙지한 상태라면, 큰 어려움 없이 답을 고를 수 있다. 그리고 밑줄이 그어진 단어의 뜻을 모를 때는 그 단어를 빈칸으로 만들고, 선지에 있는 단어를 넣어서 문맥에 자연스러운 단어를 선택해도 된다.
   * 실용문으로 문제를 구성하기 때문에, 실용문에 자주 나오는 어휘에 친숙해져 있어야 한다.

**기출 1** 다음 글을 읽고 물음에 답하시오.　　　　2025. 국가직 9급

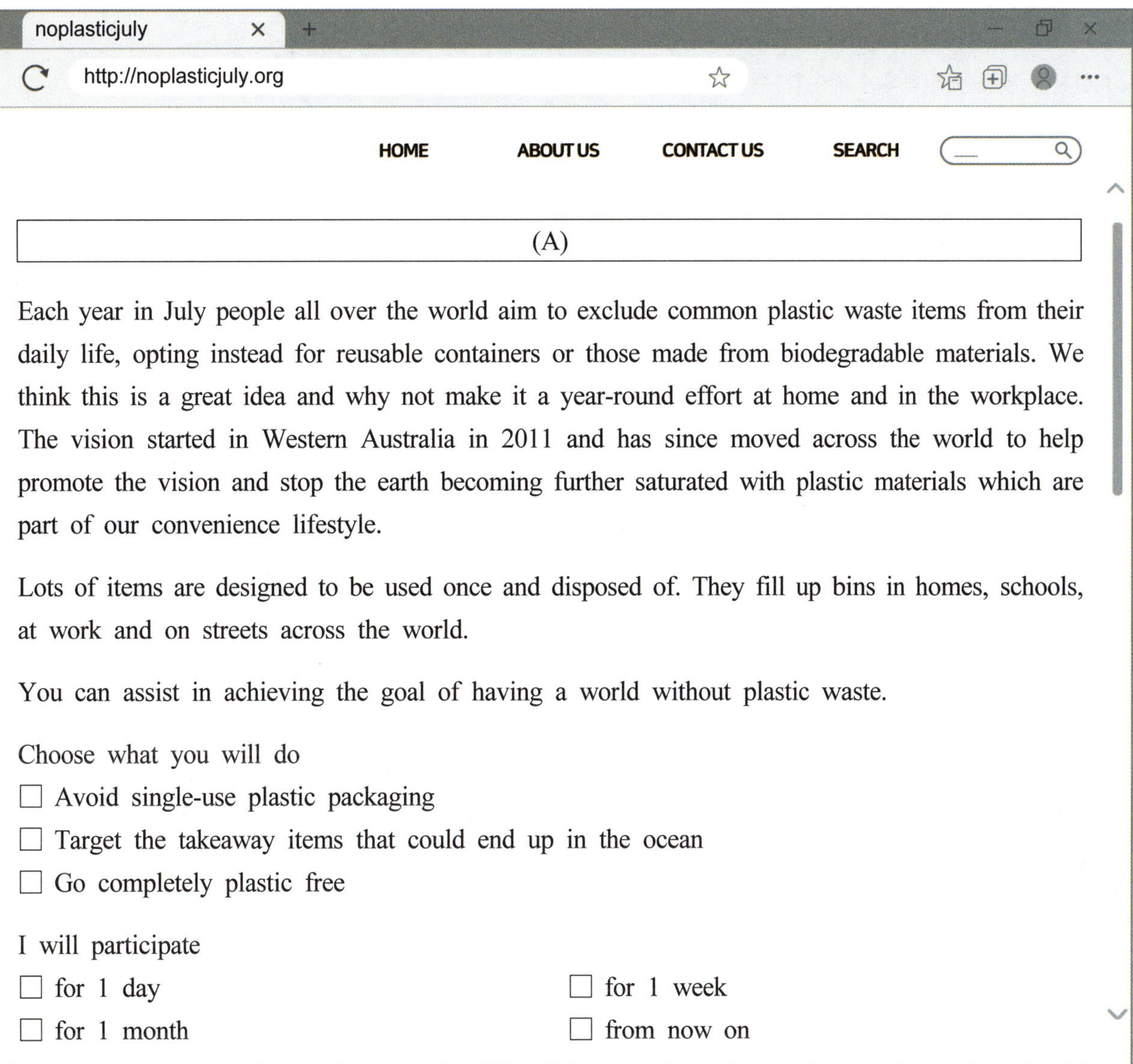


01. (A)에 들어갈 윗글의 제목으로 가장 적절한 것은?

① Development of Single-Use Items

② Join the Plastic-Free Challenge

③ How to Dispose of Plastic Items

④ Simple Ways to Save Energy

**02. 윗글에서 캠페인에 관한 내용과 일치하지 않는 것은?**

① 2011년 서호주에서 시작되었다.

② 플라스틱 과다 사용을 줄이기 위해 전 세계로 확산되었다.

③ 실천할 활동을 선택하여 참여할 수 있다.

④ 최대 한 달까지 참여할 수 있다.

**기출 2** **다음 글을 읽고 물음에 답하시오.**  2025. 국가직 9급

---

## Consular services

We welcome all feedback about our consular services, whether you receive them in the UK or from one of our embassies, high commissions or consulates abroad. Tell us when we get things wrong so that we can <u>assess</u> and improve our services.

If you want to make a complaint about a consular service you have received, we want to help you resolve it as quickly as possible. If you are complaining on behalf of someone else, we must have written, signed consent from that person allowing us to share their personal information with you before we can reply.

Send details of your complaint to our feedback contact form. We will record and examine your complaint, and use the information you provide to help make sure that we offer the best possible help and support to our customers. The relevant embassy, high commission or consulate will reply to you.

---

**01. 밑줄 친 assess의 의미와 가장 가까운 것은?**

① upgrade

② prolong

③ evaluate

④ render

**02. 윗글의 목적으로 가장 적절한 것은?**

① to give directions to the consulate

② to explain how to file complaints

③ to lay out the employment process

④ to announce the opening hours

**예제 1** 다음을 읽고 물음에 답하시오.

---

## Construction Set to Begin on Music Hall

March 25 — Construction on the long-awaited Metro City Orchestra Center is set to begin next month. The music hall has been in its planning stages for over a year and residents have been eagerly awaiting information about the five-story building. Terrance Jacobs, who has been <u>overseeing</u> the design of the building, says construction will take up to one year. The building will feature four different concert halls, each with state-of-the art acoustics. Mr. Jacobs has stated that "the hall will provide a place for music lovers to enjoy their favorite musicians' and composers' works in a comfortable and elegant atmosphere." The music hall will be located directly across from the already greatly successful Metro City Convention Center. "We decided to build the music hall nearby the convention center because of the convenience of the location and also to solidify the location as a cultural hub," said Mr. Jacobs during the recent announcement of construction. Local residents are excited to see the opening of the music hall and attendance to musical events is expected to be high. "I have a great love for classical music and it will be great to finally have somewhere to see the performances that I want," said Tracy Diaz, a local music enthusiast. If you wish to stay up to date on the progress of the construction, you can visit the Metro City Orchestra Center Web site at www.mcocenter.com.

---

01. 위 글에서 언급된 Music Hall에 대해 추론할 수 있는 것으로 가장 적절한 것은?

① It will open next month.

② It will offer classical music.

③ It is nearing completion.

④ It will be next to the convention center.

02. 밑줄 친 "overseeing"의 의미와 가장 가까운 것은?

① supervising

② allocating

③ engineering

④ processing

## 2 글의 목적

글의 목적 문제는 앞에서 배운 STS를 이용하거나, 필자의 주관(특히, 1인칭 표현)이 실린 문장을 찾으면 선지에서 답을 쉽게 고를 수 있다.

**기출 1** 다음 글의 목적으로 가장 적절한 것은?　　　　　　　　　2025. 국가직 9급

Dear Members of the Woodville City Council,

I am writing to inform you of several issues in our community that need attention. A resident, John Smith, of 123 Elm Street, has reported problems with the road conditions on Elm Street, especially between Maple Avenue and Oak Street. There are many potholes and cracks that have worsened after recent heavy rain, causing traffic disruptions and safety hazards. Even though temporary repairs have been made, the problems continue.

The resident is also concerned about poor lighting in Central Park, especially along Park Lane, because broken or missing streetlights have led to minor accidents and lowered property values. He requests that the Council repair Elm Street and improve the lighting in the park.

I urge the Council to address these issues for the safety and well-being of our community. Thank you for your attention to these matters. I trust we will work together to resolve these issues effectively.

Sincerely,

Stephen James

Head of Woodville City Council

① to express gratitude to the Council for their efforts

② to invite the Council to visit Central Park

③ to solicit the Council to deal with the community problems

④ to update the Council on recent repairs made in the area

| | Send | Preview | Save |
|---|---|---|---|
| **To** | derrick85@naver.com | | |
| **From** | martinauto@google.com | | |
| **Date** | June 6. 2025 | | |
| **Subject** | membership into our orgnization | | |

Dear Mr. Martin,

The Mechanics Association of America (MAA) would like to let you know that you are eligible for membership into our organization. As a professional mechanic, you have a lot to gain by joining us. One of the benefits is that you will receive a free subscription to Mechanics Today, the official magazine of the MAA. This magazine, which is delivered monthly, has numerous articles and tips on how to improve your skills as a mechanic.

The MAA also sponsors special events all around the country. We put on seminars that explain how to repair some of the newest cars. One of them, incidentally, will be in Columbus this year. We also sponsor conferences and other events throughout the year. If this sounds interesting to you, call me at 1-800-MECHANIC, and we can discuss your membership.

Sincerely,

Ray Brothers
Mechanics Association of America

① To encourage a person to purchase a magazine
② To make an invitation to a special seminar
③ To announce a special event to be held next month
④ To ask a person to become a member of a group

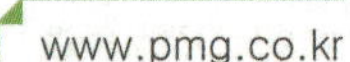

## 3  내용 일치, 불일치

1. 내용 일치, 불일치 문제는 기존의 공무원 내용 일치, 불일치 문제와 다르게 선지가 한글 선지이고, 지문과 선지의 배열이 순방향이라서 덜 어렵다.
   cf) 순방향 배열 ― 지문의 앞 내용이 선지의 ① ②번에 배치 / 지문의 중간 내용이 선지의 ② ③번에 배치 / 지문의 뒷 내용이 선지의 ③ ④번에 배치되는 형태를 말한다.
2. 기존의 일치, 불일치 문제와 다르게 실용문으로 문제를 구성하기 때문에, 실용문에 자주 나오는 어휘에 친숙해져 있어야 한다.

**기출 1**  다음 글의 내용과 일치하지 않는 것은?　　　　　　　　　　　2025. 국가직 9급

---

### KIDS SUMMER ART CAMP 2025

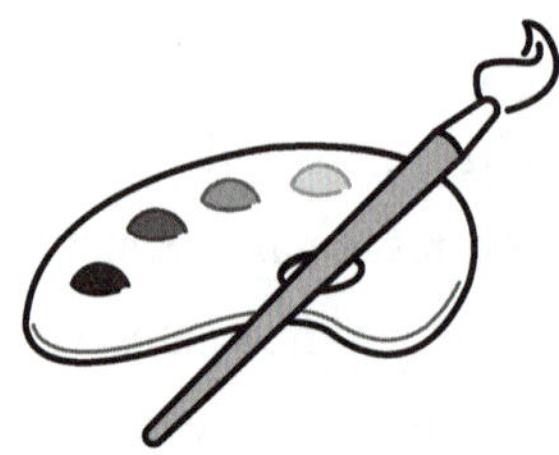

Join the Stan José Art Museum (SJAM) for a week of fun!

Campers get behind-the-scenes access to exhibitions, experiment with the artistic process, and show off their own work in a student exhibition.

**WHO**

For children ages 6 - 14

Each camper will receive individual artistic support, encouragement, and creative challenges unique to their learning style and skill level.

**WHAT**

Join SJAM for a summer art camp that pairs creative exploration of art materials and processes led by our experienced gallery teachers and studio art educators. In addition, campers will engage in interpretive art and science lessons created by Eddie Brown, a STEM consultant.

**ART CAMP EXHIBITION**

We invite families and caregivers to attend a weekly exhibition reception of campers' artwork to celebrate the artistic achievements of each participant.

**WHEN**

All camps run 9 am - 3 pm, Monday - Friday.

Monday, June 9 - Friday, July 25 (no camp the week of June 30)

---

① Campers will have opportunities to display their work in a student exhibition.

② The camp includes individual artistic support for children ages 6 - 14.

③ A STEM consultant developed interpretive art and science lessons.

④ The camp runs with no break between June 9 and July 25.

**기출 2**  다음 글의 내용과 일치하는 것은?

2025. 국가직 9급

## Department of Health and Human Services

### Mission Statement

The mission of the Department of Health and Human Services (HHS) is to enhance the health and well-being of all individuals in the nation, by providing for effective health and human services and by fostering sound, sustained advances in the sciences underlying medicine, public health, and social services.

### Organizational Structure

HHS accomplishes its mission through programs and initiatives that cover a wide spectrum of activities. Eleven operating divisions, including eight agencies in the Public Health Service and three human services agencies, administer HHS's programs. While HHS is a domestic agency working to protect and promote the health and well-being of the American people, the interconnectedness of our world requires that HHS engage globally to fulfill its mission.

### Cross-Agency Collaborations

Improving health and human services outcomes cannot be achieved by the Department on its own; collaborations are critical to achieve our goals and objectives. HHS collaborates closely with other federal departments and agencies on cross-cutting topics.

① HHS aims to improve the health and well-being of low-income families only.

② HHS's programs are administered by the eleven operating divisions.

③ HHS does not work with foreign countries to complete its mission.

④ HHS acts independently from other federal departments and agencies to achieve its goals.

**예제 1** 다음 글의 Hotel Andromeda에 대한 내용으로 가장 적절한 것을 고르시오.

### Hotel Andromeda

We are located in the downtown area, right next to Lakeshore Boulevard. Being only 10 minutes from both baseball stadium Eaton's Center and Exhibition Place, Hotel Andromeda is an ideal place for your weekend of business or pleasure. It is only 20 minutes to the region's only international airport and just minutes from multiple subway stations and bus lines. All of our rooms include mini-fridges, Wi-Fi access, cable television, and desk space. The swimming pool is available to all guests, and for no extra charge anyone staying at least two nights can enjoy our state-of-the-art fitness center.

The meeting chambers throughout the left wing of the hotel can accommodate groups from 10 to 400 people. Hotel Andromeda is an ideal venue for corporate events. Our event planner can aid your company in setting up conferences, meetings, and other events.

To book rooms of any size, please contact us at 123-458-7430, or e-mail us at andromedares@hotel.net. To contact our corporate event planner, please call 123-458-7222. You can find more information about the Andromeda Hotel, including directions to the premises, on our Web site at www.andromeda@hotel.net.

① It does not have any mass transit access.

② It has been in business for over 10 years.

③ It specializes in wedding and anniversary parties.

④ Its meeting rooms can accommodate up to 400 people.

# MEMO

장대영 영어
# Graphic 독해

# 정답 및 해설

## Chapter 01 STS(중요 문장 찾기)

### STS 1 의무/필요

| 예제 1 | ④ | 예제 2 | ① |
|---|---|---|---|

### STS 2 '중요한'의 의미를 가진 형용사

| 예제 1 | ② |
|---|---|

### STS 3 결론/요약

| 예제 1 | ② |
|---|---|

### STS 4 역접장치

| 예제 1 | ④ | 예제 2 | ② |
|---|---|---|---|

### STS 5 not 과 but 의 A B 접속사

| 예제 1 | ① |
|---|---|

### STS 6 명령문

| 예제 1 | ④ |
|---|---|

### STS 7 양보절과 주절

| 예제 1 | ④ | 예제 2 | ③ |
|---|---|---|---|

### STS 8 강조표현

#### 1. It – that 강조구문

| 예제 1 | ② |
|---|---|

#### 2. 강조의 Only / 강조의 do / the very N

| 예제 1 | ② | 예제 2 | ① |
|---|---|---|---|

#### 3. 최상급 / 비교급 강조 6

| 예제 1 | ③ | 예제 2 | ③ |
|---|---|---|---|

### STS 9 1인칭의 활용

| 예제 1 | ④ |
|---|---|

### STS 10 필자의 판단 주입 어휘와 표현의 이용

| 예제 1 | ① | 예제 2 | ② |
|---|---|---|---|

### STS 11 The + 비교급, the + 비교급

| 예제 1 | ② | 예제 2 | ④ |
|---|---|---|---|

## Chapter 02 MDTS(글의 전개 방식)

### 1 연구 – 실험의 인용

| 예제 1 | ④ |
|---|---|

### 2 권위자

| 예제 1 | ③ | 예제 2 | ① |
|---|---|---|---|
| 예제 3 | ① | | |

### 3 의문문의 활용

#### 1. 첫 문장이 의문문 / 2. 중간 의문문

| 예제 1 | ④ | 예제 2 | ③ |
|---|---|---|---|

#### 3. 마지막 문장이 의문문

| 예제 1 | ① |
|---|---|

### 4 통념비판의 원리

| 예제 1 | ③ | 예제 2 | ③ |
|---|---|---|---|

### 5 문제점 발생 – 해결책 제시

| 예제 1 | ① | 예제 2 | ② |
|---|---|---|---|

### 6 시간상의 대조

| 예제 1 | ③ | 예제 2 | ④ |
|---|---|---|---|

### 7 예시

| 예제 1 | ① | 예제 2 | ③ |
|---|---|---|---|
| 예제 3 | ① | 예제 4 | ④ |
| 예제 5 | ③ | 예제 6 | ④ |
| 예제 7 | ② | | |

### 8 Story / 일화

| 예제 1 | ② | 예제 2 | ① |
|---|---|---|---|

### 9 설명문

| 예제 1 | ① | 예제 2 | ② |
|---|---|---|---|

### 10 열거

| 예제 1 | ③ | 예제 2 | ① |
|---|---|---|---|

## 11 나열식 구조

| 예제 1 | ④ | 예제 2 | ② |
|---|---|---|---|
| 예제 3 | ② | | |

## 12 인과관계

| 예제 1 | ① |
|---|---|

## Chapter 03 CLUES(문장 간의 연결 관계)

### 1 연결사

| 예제 1 | ④ | 예제 2 | ② |
|---|---|---|---|
| 예제 3 | ④ | 예제 4 | ① |
| 예제 5 | ② | 예제 6 | ③ |
| 예제 7 | ① | 예제 8 | ② |

### 3 지시사

| 예제 1 | ③ | 예제 2 | ② |
|---|---|---|---|

## Chapter 04 TYPES(유형별 접근)

### 1 주제/제목/요지/주장 Application

| 예제 1 | ② | 예제 2 | ④ |
|---|---|---|---|
| 예제 3 | ③ | 예제 4 | ① |
| 예제 5 | ② | 예제 6 | ③ |
| 예제 7 | ① | 예제 8 | ④ |
| 예제 9 | ① | 예제 10 | ② |

### 2 빈칸

#### 1. Types

| 예제 1 | ① | 예제 2 | ③ |
|---|---|---|---|
| 예제 3 | ① | 예제 4 | ③ |

#### 2. 활용

| 예제 1 | ④ | 예제 2 | ② |
|---|---|---|---|
| 예제 3 | ③ | 예제 4 | ① |
| 예제 5 | ④ | 예제 6 | ② |
| 예제 7 | ③ | 예제 8 | ③ |
| 예제 9 | ① | | |

### 3-1 순서 배열 Warming Up!

| 예제 1 | ③ | 예제 2 | ② |
|---|---|---|---|
| 예제 3 | ② | | |

### 3-2 순서 배열 Application

| 예제 1 | ② | 예제 2 | ② |
|---|---|---|---|
| 예제 3 | ① | 예제 4 | ② |

### 4-1 문장 삽입 Warming Up!

| 예제 1 | ④ | 예제 2 | ④ |
|---|---|---|---|
| 예제 3 | ③ | | |

### 4-2 문장 삽입 Application

| 예제 1 | ③ | 예제 2 | ③ |
|---|---|---|---|
| 예제 3 | ③ | 예제 4 | ① |

### 5-1 문장 제거 Warming Up!

| 예제 1 | ② | 예제 2 | ④ |
|---|---|---|---|
| 예제 3 | ③ | | |

### 5-2 문장 제거 Application

| 예제 1 | ③ | 예제 2 | ② |
|---|---|---|---|
| 예제 3 | ④ | 예제 4 | ③ |

## Chapter 05 실용문

### 1 복합지문

| 기출 1 | 01. ② 02. ④ | 기출 2 | 01. ③ 02. ② |
|---|---|---|---|
| 예제 1 | 01. ② 02. ① | | |

### 2 글의 목적

| 기출 1 | ③ | 예제 1 | ④ |
|---|---|---|---|

### 3 내용 일치, 불일치

| 기출 1 | ④ | 기출 2 | ② |
|---|---|---|---|
| 예제 1 | ④ | | |

**예제 1**  다음 글의 주제로 가장 적절한 것은?  **정답** ④ 

The New Shorter Oxford English Dictionary defines a market as "a meeting or gathering place of people for the purchase and sale of provisions or livestock" and as "the action or business of buying and selling" But markets aren't merely meeting places or a series of transactions; they are social institutions that must be built up and maintained. Initially markets may be thrown up spontaneously, but in the end they are socially sustained; all markets depend for their operation on a complex of social, cultural, and legal institutions. In order for exchanges to constitute the structure of a market many elements have to be in place: property rights need to be defined and protected, rules for making contracts need to be specified and enforced, information needs to flow smoothly, and people need to be induced through internal and external mechanisms to behave in a trustworthy manner.

① problems with the modern market economy
② controversy over the role of markets
③ strength of the modern market economy
④ elements of a market as a social system

**해석** The New Shorter Oxford English Dictionary는 시장을 '식량이나 가축을 사고팔기 위하여 사람들이 만나거나 모이는 장소'와 '사고파는 활동이나 업무'라고 정의한다. 그러나 시장은 만나는 장소나 일련의 거래일 뿐만이 아니라, 개발되고 유지되어야 하는 사회적 제도이다. 처음에 시장은 자연적으로 갑자기 만들어질지도 모르지만, 결국 그것들은 사회적으로 유지되고, 모든 시장은 그 운용을 사회적, 문화적, 그리고 법률적 제도의 복합체에 의존한다. 교역이 시장의 구조를 구성하기 위하여, 많은 요소들이 준비되어야 하는데 즉, 재산권이 정의되고 보호되어야 하고, 계약을 맺기 위한 규칙들이 명시되고 실시되어야 하며, 정보가 순조롭게 순환되어야 하고, 사람들이 신뢰할 수 있는 방식으로 행동하도록 내적, 외적 구조를 통하여 유도되어야 한다.
① 현대 시장 경제의 문제점들
② 시장에 역할에 대한 논쟁들
③ 현대 시장 경제의 장점
④ 사회적 시스템으로서의 시장이 갖춰야 할 요인들

**해설** STS 'But / not merely A ; B / must'가 들어간 문장 — But markets aren't merely meeting places or a series of transactions; they are social institutions that must be built up and maintained.
+
STS 'have to'가 들어간 문장 — In order for exchanges to constitute the structure of a market many elements have to be in place.
이 두 문장이 답 도출 근거 문장들이다.

**어휘** define 정의를 내리다, 정의하다  provision 마련, 공급  merely 그저  transaction 거래  institution 제도  sustain 지속시키다  enforce 실시하다, 억지로 시키다  induce 유도하다

**예제 2** 다음 글의 요지로 가장 적절한 것은?   **정답** ①

CHAPTER 01

---

If the listener is to appreciate the form and beauty of symphony, it is imperative that he should understand such the structure of symphony. A symphony has normally four movements. The opining movement of the symphony takes the sonata form, and has at least two important themes. Each theme is usually introduced early in the introductory section. While the first movement of a symphony is usually the most important, the other three may be equally beautiful. The second movement is slow. This is in contrast to the quicker tempos of the first. The third movement is traditionally faster; in classical symphony it was a minuet. The finale is the fourth movement of the symphony and usually balances the mood and pace of the first movement.

---

① 심포니는 일정한 구조를 이해하는 것이 그 감상을 위해 필요하다.
② 심포니는 다른 무엇보다도 각 악기들의 조화와 균형을 가장 중요시한다.
③ 현대의 심포니는 고전적 심포니의 형식과는 완전히 다르게 발전하고 있다.
④ 심포니는 대체적으로 보통 사람들이 이해하기 어려운 음악 형식으로 되어 있다.

**해석** 만일 청취자가 심포니의 형식과 아름다움을 이해하고자 한다면, 심포니의 그러한 구조에 대해서 이해하는 일은 필수적이다. 심포니는 통상적으로 4개의 악장을 갖고 있다. 심포니의 시작 악장은 소나타의 형식을 취하고, 적어도 두 개의 중요한 주제가 있다. 각 주제는 일반적으로 초기의 도입 섹션에서 소개되게 된다. 심포니의 제1장은 보통 가장 중요한데, 반면 다른 세 개의 악장은 동등하게 아름답다. 두 번째 악장은 느리다. 이것은 보다 빠른 제1악장과 대조된다. 세 번째 악장은 전통적으로 더 빠르다. 고전 심포니에 있어서는 그것은 미뉴엣이다. 피날레는 제4악장이고 보통 제1악장의 분위기와 속도를 조율한다.

**해석** STS 'imperative / should'가 들어간 문장 — If the listener is to appreciate the form and beauty of symphony, it is imperative that he should understand such the structure of symphony.
이 문장이 답 도출 근거 문장이다.

**어휘** imperative 피할 수 없는   introductory 입문

## STS 2 '중요한'의 의미를 가진 형용사

**예제 1** 다음 글의 주제로 가장 적절한 것은?   정답 ②

More and more parents believe that their children don't have to participate in physical activity if they don't want to. However, physical education (PE) is an important part of holistic schooling. It is about educating the whole person, a holistic education betters us in an all-round sense, rather than a merely academic experience. Some aspects of physical education are vital for future well-being, for example, being able to swim and learning to lift heavy weights safely. Arguments about cost seem petty when compared to this aim and also misguided, since PE departments would continue to exist to serve those that chose to study PE voluntarily, even if the subject were no longer compulsory. I believe that PE is a crucial element of all round schooling and our society's well-being.

① 체육 교육 예산을 다른 과목에 투입해야 한다.
② 체육 교육이 중요한 만큼 지속적으로 실시되어야 한다.
③ 부모들은 학교의 교육 방식에 관여하지 말아야 한다.
④ 교내 체육 활동은 세분화되고 다양성을 확보해야 한다.

**해석** 점점 더 많은 부모들이 그들의 자녀들이 원하지 않는다면 체육 활동에 참여하지 않아도 된다고 믿고 있다. 그러나 체육은 전인 교육의 중요한 일부분이다. 체육은 단순히 학문적인 경험이라기보다는 전인적인 인간을 교육하는 것, 우리를 전반적인 의미에서 더 향상시켜 주는 전인 교육과 관련이 있다. 체육의 몇몇 측면들은, 예를 들자면, 수영을 할 수 있다거나 바벨을 안전하게 들어 올리는 방법을 배우는 것처럼 미래의 복지에 필수적이다. 비용에 대한 논쟁도 이러한 목표에 비하면 하찮기 그지없고, 또한 잘못 이해하고 있는 것처럼 보이는데, 왜냐하면 그 과목(체육)이 더 이상 필수 과목이 아니게 된다 해도 체육을 자발적으로 배우기로 한 학생들의 요구에 부응하기 위해 체육부서는 계속 존재할 것이기 때문이다. 나는 체육이 다방면에 걸친 학교 교육과 우리 사회의 복지를 위해서 아주 중대한 요소라고 믿고 있다.

**해설** STS 'However / important'가 들어간 문장 — However, physical education (PE) is an important part of holistic schooling.
+
STS 'I believe / crucial'이 들어간 문장 — I believe that PE is a crucial element of all-round schooling and our society's well-being.
이 두 문장이 답 도출 근거 문장들이다.

**어휘** holistic 전체적인   compulsory 강제적인, 의무적인, 필수

## STS 3 결론/요약

### 예제 1 다음 글의 제목으로 가장 적절한 것은?　　　　　　　정답 ②

The challenges for us today are the same as they were during the days of the Romans; we just have more advanced methodologies and technologies to apply to the water loss problem. We can look back at past efforts and smile and think that we are so much better, but to be honest we just have better tools. An open mind, an unwillingness to accept existing inefficiencies, and a wish to improve are the basic skills that we need to have today. The rest can be obtained as work progresses. Water loss control programs will only be successful if we are willing to accept what we find and act on it openly. Therefore, it is critical that we understand the extent and impact of water loss, and the control of water loss holds a priority of paramount importance.

① Understanding the Steps of Water Loss
② What Needs to Be Done to Decrease Water Loss?
③ The Occurrence and Bad Influence of Water Loss
④ How Much Water Are We Wasting in Our Daily Lives?

**해석** 오늘날 우리에게 닥친 도전들은 로마 시대 동안의 그것들과 같다. 우리는 단지 물 손실 문제들에 적용할 더 진보된 방법론들과 기술들을 갖고 있을 뿐이다. 우리는 과거의 노력들을 되돌아보고 우리가 훨씬 더 낫다고 생각하며 미소 지을 수도 있지만, 정직하게 말하면 우리는 단지 더 좋은 기술들을 갖고 있을 뿐이다. 개방된 마음, 현재의 비효율을 받아들이려 하지 않는 마음, 그리고 개선하려는 소망이 오늘날 우리가 지닐 필요가 있는 기본적인 자질들이다. 나머지는 일이 진행됨에 따라서 얻을 수 있다. 물 손실 관리 프로그램들은 우리가 발견하는 것을 기꺼이 인정하고 숨김없이 그것에 따라 행동한다면 성공을 거둘 것이다. 그러므로 우리가 물 손실의 정도와 영향을 이해해야 하는 것이 아주 중요하고, 물 손실의 통제가 최고로 중요한 우선권을 갖는다.
① 물 손실의 단계를 이해하기
② 물 손실을 줄이기 위하여 무엇을 행동에 옮겨야 할 것인가?
③ 물 손실의 발생과 나쁜 영향
④ 우리의 일상 생활에서 우리는 얼마나 많은 물을 낭비하고 있는가?

**해설** STS 'Therefore / critical / priority / of paramount importance'가 **들어간 문장** – Therefore, it is critical that we understand the extent and impact of water loss, and the control of water loss holds a priority of paramount importance
이 문장이 답 도출 근거 문장이다.

**어휘** methodology 방법론　unwillingness 내키지 않음　obtain 얻다　extent 정도　priority 우선순위　paramount 최고의, 주요한 occurrence 발생

## STS ④ 역접장치

**예제 1** 다음 글의 요지로 가장 적절한 것은?    정답 ④

> I was thrilled when your establishment moved into our neighborhood. I appreciate the convenience that your family-run business provides. Your store is always clean and well-stocked, and your workers are always attentive and knowledgeable. But I would like to bring one consideration to your attention, and that is the cost of your merchandise. I realize that a family-run business will be more expensive than a chain store, and I've been willing to pay that difference. Frequently, however, your prices are nearly double what I would have paid at other stores. I want to continue shopping at your store, but I'm not sure I can consistently afford to pay such high prices.

① 상점의 이용이 편리하다.
② 상품이 아주 잘 진열되어 있다.
③ 상점 운영시간이 지나치게 짧다.
④ 상점의 물건 값이 너무 비싸다.

**해석** 저는 당신의 시설물(가게)이 우리 이웃(근처)으로 이사 올 때 너무 좋았어요. 저는 당신의 가족들이 운영하는 가게에서 제공하는 편리함을 높이 평가했습니다.('고맙게 생각했습니다'로 해석해도 됨.) 당신의 가게는 늘 깨끗하고, 물건들이 잘 갖추어져 있고, 또 일하시는 분들이 늘 친절하고 식견이 풍부하십니다. 하지만 저는 한 가지 고려해야 할 문제를 당신께 전하고 싶은데, 그건 다름이 아니고 당신 물건들의 가격입니다. 저는 가족들이 운영하는 가게가 체인점 가게보다 더 비싸게 받는 것을 이해합니다, 그리고 그 차액을 기꺼이 지불해 왔습니다. 그런데, 종종(자주) 당신 가게의 가격들이 다른 가게에서 제가 지불했던 것보다 거의 두 배 입니다. 저는 당신의 가게에서 계속 물건을 구매하고 싶지만, 제가 그렇게 비싼 가격들을 지속적으로 지불할 수 있을지 확신할 수 없습니다.

**해설** STS 'But / I would like to'가 들어간 문장 — But I would like to bring one consideration to your attention, and that is the cost of your merchandise.
+
STS 'however'가 들어간 문장 — Frequently, however, your prices are nearly double what I would have paid at other stores.
이 두 문장이 답 도출 근거 문장들이다.

**어휘** attentive 친절한   knowledgeable 지식이 풍부한

**예제 2** 다음 글의 주제로 가장 적절한 것은?   **정답** ②



To many people, television is just flickering wallpaper, moving pictures in the corner of the room. As a medium, television is extremely easy to watch without, apparently, requiring a great deal of effort from the viewer. However, while it is easy to watch television, it is hard to write analytically about it. If you are studying communications, media studies, social studies, humanities or English, you will probably need either to write about a television programme, or to prepare and present a project about television at some point in the course of your studies. Most students find this very difficult. Precisely because television is so easy to watch, it seems to resist our efforts to analyze it critically.

① 텔레비전 매체의 파급력
② 텔레비전 분석의 까다로움
③ 텔레비전의 기술적인 발전
④ 텔레비전 연구의 최근 동향

**해석** 많은 사람들에게 텔레비전은 그저 깜빡이는 벽지이자, 방구석에서 움직이는 사진[활동사진]일 뿐이다. 매체로서의 텔레비전은 시청자들에게 많은 노력을 요구하지 않는 것이 분명하므로 시청하기에 매우 쉽다. 그러나 텔레비전을 시청하기가 쉽기는 하지만, 그에 관해서 분석적으로 글을 쓰는 것은 어렵다. 커뮤니케이션학, 미디어학, 사회학, 인문학 또는 영어를 공부하고 있다면, 아마도 여러분은 텔레비전 프로그램에 관한 글을 쓰거나, 또는 학업 과정의 어느 시점에서 텔레비전에 관한 과제를 준비해서 제출해야 할 것이다. 대부분의 학생들은 이것을 매우 어려워 한다. 텔레비전은 시청하기가 매우 쉽다는 바로 그 이유 때문에 그것을 비판적으로 분석하려는 우리의 노력을 받아들이지 않는 듯하다.

**해설** STS '**However / 양보절과 주절**'이 들어간 문장 — However, while it is easy to watch television, it is hard to write analytically about it.
이 문장이 답 도출 근거 문장이다.

**어휘** flickering 깜박거리는   medium 매개물   analytically 분석적으로   humanities 인문학

## STS **5** not과 but의 A B 접속사

**예제 1** 다음 글의 요지로 가장 적절한 것은?    정답 ①

Futurists are not prophets. They do not "predict" what will happen. They employ devices, ranging from extremely simple to highly sophisticated, to detect trends. However, their output is **not** a "fine" projection **but** an array of possibilities — a multiple series of alternatives, **not** a fixed singularity. Besides, futurists are **not so much** interested in predicting **as** in creating desirable futures; the stress is **not** on what it will be **but** what it can or should be. Futurists leap ahead to the future **not** so that they may stay in an escapist never-never land, **but** so that they can lure that future into the present and negotiate with it while the options are chosen rather than imposed. If there is indeed the prospect of future shock, then dealing with it now may transform future shock into something less intimidating.

① 미래학자는 올바른 미래의 방안을 선택하도록 이끈다.

② 미래학자는 미래에 대한 정확한 예측을 해내는 사람이다.

③ 미래학자는 우리가 미래에 갖춰야 할 행동양식을 연구한다.

④ 미래학자는 절대 미래 사건에 대해 가치 판단을 내리지 않는다.

**해석** 미래학자는 예언자가 아니다. 그들은 무엇이 일어날지 "예측"하지 않는다. 그들은 극도의 단순한 것에서부터 고도의 정교한 것에 이르는 장치를 사용해서 경향을 추적한다. 그러나 그들의 결과물은 "정교한" 예측이 아니라 가능성의 조합이며 고정된 하나가 아니라 다양한 연속의 대안이다. 게다가 미래학자는 예측하는 데 관심이 있기보다는 바람직한 미래를 만드는 데 관심이 있다. 강조점은 미래에 나타날 모습이 아니라 미래에 가능하고 되어야 하는 모습이다. 미래학자들은 현실 도피의 이상향에 머무르기 위해서가 아니라 그 미래를 현재로 끌어들여 그것과 타협하여, 선택권이 부여되는 게 아니라 선택되도록 하기 위해서 미래를 내다본다. 미래의 충격에 대한 가능성이 실제 있다면 지금 그것을 해결하는 것은 미래의 충격을 덜 위협적인 것으로 바꾸어 줄 수 있다.

**해설** STS 'However / not A but B / B, not A'가 들어간 문장 — However, their output is not a "fine" projection but an array of possibilities — a multiple series of
alternatives, not a fixed singularity.
+

STS 'not so much A as B / not A but B'가 들어간 문장 — Besides, futurists are not so much interested in predicting as in creating desirable futures; the stress is not on what it will be but what it can or should be.
+

STS 'not A but B'가 들어간 문장 — Futurists leap ahead to the future not so that they may stay in an escapist never-never land, but so that they can lure that future into the present and negotiate with it while the options are to chosen rather than imposed.

이 세 문장이 답 도출 근거 문장들이다.

**어휘** futurist 미래학자    prophet 예언자    employ 고용하다, 쓰다    ranging from ~에 이르기까지    singularity 특이, 단독
leap 뛰다    escapist 현실도피의, 현실도피주의의    lure 미끼, 유인하다    impose 강요하다, 도입하다    intimidate 위협하다

## STS **6** 명령문

**예제 1** 다음 글의 제목으로 가장 적절한 것은?    정답 ④

> Allow me to give you a little advice about writing fiction. First, make your characters believable. In real life, everyone is unique. If all your characters speak the same way and react to things in the same way, you'll lose your readers from the start. Once your readers believe in your characters, you must get them to care. Each reader must be able to identify with at least one character, to almost become that character in his or her mind. You can do this by developing characters with genuine human traits, both good and bad. Now it's time to weave your tale, to create a plot. Your readers are part of the story now; they are involved. One last thing is, your story must touch the readers' emotions. If you can make them laugh and cry along with your characters, you will be a successful writer.

① The Three Elements for a Storyline
② Investigation on Unique Human Traits
③ Identification with Characters of a Story
④ Some Useful Tips for Writing a Novel

**해석** 소설 쓰기에 대한 약간의 충고를 좀 하고 싶다. 우선, 당신의 등장인물들을 믿을 만하게 만들어라. 실제 생활에서 모든 사람들은 독특하다. 만일 모든 등장인물들이 똑같은 방식으로 말하고 똑같은 방식으로 어떤 일에 반응한다면, 당신은 시작부터 독자들을 잃게 될 것이다. 일단 독자들이 당신의 인물들을 믿게 되면, 그들이 (계속해서) 관심을 가지도록 해야 한다. 각각의 독자가 적어도 하나의 인물과 공감대를 형성해서, 자신의 마음속에서 거의 그 인물이 될 수 있어야 한다. 당신은 좋든 나쁘든 진정한 인간의 특징을 가진 인물을 만들어 냄으로써 이것을 할 수 있다. 이제 당신의 이야기를 짜고 줄거리를 만들어 낼 시간이다. 당신의 독자들은 이제 이야기의 일부가 된다. 그들은 몰입해 있는 것이다. 마지막으로 당신의 이야기는 독자들의 감정을 감동시켜야 한다. 만일 당신이 그들을 당신의 인물들과 함께 웃고 울게 만들 수 있다면, 당신은 성공적인 작가인 것이다.
① 줄거리의 세 가지 요인들
② 독특한 인간의 성향에 관한 조사
③ 이야기의 등장인물들과 동일시하기
④ 소설 쓰기를 위한 몇 가지 유용한 조언들

**해설** STS '명령문'이 들어간 문장 — Allow me to give you a little advice about writing fiction.
이 문장이 답 도출 근거 문장이다.

**어휘** genuine 진실한   trait 특성   weave 짜다

## STS 7 양보절과 주절

**예제 1** 다음 글의 제목으로 가장 적절한 것은?  　　　　　　　　　　정답 ④

> Prior to the 19th century, the major role of children in a capitalist economy was to work. There were few industries that did not employ children at some level, and there were few families whose children did not contribute economically through either farm or factory labor. In 20th-century America, this began to change. Social movements that for decades worked to restrict child labor finally convinced state and federal legislatures to pass laws making child labor illegal. These developments signaled a transformation of children from workers to consumers. Although this may not have been the intent of the reformers, children were to contribute far more to the national economy as consumers than they ever did as laborers.

① The High Increase in Juvenile Labor in Factories
② The Significance of Children in the Future Economy
③ The Horrible Realities of Children in Modern Economy
④ The Roles of American Children: Laborers or Consumers

**해석** 19세기 이전에는, 자본주의 경제에서의 아동의 주된 역할은 노동하는 것이었다. 어떤 수준에서든 아이들을 고용하지 않은 산업체는 거의 없었고, 아이들이 농장이나 공장 노동을 통하여 경제적으로 기여하지 않은 가정은 거의 없었다. 20세기 미국에서 이것은 변하기 시작했다. 수십 년 동안 아동 노동을 제한하기 위해 노력을 했던 사회 운동들은 마침내 아동 노동을 불법으로 만드는 법안들을 통과시키도록 주와 연방의 입법부를 설득시켰다. 이런 발전들은 노동자에서 소비자로서의 아동의 변화의 전조가 되었다. 비록 이것이 개혁가들의 의도는 아니었을지라도, 아동들은 이전에 노동자로서 했던 것보다 소비자로서 국가 경제에 훨씬 더 많이 기여할 수 있게 되었다.
① 공장에서의 청소년 노동의 높은 증가
② 미래 경제에서 아동의 중요성
③ 현대 경제에서 아동의 끔찍한 현실들
④ 미국 아동의 역할: 노동자 또는 소비자

**해설** STS '양보절과 주절'이 들어간 문장 – Although this may not have been the intent of the reformers, children were to contribute far more to the national economy as consumers than they ever did as laborers.
이 문장이 답 도출 근거 문장이다.

**어휘** prior to 앞서서　capitalist economy 자본주의　contribute 기여하다　restrict 얽매다　convince 확신시키다, 설득하다
federal legislature 연방 입법부　signal 신호하다　intent 의지　reformer 개혁가

**예제 2** 다음 글의 주제로 가장 적절한 것은?    정답 ③

> While e-books have yet to make a big impact on the general public, they have become a major aspect of library collections over the past several years. E-books have been quietly taking their place beside more traditional materials, and many academic libraries now count hundreds of thousands of electronic books as part of their collections. E-books offer many advantages; they cannot be lost, stolen, or mutilated, and they are particularly valuable to distance-learning students, 24 hours a day. Depending upon what licensing arrangements are made, e-books can be made available to multiple users at once. Libraries that have suffered major physical disasters such as fires or floods can continue to offer large parts of their collection online. E-books may also offer a level of search-ability completely beyond what could be accomplished with more traditional printed text.

① 전자책의 종류
② 전자책의 역사
③ 전자책의 이점
④ 전자책의 검색 절차

**해석** 전자책이 아직 일반 대중에게까지 큰 영향력을 행사하지는 않지만, 지난 몇 년간 도서관 소장의 주요한 측면이 되었다. 전자책은 기존의 전통적인 자료들 옆에 조용히 자리를 잡아가고 있으며, 많은 학문 도서관들이 현재 소장 서적의 일부로 수십 만 권의 전자책을 가지고 있다. 전자책은 많은 장점을 제공한다. 분실되거나 도난당하거나 훼손되지 않으며, 특히 원격 학습 학생에게는 24시간 이용 가능하다. 어떤 저작권 협의를 했는지에 따라 전자책은 동시에 여러 명의 사용자가 이용할 수도 있다. 화재나 홍수와 같은 큰 물리적 재해를 입은 도서관들도 계속적으로 소장 도서의 상당 부분을 온라인으로 제공할 수 있다. 또한 전자책은 전통적인 인쇄 도서와 비교할 수 없을 만큼의 검색력을 제공한다.

**해설** STS '양보절과 주절 / major'가 들어간 문장 — While e-books have yet to make a big impact on the general public, they have become a major aspect of library collections over past several years.
이 문장이 답 도출 근거 문장이다.

**어휘** mutilated 훼손된

## STS ⑧ 강조표현

### 1 It-that 강조구문

**예제 1** 다음 글의 제목으로 가장 적절한 것은?　　　　　　　　　　　　　　　**정답** ②

> As millions of men left to fight in World War I, women took over their jobs and kept national economies going. Many women worked in war industries, manufacturing weapons and supplies. Others joined women's branches of the armed forces. When food shortages threatened Britain, volunteers in the Women's Land Army went to the fields to grow their nation's food. Nurses shared the dangers of the men whose wounds they tended. At aid stations close to the front lines, nurses often worked around the clock. War work gave women a new sense of pride and confidence. They challenged the idea that women could not handle demanding and dangerous jobs. In many countries, including Britain, Germany, and the United States, it was women's support for winning the war that helped them finally win the right to vote.

① How the British Won World War I
② Improved Rights through Women's War Effort
③ Responsibilities of Women in Maintaining Society
④ Women as Victims of Long-standing Discrimination

**해석** 수백만의 남성들이 제 1차 세계대전에서 싸우기 위해 떠남에 따라 여성들은 그들의 일자리를 이어받아 국가 경제가 계속 유지되게 했다. 많은 여성들은 무기와 보급품들을 제조하면서 전쟁 산업에서 일을 했다. 다른 여성들은 군대의 여성분과에 합류했다. 식량 부족이 영국을 위협하자 농업 자원 부인회는 들판으로 가서 그들 나라의 식량을 재배했다. 간호사들은 그들이 부상을 돌본 남성들의 위험을 공유했다. 전선에서 가까운 응급 치료소에서 간호사들은 흔히 24시간 내내 일했다. 전쟁 관련 일은 여성들에게 새로운 의미의 자부심과 자신감을 심어줬다. 그들은 여성들은 고되고 위험한 일들을 처리할 수 없다는 생각에 도전했다. 영국, 독일, 그리고 미국을 포함해서 많은 나라들에서 여성들이 마침내 투표권을 쟁취하는 데 도움을 준 것은 전쟁에서 이기기 위한 여성들의 지원이었다.
① 영국이 1차 세계대전에서 승리한 방법
② 여성의 전쟁에서의 노력을 통한 향상된 권리들
③ 사회를 유지하는 데 있어서 여성의 책임감들
④ 오랫동안 계속된 차별의 희생자로서의 여성들

**해설** STS 'It-that 강조구문'이 들어간 문장 — In many countries, including Britain, Germany, and the United States, it was women's support for winning the war that helped them finally win the right to vote.
이 문장이 답 도출 근거 문장이다.

**어휘** branch 가지, 지사, 지점　food shortage 식량 부족　wound 상처　tend 돌보다, 간호하다　around the clock 24시간　demanding 요구가 지나친, 큰 노력을 요하는

**'2 강조의 Only / 강조의 do / the very N**

**예제 1** 다음 글의 제목으로 가장 적절한 것은?          정답 ②



To some degree, biology is destiny when it comes to communication style. Studies of identical and fraternal twins suggest that traits including sociability, anger, and relaxation seem to be partially a function of our genetic makeup. Fortunately, biology isn't the only factor that shapes how we communicate: Communication is a set of skills that anyone can learn. As children grow, their ability to communicate effectively develops. For example, older children can produce more sophisticated persuasive attempts than can younger ones. Along with maturity, systematic education (such as the class in which you are now enrolled) can boost communicative competence. Even a modest amount of training can produce dramatic results. After only thirty minutes of instruction, one group of observers became significantly more effective in detecting deception in interviews.

① Communication Leading to Success in Life
② Communicative Competence Can Be Learned
③ Learning Requires Communicative Competence
④ Relaxation as A Major Part of Communication

**해석** 어느 정도는 의사소통 스타일에 관한 한 생물학은 숙명이다[유전적인 특질이 결정한다]. 일란성 쌍둥이와 이란성 쌍둥이에 대한 연구는 사교성, 분노, 그리고 느긋함을 포함하는 특성들이 부분적으로는 우리의 유전적인 구성의 작용으로 보인다는 점을 시사한다. 다행히도, 생물학[유전적인 특질]만이 우리가 의사소통하는 방식을 형성하는 유일한 요소는 아니다. 의사소통은 누구나 배울 수 있는 일련의 기술이다. 성장해감에 따라 효과적으로 의사소통하는 아동의 능력은 발달한다. 예를 들어, 나이가 더 많은 아이들은 나이가 더 적은 아이들보다 더 수준 높고 설득력 있는 시도를 할 수 있다. 나이를 먹는 것과 함께 (여러분이 현재 등록된 수업과 같은) 체계적인 교육도 의사소통 능력을 향상할 수 있다. 그리 많지 않은 양의 훈련이라도 대단한 결과를 만들어 낼 수 있다. 불과 30분간의 지도를 받은 후에, 한 집단의 참관자들은 인터뷰에서 속임수를 탐지하는 데 상당히 더 능숙해졌다.
① 인생에서 성공의 결과를 가져다준 의사소통
② 의사소통 능력은 학습될 수 있다.
③ 학습은 의사소통 능력을 요구한다.
④ 의사소통의 중요한 부분으로서의 긴장 완화

**해설** STS '**Fortunately / only**'가 들어간 문장 — Fortunately, biology isn't the only factor that shapes how we communicate
+
STS '**only / effective**'가 들어간 문장 — After only thirty minutes of instruction, one group of observers became significantly more effective in detecting deception in interviews.
이 두 문장이 답 도출 근거 문장들이다.

**어휘** fraternal twins 이란성 쌍둥이   sociability 사교성   relaxation 기분 전환, 느슨함   partially 부분적으로
genetic makeup 유전적 구성   persuasive 설득력 있는   maturity 성숙함   systematic education 체계적인 교육
communicative 의사소통의   competence 능력   modest 보통의

**예제 2** 다음 글의 요지로 가장 적절한 것은?   정답 ①

Science is all about possibilities. We propose theories, conjectures, hypotheses, and explanations. We collect evidence and data, and we test the theories against this new evidence. If the data contradict our theory, then we change the theory. In this way science advances, and we gain greater and greater understanding. But there is always the possibility of new evidence arising which contradicts the existing theories. It's the very essence of science that its conclusions can change, that is, that its truths are not absolute. The intrinsic good sense of this is contained within the remark reportedly made by the distinguished economist John Maynard Keynes, responding to the criticism that he had changed his position on monetary policy during the 1930s Depression: "When the facts change, I change my mind. What do you do, sir?"

① 과학 이론은 새로운 증거에 의해 늘 변할 수 있다.
② 과학 이론에서 자료의 해석이 수집보다 더 강조된다.
③ 과학의 발전에 경제적 안정이 긍정적 영향을 미쳐 왔다.
④ 과학자들은 절대불변의 과학적 이론 확립을 위해 노력한다.

**해석** 과학은 온통 가능성에 관한 것이다. 우리는 이론과 추측, 가설, 그리고 설명을 제안한다. 우리는 증거와 자료를 수집하고 이러한 새로운 증거와 대조하여 이론을 검증한다. 만약 자료가 이론과 모순되면 그러면 우리는 이론을 변경한다. 이러한 방식으로 과학은 진보하고 우리는 점점 더 잘 이해하게 된다. 그러나 기존의 이론과 모순되는 새로운 증거가 나타날 가능성은 항상 있다. 결론이 바뀔 수 있다는 것, 즉 진리가 절대적이지 않다는 것이 바로 과학의 본질이다. 이것의 본질적인 진정한 의미는 저명한 경제학자 John Maynard Keynes가 1930년대의 대공황 시기에 통화정책에 대한 자신의 입장을 바꿨던 것에 대한 비판에 대응하면서 했다고 전해지는 그의 논평에 드러나 있다 "사실이 달라지면 나는 내 생각을 바꾸죠. 당신은 어떻게 하시나요?"

**해설** STS 'But'이 들어간 문장 — But there is always the possibility of new evidence arising which contradicts the existing theories.
+
STS 'It—that 강조구문 / the very N'가 들어간 문장 — It's the very essence of science that its conclusions can change.
이 두 문장이 답 도출 근거 문장들이다.

**어휘** conjecture 추측   hypothesis 가설   intrinsic 본질적인   reportedly 전하는 바에 따르면

**CHAPTER 01**

## `3` 최상급/비교급 강조 6

**예제 1**  다음 글의 주제로 가장 적절한 것은?　　　　　정답 ③

Suppose we need to measure the temperature in a vineyard. If we have only one temperature sensor for the whole plot of land, we must make sure it is accurate and working at all times; no messiness allowed. In contrast, if we have a sensor for every one of the hundreds of vines, we can use cheaper, less sophisticated sensors (as long as they do not introduce a systematic bias). Probably, at some points, a few sensors may report incorrect data, creating a less exact, or "messier," dataset than the one from a single precise sensor. Any particular reading may be incorrect, but the collection of many readings will provide a more comprehensive picture. Because this dataset consists of more data points, it offers far greater value that likely compensates for its messiness.

① forms of sensors appropriate for vineyards
② elements influencing the worth of the dataset
③ the advantage of acquiring a large set of data
④ the influences of technology on farming grape

**해석** 우리가 포도밭에서 온도를 측정해야 한다고 가정하자. 만약 우리가 땅의 전체 구획에 대해서 오직 하나의 온도 감지기만 가지고 있다면, 우리는 그것이 정확하고 항상 작동하고 있는지 확인해야 한다. 혼란스러움은 허용되지 않는다. 반면에, 만약 우리가 수백 그루의 포도나무 한 그루마다 감지기를 가진다면, 우리는 더 저렴하고 덜 정교한 감지기를 사용할 수 있다.(그 감지기들이 일관되게 편의[편중된 결과]를 보이지 않는 한). 어쩌면, 어느 순간에는, 몇몇 감지기들이 부정확한 자료를 보일 수 있고, 그래서 하나의 정확한 감지기로부터 얻은 자료 집합보다 덜 정확하고, 혹은 '더 혼란스러운' 자료 집합을 만들어 낼 수 있다. 어떤 특정한 측정치는 부정확할 수도 있지만, 많은 측정치의 수집은 더 종합적인 모습을 제공할 것이다. 이 자료 집합은 더 많은 측정치로 구성되어 있기 때문에, 어쩌면 그것은 혼란스러움을 보상해 줄 수도 있을 훨씬 더 유용한 가치를 제공해 준다.
① 포도밭에 적절한 센서의 형태들
② 자료 집합의 가치에 영향을 미치는 요인들
③ 커다란 자료 집합을 얻는 것의 장점
④ 기술이 포도 농사에 미치는 영향들

**해설** STS '비교급 강조 far/value'가 들어간 문장 — Because this dataset consists of more data points, it offers far greater value that likely compensate for its messiness.
이 문장이 답 도출 근거 문장이다.

**어휘** vineyard 포도밭, 포도원　vine 덩굴　comprehensive 포괄적인　likely ~할 것 같은　compensate 보상하다

**예제 2**  다음 글의 요지로 가장 적절한 것은?                    정답 ③

It's striking to me that in all the heated debate about health care reform, one basic fact is rarely discussed, and that is the one thing that could dramatically bring down the costs of health care while improving the health of our people. Studies have shown that 50 to 70 percent of the nation's health care costs are preventable, and the single most effective step most people can take to improve their health is to eat a healthier diet. If we were to stop overeating, to stop eating unhealthy foods and to instead eat foods with higher nutrient densities and cancer protective properties, we could have a more affordable, sustainable, and effective health care system. And more importantly, we'd be less dependent on insurance companies and doctors, and more dependent on our own health-giving choices.

① 사람에 따라 일일 권장 섭취량은 다를 수 있다.

② 의료 혁신을 위해 다방면의 의견을 수용할 필요가 있다.

③ 식생활 개선을 통해 건강을 증진하고 의료비를 절감할 수 있다.

④ 현대에는 치료가 아닌 예방을 중시하는 의료 시스템이 더 효과적이다.

**해석** 의료 개혁에 대한 모든 열띤 토론 속에서 한 가지 기본적인 사실이 좀처럼 논의되지 않는 것은 나에게 놀라운데, 그것은 우리 국민의 건강을 증징하면서 의료비를 극적으로 절감할 수 있는 하나[한 가지 방안]이다. 국가 의료비의 50~70%는 지출을 막을 수 있으며, 대부분의 사람이 자신들의 건강을 향상하기 위해 취할 수 있는 한 가지 가장 효과적인 조치는 건강에 더 좋은 음식을 먹는 것임을 여러 연구에서 입증해왔다. 우리가 과식하지 않고, 건강에 좋지 않은 음식을 먹지 않으며, 대신에 더 놓은 영양 밀도와 암 예방 성분을 함유한 음식을 먹는다면 우리는 좀 더 가격이 알맞고, 지속 가능하며, 효과적인 의료 체계를 가질 수 있을 것이다. 그리고 더 중요한 것은 우리는 보험회사와 의사에게 덜 의존하고 건강하게 만드는 우리 자신의 선택에 더 의존할 것이다.

**해설** STS '**연구의 결과 / the single most effective**'가 들어간 문장 — Studies have shown that 50 to 70 percent of the nation's health care costs are preventable, and the single most effective step most people can take to improve their heath is to eat a healthier diet.

**어휘** striking 인상적인    preventable 예방 가능한

CHAPTER 01

## STS ⑨ 1인칭의 활용

**예제 1** 다음 글의 요지로 가장 적절한 것은?    정답 ④

I believe that it is a variety of responses that are most effective in dealing with the real social dilemmas. This is true of handling computerized information in this country. We need extensive information to manage rational and humane society, but what is needed is a ban by law on any computerized data banks that are so dangerous perse that they should not be allowed. Among other possible responses, we might convene hearings before legislatures and regulatory commissions so that government agencies may present their plans for computerized systems and demonstrate necessary safeguards before they are allowed to computerize sensitive files containing personal information. Within the computerized systems, we can reexamine existing rules, such as those which pertain to the confidential nature of data.

① 공익을 위해 어느 정도 개인의 신상 정보 공개는 용납될 수 있다.
② 처음부터 컴퓨터로 개인의 신상 정보를 다루는 것을 금지해야 한다.
③ 정부기관이 개인 신상 정보를 다루는 경우에는 사전 승인을 받도록 해야 한다.
④ 다양한 접근방법을 시도해 봄으로써 컴퓨터 처리된 개인 정보를 다뤄 볼 수 있다.

**해석** 현실적인 사회적 딜레마를 해결하는 데 있어서 가장 효과적인 것은 다양한 반응들이다. 이러한 사실은 우리나라에 있어서 컴퓨터 처리 정보를 다룸에 있어서도 역시 진실이다. 우리는 이성적이고도 인간적인 사회를 관리하기 위하여 광범위한 정보를 필요로 한다. 그러나 필요한 것은 그 자체로도 너무나 위험하여 허용되지 말아야 할 그 어떤 컴퓨터 처리 데이터 뱅크에 대한 법률에 의한 금지조치인 것이다. 다른 가능한 반응들 중에서 우리는 입법부 및 규제 위원회 앞에서의 청문회를 소집하는 것인데, 그것은 정부 기관들이 컴퓨터 체계에 대한 계획을 제시하고, 개인 정보를 포함하는 민감한 파일을 컴퓨터 처리하는 것이 허용되기 전에 필요한 안전장치를 증명하기 위한 것이다. 컴퓨터 체계 내부에서, 우리는 자료의 기밀에 속하는 것들과 같은 현존하는 법칙을 다시 점검할 수 있다.

**해설** STS 'I believe / It–that 강조구문 / most effective'가 들어간 문장 — I believe that it is a variety of responses that are most effective in dealing with the real social dilemmas.
+
**위 문장을 가리키는 This 시작해서 보충 설명해 주는 문장** — This is true of handling computerized information in this country.
이 두 문장이 답 도출 근거 문장들이다.

**어휘** extensive 광범위한   humane 인도적인   perse 그 자체로   legislature 입법부   regulatory 규제   reexamine 재검토   pertain 관련

## STS 10 필자의 판단 주입 어휘와 표현의 이용

**예제 1** 다음 글의 주제로 가장 적절한 것은?  정답 ①

Our expectations are constructed through our value systems, upbringing, and past experiences and can be very different from those of others. These expectations can become major sources of frustration when not met by others' behavior, such as that of our tutees. The best thing to do is to try to enter tutoring without any expectations at all. This, of course, includes giving up expectations you may have of your future students and their personalities, their academic skills or progress, and their motivation and attitude toward you. All children are different. They have different backgrounds, different strengths, and different weaknesses. Some may be thrilled to be tutored; others may be suspicious. At the first meeting, a tutor's conception of a student should be a blank slate. Tutors must be prepared to accept and to work with any students to whom they are assigned.

① need for a tutor to accept a tutee as it is
② benefits of having tutees of diverse backgrounds
③ how to make children be responsible for their own learning
④ advantages of a group-based tutoring program for children

**해석** 우리의 기대는 우리의 가치 체계, 가정교육, 과거 경험을 통해 형성되며 다른 사람들의 것(기대)와 매우 다를 수 있다. 이러한 기대는 (우리가 가르치는) 학생들의 행동과 같은 다른 사람들의 행동에 의해 충족되지 않을 때 좌절감의 주요 원인이 될 수 있다. 가장 최선은 아무런 기대를 갖지 않고 대인 지도를 시작하려고 노력하는 것이다. 물론 이것은 미래의 학생과 그들의 성격, 학업 능력이나 (학업) 향상, 그들의 동기와 여러분을 향한 태도에 대해 여러분이 가질 수 있는 기대를 포기하는 것을 포함한다. 모든 아이는 서로 다르다. 그들은 서로 다른 배경, 서로 다른 강점, 서로 다른 약점을 가지고 있다. 어떤 아이들은 개인 교습을 받는 것에 대해 신이날 수도 있고, 또 어떤 아이들은 못 미더워할 수도 있다. 첫 만남에서 학생에 대한 개인 지도 교사의 생각은 백지 상태이어야 한다. 개인 지도 교사는 자신에게 배정된 어떤 학생도 받아들이고 같이 하려는 준비가 되어 있어야 한다.
① 교사가 학생을 있는 그대로 받아들일 필요성
② 다양한 배경을 가진 학생을 갖는 것의 장점들
③ 아이들에게 자신의 학습을 책임지게 만드는 방법
④ 아이들을 위한 집단에 기반을 둔 교수 프로그램의 장점들

**해설** STS 'The best'가 들어간 문장 — The best thing to do is to try to enter tutoring without any expectations at all.
+
STS 'should'가 들어간 문장 — At the first meeting, a tutor's conception of a student should be a blank slate.
+
STS 'must'가 들어간 문장 — Tutors must be prepared to accept and to work with any students to whom thay are assigned.
이 세 문장이 답 도출 근거 문장들이다.

**어휘** upbringing 교육   tutee 지도를 받고 있는 사람   assigned 할당된

**예제 2** 다음 글에서 필자가 주장하는 바로 가장 적절한 것은?  정답 ②

All kinds of high-tech devices exist to test meat for microbial infestations like salmonella. The government is too cheap to invest in these, however, so federal food inspectors continue to inspect meat visually, as it rolls past on a conveyor belt. Micro-organisms are invisible and you can imagine how attentively a low-paid federal food inspector is going to be looking at each of 18,000 identical chickens sliding past him. By the government's own admission, as much as 20 percent of all chicken and 30 percent of turkey is contaminated. It is thought that as many as 10 million people may get sick each year from factory contaminated food, costing the economy about $2 billion in additional health care costs, lost productivity, and so on. Given all this, why doesn't the government turn to high-tech devices? It is high time that we should let the government be able to keep food safe for consumers by increasing its budget.

① 전염병을 예방하기 위해 가축 방역을 확대하자.
② 식품 안전 강화를 위해 더 많은 예산을 투입하자
③ 수입 육류에 대한 효율적 검역 시스템을 마련하자.
④ 식품 검사관의 열악한 근무 조건 개선책을 마련하자.

**해석** 살모넬라 같은 미생물의 침입이 있는지 육류를 검사하기 위한 모든 종류의 첨단 장치들이 존재한다. 그러나 정부는 이런 것들에 투자하기에는 너무 인색하다. 그래서 연방 식품 검사관들은 계속해서 육류가 컨베이어 벨트에서 굴러 지나갈 때 고기를 눈으로 검사한다. 미생물은 눈에 보이지 않고, 당신은 박봉의 연방 식품 조사관이 그를 지나 미끄러져가는 1만 8천 마리나 되는 똑같은 닭고기 각각을 얼마나 주의 깊게 살펴볼 것인지 상상할 수 있을 것이다. 그리고 정부가 스스로 인정하는 바에 따르면 모든 닭고기의 20퍼센트, 그리고 칠면조 고기의 30퍼센트가 오염이 되어 있다. 그리고 1천만 명 정도 되는 사람들이 매년 공장에서 오염된 식품 때문에 아프게 될 수 있으며, 그리하여 추가적인 의료보호 비용, 손실된 생산성 등등으로 경제에 약 20억 달러의 비용이 들게 한다고 생각된다. 이 모든 것을 고려했을 때, 왜 정부는 첨단 장치들에 의존하지 않는가? 이제 정부가 예산을 증가시킴으로써 소비자들을 위해 식품을 안전하게 유지시킬 수 있도록 할 때이다.

**해설** STS 'It is high time'이 들어간 문장 — It is high time that we should let the government be able to keep food safe for consumers by increasing its budget.
이 문장이 답 도출 근거 문장이다.

**어휘** microbial infestations 미생물 침입   inspector 검사관   attentively 주의 깊게   contaminated 오염된

## STS 11 The + 비교급, the + 비교급

**예제 1** 다음 글의 주제로 가장 적절한 것은?　　　　　　　　정답 ②

It doesn't really matter whether we share a first name, a birthday, a home state, or a rare fingerprint pattern — similarity can help to create an in-group dynamic that brings people together. The more we can zero in on and accentuate the similarities we have with someone else, the more likely we are to get along with that person. This is especially useful in trying to connect with someone who seems very different from us. If the person is from a different cultural background or a different profession or industry, focus on the ways in which you are similar — music, sports, humor. You're more likely to create a connection.

① the chance of unexpected meetings
② the similarity-based relationship-building
③ the effect of hobbies on communication
④ the understanding of diversity of culture

**해석** 우리가 이름, 생일, 고향, 혹은 희귀한 지문 형태를 공유하고 있는지는 실제로 중요하지 않지만, 유사성은 사람들을 결합하는 집단 내의 역동성을 만드는 데 도움을 줄 수 있다. 우리가 다른 어떤 사람과 함께 공유하고 있는 유사성에 초점을 맞추고 강조하면 할수록 우리는 그 사람과 사이좋게 지낼 가능성이 더욱더 많아진다. 이것은 우리와 매우 달라 보이는 누군가와 사귀려고 애쓸 때 특히 유용하다. 만약 그 사람이 문화적 배경, 직업이나 일의 분야가 다르다면, 여러분이 (서로) 유사한 방식 즉 음악, 스포츠, 유머에 초점을 맞추어라. (그러면) 여러분은 (그 사람과) 유대관계를 맺을 가능성이 좀 더 많아질 것이다.
① 예측하지 못한 만남의 기회
② 유상성에 기반을 둔 관계 형성
③ 취미가 의사소통에 미치는 영향
④ 문화의 다양성에 대한 이해

**해설** STS 'The + 비교급, the + 비교급'이 들어간 문장 — The more we can zero in on and accentuate the similarities we have with someone else, the more likely we are to get along with that person.
+
STS '명령문'이 들어간 문장 — focus on the ways in which you are similar — music, sports, humor.
+
위 문장을 보충 설명하는 문장 — You're more likely to create a connection.
이 세 문장이 답 도출 근거 문장들이다.

**어휘** zero in on 초점을 맞추다, 겨냥하다　accentuate 강조하다

**예제 2**  다음 글에서 필자가 주장하는 바로 가장 적절한 것은?  **정답** ④

CHAPTER 01

> States that previously lowered the drinking age to 18, such as Massachusetts, Michigan, and Maine, experienced an increase in alcohol-related crashes among the 18 to 20 age group. Lowering drinking ages to 16, 17, or 18 like the MLDA (Minimum Legal Drinking Age) in some European countries is inappropriate for US standards because American teens generally start driving at earlier ages and drive more often than their European counterparts. American teens are thus much more likely to drive under the influence of alcohol if the drinking age is lowered in the US. Moreover, the earlier a person begins alcohol use, the greater the chances are of that person becoming an alcoholic later in life and suffering negative physical withdrawal symptoms.

① 청소년 대상 음주 문화 교육을 강화해야 한다.

② 알코올음료 광고의 시간대 제한이 도입되어야 한다.

③ 청소년들의 음주는 법률적으로 전면 금지되어야 한다.

④ 지금보다 음주 가능 최저 연령을 더 낮추어서는 안 된다.

**해석** Massachusetts, Michigan, Maine 주처럼 전에 음주 연령을 18세로 낮췄던 주들은 18~20세의 연령층에서 음주 관련 충돌 사고의 증가를 겪었다. 유럽의 몇몇 국가들처럼 법적 최저 음주 연령을 16, 17, 18세로 낮추는 것은 미국의 표준에 맞지 않는데, 이것은 미국의 십대들이 일반적으로 유럽의 십대들보다 좀 더 어린 나이에 운전을 시작하고, 더 자주 운전을 하기 때문이다. 따라서 음주 연령이 미국 내에서 낮아지게 되면 미국의 십대들이 음주 운전을 할 가능성은 훨씬 더 커지게 된다. 게다가 음주를 더 일찍 시작하면 할수록 그 사람은 나중에 알코올 중독 자가 되어 부정적인 신체적인 금단 증상을 앓게 될 가능성이 더 크다.

**해설** STS 'The + 비교급, the + 비교급'이 들어간 문장 − Moreover, the earlier a person begins alcohol use, the greater the chances are of that person becoming an alcoholic later in life and suffering negative physical withdrawal symptoms.
이 문장이 답 도출 근거 문장이다.

**어휘** crashes 차 사고  withdrawal symptoms 금단증상

# MDTS(글의 전개 방식)

## 1 연구 − 실험의 인용

**예제 1** 다음 글의 요지로 가장 적절한 것은?　　　　　　　　　　　정답 ④

Psychologists have frequently tested the notion that people's personalities cause them to exhibit consistently the same behavioral patterns in a variety of situations. In one study, for example, counselors working at a summer camp for teenage boys were asked to secretly note down the degree to which the boys displayed various forms of extroverted behavior, such as talking during mealtimes, seeking the limelight, and initiating conversations. The researchers then carefully analyzed the data by comparing the boys' level of extroversion on odd and even days. The 'personality causes behavior' theory predicts there would be a high level of consistency in the boys' actions, with the extroverted teenagers constantly chatting away and the introverted ones repeatedly hiding away in the corner. In fact, the results failed to show any evidence of such consistency. On one day, one of the boys would be full of beans and very chatty, while on the next day the very same boy was quiet and withdrawn.

① 사람은 상황에 따라서 다른 행동을 보일 수 있다.
② 사람의 특정한 행동은 성격으로부터 나온다.
③ 사람의 타고난 성격은 어떠한 상황에서도 변하지 않는다.
④ 사람의 성격으로부터 일관성 있는 행동이 나온다는 증거는 없다.

**해석** 심리학자들은 사람들의 성격이 그들로 하여금 다양한 상황에서 동일한 행동 양식을 일관되게 보이게 한다는 개념을 자주 시험해왔다. 예를 들어 한 연구에서 십 대 소년들을 위한 여름 캠프에서 일하는 지도자들은 그 소년들이 식사 시간 중에 말하는 것, 이목을 끌려고 하는 것, 그리고 대화를 시작하는 것과 같이 다양한 형태의 외향적인 행동을 보인 정도를 은밀히 적어둘 것을 요청받았다. 그 연구자들은 그다음에 홀숫날과 짝숫날에 그 소년들의 외향성의 정도를 비교하여 그 자료를 신중히 분석했다. '성격이 행동을 야기한다'는 이론은 외향적인 십 대들은 끊임없이 수다를 떨고 내성적인 십 대들은 반복하여 구석에 몸을 숨기면서 그 소년들의 행동에 높은 수준의 일관성이 있을 것이라고 예측한다. 사실 그 결과는 그러한 일관성에 대한 어떤 증거도 보여주지 못했다. 어느 날에는 그 소년들 중 한 명이 원기 왕성하고 매우 수다스럽곤 했는데, 다음 날에는 바로 그 똑같은 소년이 조용하고 집 안에 틀어박혔다.

**해설** STS '연구의 결과를 나타내는 표현 − **the results failed to show**'가 들어간 문장 − In fact, the results failed to show any evidence of such consistency.

＋

**위 문장에 대한 부연 설명을 하는 문장** − On one day, one of the boys would be full of beans and very chatty, while on the next day the very same boy was quiet and withdrawn.
이 두 문장이 답 도출 근거 문장들이다.

**어휘** extrovert 외향적인　limelight 라임라이트(주요 인물을 집중적으로 비추는 강한 백색광)　initiate 시작하다, 개시하다
extroversion 외전, 외향성　consistency 일관성

## 2  권위자

**예제 1**  다음 글의 제목으로 가장 적절한 것은?　　　　　**정답** ③

Some people believe that when they are alone they are lonely. However, if we accept our aloneness, we can give ourselves to our projects and our relationships out of our freedom instead of running to them out of our fear. In writing about solitude, Father William McNamara says that it is a misunderstanding to equate solitude with isolation. In his view, the opposite is true. When we enter into genuine solitude, we then have the ability to enter into the center of our being and connect in a meaningful way with others. Silence and solitude provide a means for coming to know ourselves better, for becoming centered, and for forming meaningful relationships. The Dalai Lama stresses that to make changes in our lives we need solitude, by which he means "a mental state free of distractions, not simply time alone in a quiet place."

① Solitude: What Must Be Overcome
② Being Alone: The Grave of a Relationship
③ Positive Aspects of Solitude
④ Solitude vs Isolation: Which is worse?

**해석** 어떤 사람들은 혼자 있을 때 외롭다고 생각한다. 그러나 혼자인 것을 받아들이면, 우리는 두려움 때문에 일과 관계에 달려가는 것이 아니라 자유로운 선택에 따라 그것들에 전념할 수 있다. 고독에 관해 쓰면서 William McNamara 신부는 고독과 고립을 동일시하는 것은 오해라고 말한다. 그의 관점에서는 그 반대가 맞다. 진정한 고독에 들어갈 때, 우리는 그때 우리 존재 중심에 들어가서 다른 사람들과 의미 있는 방식으로 관계를 맺을 능력을 가진다. 침묵과 고독은 우리 자신을 더 잘 알게 되고, 집중하게 되고, 의미 있는 관계를 형성하기 위한 수단을 제공한다. Dalai Lama는 인생에서 변화를 일으키기 위해서는 우리가 고독을 필요로 한다는 것을 강조하는데, 여기에서 그가 의미하는 고독은 단지 "조용한 곳에 혼자 있는 시간이 아니라 산만함이 없는 정신 상태"이다.
① 고독: 극복해야만 하는 것
② 혼자 있는 것: 관계의 무덤
③ 고독의 긍정적인 측면들
④ 고독 vs 고립: 어떤 것이 더 나쁜 것인가?

**해설** STS '권위자의 말 – Father William McNamara says that'이 들어간 문장 – Father William McNamara says that it is a misunderstanding to equate solitude with isolation.
+
STS '권위자의 주장 – The Dalai Lama stresses that'이 들어간 문장 – The Dalai Lama stresses that to make changes in our lives we need solitude, by which he means "a mental state free of distractions, not simply time alone in a quiet place." 이 두 문장이 답 도출 근거 문장들이다.

**어휘** aloneness 외로움　solitude 고독　equate 같게 하다

**예제 2** 다음 글의 빈칸 (A), (B)에 들어갈 말로 가장 적절한 것을 고르시오.　　정답 ①

The people who do become top-level achievers are rarely child prodigies. That is certainly true in business; the early lives of the Welches, Ogilvies, and Rockefellers almost never hint at the success to come. Looking at more scientific research, this is one of the most notable findings in Benjamin Bloom's large study, which examined performers at the highest level — people who had achieved national or international recognition before age forty. ＿＿＿(A)＿＿＿, all of the twenty-four pianists studied — each a finalist in at least one major international competition — had had lessons "forced upon them," in the words of the study, just the opposite of the kids who seemed driven to sit at the piano as toddlers. ＿＿＿(B)＿＿＿, in no case did the parents of the future champion swimmers foresee their child's eventual achievements. Time and again the story is the same: Even by age eleven or twelve it would have been difficult to predict who the future exceptional performers would be.

|  | (A) | (B) |
|---|---|---|
| ① | For instance | Similarly |
| ② | For instance | Thus |
| ③ | However | Likewise |
| ④ | However | Thus |

**해석** 정말 최고 수준으로 성공하게 된 사람들이 신동인 경우는 거의 없다. 그것은 사업에서 확실히 적용되는데, Welch 가문, Ogilvy 가문, Rockefeller 가문 사람들의 어린 시절의 삶은 다가올 성공을 거의 절대 암시하지 않는다. 더 과학적인 연구를 보면, 이것은 Benjamin Bloom의 광범위한 연구에서 가장 주목할 만한 연구 결과 중 하나인데, 그 연구에서는 최고 수준의 연주자들, 즉 40세 이전에 전국적이거나 국제적인 인정을 받았던 사람들을 조사하였다. 예를 들어 연구 대상인 24명의 피아니스트 각각은 적어도 한 개의 주요 국제 대회의 결승 진출자였는데, 그들 모두 연구에서 표현된 말로, '그들에게 강요된'수업을 받았고, 그것은 유아 때부터 의욕에 사로잡혀 피아노에 앉은 것 같은 아이들과는 정반대였다. 마찬가지로, 어떤 경우에도 미래의 수영 챔피언들의 부모들은 그들 자녀의 궁극적인 업적을 예견하지 못했다. 몇 번이고 이야기는 같은데, 11세나 12세 무렵조차 미래의 특출한 성과를 이루어 내는 사람이 누구일 것인지 예측하는 것은 어려웠을 것이다.

**해설** (A)를 기준으로 위 문장에서 등장한 '상위개념 — performers at the highest level'과 (A)를 기준으로 뒤 문장에서 등장한 '하위개념 — the twenty-four pianists'를 연결시켜 주는 예시의 연결사 'For instance'가 (A)의 위치에 적절하다.
　+
(B)를 기준으로 위 문장에서 등장한 '국제 경연에 결승전까지 올라간 피아니스트들의 사례'와 (B)를 기준으로 뒤 문장에서 등장한 '수영 챔피언들의 사례'가 유사한 사례들이므로, 'Similarly'가 (B)의 위치에 적절하다.

**어휘** achiever 성취자　prodigy 신동　notable 주목할 만한　recognition 인식　finalist 결선 진출자　foresee 예견하다　eventual 어쩌면 일어날 수도 있는

**예제 3** 다음 글에 드러난 Boon Huat의 심경으로 가장 적절한 것은?　　　　　정답 ①

> Boon Huat was outside the conference room waiting to be interviewed for the post of sales manager. His mind began to race as a hundred thoughts went through his mind at once. "What would they expect of me as a sales manager? Would they be kind, and would I be able to impress them, or make a fool of myself instead?" He kept his eyes fixed on the door, waiting for it to be opened any moment. Each time a telephone nearby rang, he was startled. His heart began beating faster and faster as he listened to his shallow and rapid breathing. His mouth felt dry. Quickly he rushed to the toilet. And looking into the mirror, he realized that he was sweating in the cold air-conditioned room. His hands trembled as he inspected his hair and adjusted his tie.

① nervous
② irritated
③ furious
④ sorrowful

**해석** Boon Huat은 회의실 밖에서 판매부장직을 위한 면접을 기다리고 있었다. 백 가지나 되는 생각이 한꺼번에 그의 머릿속을 지나가면서 그의 마음은 바쁘게 돌아가기 시작했다. '그들은 나에게 판매부장으로서 무엇을 기대할까? 그들은 친절할까, 그리고 내가 그들에게 감명을 줄 수 있을까, 아니면 그렇지 않고 내 자신을 웃음거리로 만들게 될까?' 그는 시선을 문에 계속 고정시킨 채로, 어느 순간에라도 그 문이 열리기를 기다렸다. 가까운 곳에 있는 전화기가 울릴 때마다, 그는 깜짝 놀랐다. 그가 자신의 얕고 빠른 호흡에 귀를 기울이면서 그의 심장은 점점 더 빠르게 뛰기 시작했다. 그의 입은 말랐다. 재빨리 그는 화장실로 달려갔다. 거울을 들여다보면서 그는 냉방이 되는 차가운 실내에서 자신이 땀을 흘리고 있다는 것을 깨달았다. 머리 상태를 점검하고 넥타이를 바로 맬 때 그의 손은 떨렸다.

**해설** His mind began to race / he was startled / His heart began beating faster and faster as he listened to his shallow and rapid breathing / His mouth felt dry / he was sweating / His hands trembled등에서 이야기의 주인공 Boon Huat의 심경으로 적절한 것은 nervous(긴장한)이다.

**어휘** tremble 떨림　inspect 검사　adjust 조정

## 3  의문문의 활용

### `1  첫 문장이 의문문 / `2  중간의문문

**예제 1**  다음 글의 요지로 가장 적절한 것은?    **정답** ④

---

Arachnophobia, or fear of spiders, seems to be a universal human dread, especially in children. The biologist Tim Flannery asks, "Why do so many of us react so strongly, and with such primal fear, to spiders? The world is full of far more dangerous creatures that appear to barely worry most people." Flannery guesses that a Darwinian story connects human arachnophobia to our African prehistory. Homo sapiens emerged in Africa. Africa is the place where the human mind acquired many of its useful instincts. If humans evolved in an environment with poisonous spiders, a phobia could have been advantageous for human survival and could be expected to gain greater frequency in the larger human population. The six-eyed sand spider of western and southern Africa actually fits that guess very well. It is a crab-like spider that hides in the sand and leaps out to capture prey; its poison is extremely harmful to children. One can see how a fear of spiders would have been highly advantageous in this context.

---

① 인간은 생존을 위해 거미 공포증을 극복해 왔다.

② 거미는 전래동화 속에서 자주 등장하는 소재들 중 하나이다.

③ 치명적인 독을 가지고 있는 거미의 종류는 생각보다 많지 않다.

④ 거미에 대한 공포의 유래는 아프리카 선사시대에서 찾을 수 있다.

**해석**  Arachnophobia(거미 공포증), 즉 거미에 대한 공포는, 특히 아동에게, 보편적인 인간의 두려움인 것처럼 보인다. 생물학자인 Tim Flannery는 "왜 우리 중 그렇게 많은 사람들이 거미에 그토록 강하게, 그리고 그런 원시적 공포로 반응하는가? 세상은 대부분의 사람들을 거의 걱정시키지 않는 듯이 보이는 훨씬 더 위험한 생물들로 가득 차 있는데"라고 질문한다. Flannery는 다윈설에 따른 한 이야기가 인간의 거미 공포증을 우리의 아프리카 선사시대로 연결해 준다고 추측한다. 호모 사피엔스는 아프리카에서 출현했다. 아프리카는 인간의 정신이 유용한 본능들 중 많은 것을 습득했던 곳이다. 인간이 유독한 거미가 있는 환경에서 진화했다면, 공포증은 인간 생존에 이로웠을 수 있으며, 인구가 더 많은 곳에서 더욱 빈번하게 발생한다고 예상할 수 있다. 서부와 남부 아프리카의 눈이 여섯 개인 모래 거미는 실제로 그런 추측과 매우 잘 부합한다. 그 거미는 모래에 숨어 있다 먹이를 잡기 위해 뛰어 나오는, 게와 유사한 거미인데, 그것의 독은 아이들에게 몹시 해롭다. 우리는 이런 상황에서 거미에 대한 공포가 어떤 식으로 매우 이로웠을지를 알 수 있다.

**해설**  STS '의문문 (The biologist Tim Flannery asks, "Why do so many of us react so strongly, and with such primal fear to spiders?) 에 대한 답변'에 해당하는 문장 — Flannery guesses that a Darwinian story connects human arachnophobia to our African prehistory.
이 문장이 답 도출 근거 문장이다.

**어휘**  arachnophobia 거미 공포증   dread 공포   primal 원시   prehistory 선사시대   leap 도약

**예제 2** 다음 글의 내용을 한 문장으로 요약할 때 빈칸 (A)와 (B)에 들어갈 말로 가장 적절한 것은? **정답** ③



Often, you may have observed students reading a passage very slowly and vocalizing (i.e. reading every word aloud) and re-reading sentences they have already read earlier because they have not comprehended the passage. When tested for comprehension, they score very low. Why does it happen? Why do students score low on comprehension when they have read a passage repeatedly? This happens because in reading the passage very slowly and very carefully the students have concentrated so much on the individual words and created so many fixations that they have failed to get the overall meaning of the passage. It is like seeing a film slowly, frame by frame. Ask the people who read fast and they will testify that there is no need to read slowly. Reading slowly interferes with one's comprehension because it causes too many artificial breaks and fixations which only block the smooth intake of ideas.

Reading _____(A)_____ is a bad idea because it makes the readers get stuck on the _____(B)_____.

|     | (A)     | (B)      |
|-----|---------|----------|
| ①   | quickly | plot     |
| ②   | slowly  | point    |
| ③   | slowly  | details  |
| ④   | fast    | specifics |

**해석** 종종 여러분은 학생들이 어떤 구절을 매우 느리게 읽고, 소리 내어 읽고 (즉, 모든 단어들을 큰 소리로 읽고), 그 구절을 이해하지 못했기 때문에 이미 앞서 읽은 문장들을 다시 읽는 것을 보았을 것이다. 이해도를 시험해 보면 그들은 매우 낮은 점수를 받는다. 왜 그런 일이 일어날까? 왜 학생들은 지문을 되풀이하여 읽었는데 이해도에 대한 점수를 낮게 받을까? 그 구절을 매우 천천히 그리고 매우 주의하여 읽으면서 학생들이 개개의 단어들에 너무나도 집중하고 너무나도 많이 집착하여 그 구절의 전체적인 의미를 이해하지 못했기 때문에 이런 일이 일어난다. 그것은 영화를 한 장면씩 천천히 보는 것과 같다. 빠르게 읽는 사람들에게 물어보면 천천히 읽을 필요가 없다고 증언해 줄 것이다. 천천히 읽는 것은, 아이디어의 부드러운 수용을 방해하기만 하는 너무 많은 인위적인 멈춤과 집착을 초래하기 때문에 이해를 방해한다.

[요약문] 느리게 읽는 것은 읽는 사람으로 하여금 <u>세부사항</u>에 얽매이게 하기 때문에 좋지 않은 생각이다.

**해설** STS '의문문 (Why do students score low on comprehension when they have read a passage repeatedly?)에 대한 답변'에 해당하는 문장 – This happens because in reading the passage very slowly and very carefully the students have concentrated so much on the individual words and created so many fixations that they have failed to get the overall meaning of the passage. 이 문장이 답 도출 근거 문장이다.

**어휘** vocalizing 발성  fixation 고정  intake 섭취

## `3` 마지막 문장이 의문문

**예제 1** 다음 글의 제목으로 가장 적절한 것은?　　　　　　　　　　**정답** ①

> How can young people help to solve social problems, even though they don't have enough power and resources? Youngsters learn by digging in and finding out what the issue are all about. And by being informed, they can influence adults through direct action. In fact, given an opportunity, young people many times have brought their thinking about significant issues to the attention of public officials. Thanks to the actions of young people, historical sites have been saved, and several kinds of endangered species have been preserved. How can we solve social problems without such actions of young people?

① Need for Young People in Solving Social problems
② The Impact of Social Problems on Young People
③ Adult's Intervention in Young People's Problem
④ The Significance of Data Conservation in the Information Age

**해석** 청소년들이 충분한 힘과 자원 없이 문제를 해소하는 데에 이바지하는 방법은 무엇일까? 청소년들은 파고들어가서 이슈가 무엇인지 알게 되면서 배운다. 그리고 정보가 제공되면 그들은 직접 행동함으로써 어른들에게 영향을 끼칠 수 있다. 사실 청소년들에게 기회가 주어진 경우 중대한 이슈에 대한 그들의 생각을 공직자들이 관심을 갖도록 하게 한 경우도 여러 차례 있었다. 청소년들의 행동으로 말미암아 역사적인 유적이 보존되었고, 여러 멸종 위기에 처한 동물들이 구해졌다. 이런 청소년들의 행위 없이 사회적 문제를 어떻게 해소할 수 있겠는가?
① 사회 문제 해결에 있어서 젊은 사람들의 필요성
② 사회 문제가 젊은 사람들에게 미치는 영향
③ 젊은 사람들의 문제점에 성인들의 간섭
④ 정보 시대에 데이터 보존의 중요성

**해설** **마지막 문장에 쓰인 수사의문문에 해당하는 문장** – How can we solve social problems without such actions of young people? 이 문장이 답 도출 근거 문장이다.

**어휘** youngster 젊은이, 어린이　　dig in 열심히 공부하다

## 4 통념비판의 원리

**예제 1** 다음 글의 주제로 가장 적절한 것은?    **정답** ③

> Many people believe that they will be free of their anger if they express it, and that their tears will release their pain. This belief derives from a nineteenth-century understanding of emotions, and it is no truer than the flat earth. It sees the brain as a steam kettle in which negative feelings build up pressure. But no psychologist has ever succeeded in proving the unburdening effects of the supposed safety valves of tears and anger. On the contrary, over forty years ago, controlled studies showed that fits of anger are more likely to intensify anger, and that tears can drive us still deeper into depression. Our heads do not resemble steam kettles, and our brains involve a much more complicated system than can be accounted for by images taken from nineteenth-century technology.

① 19세기 과학의 발전이 뇌 연구에 미친 영향
② 감정의 종류와 뇌 구조의 상관관계
③ 감정을 표현하는 것에 대한 사람들의 오해
④ 눈물과 분노를 담당하는 뇌의 영역

**해석** 많은 사람들은 분노를 표현하면 분노로부터 자유로워질 것이며 눈물이 고통을 덜어줄 것이라고 믿고 있다. 이런 믿음은 감정에 대한 19세기의 이해에 그 기원이 있는데 이 믿음은 평평한 지구라는 생각처럼 사실이 아니다. 이 믿음에 따르면 뇌는 부정적인 감정이 압력을 키우는 증기 주전자로 간주된다. 하지만 어떤 심리학자도 지금까지 눈물과 분노의 안전밸브로 추정되는 것의 부담경감의 효과를 입증하는 데 성공하지 못했다. 오히려 40년이 넘는 동안의 통제된 연구의 결과에 따르면, 분노의 폭발이 분노를 강화시킬 가능성이 더 많으며 눈물이 우리를 훨씬 더 깊은 우울증으로 몰고 갈 수 있다고 한다. 우리의 머리는 증기 주전자를 닮지 않았으며 우리의 뇌는 19세기 과학기술이 이끌어낸 이미지에 의해 설명될 수 있는 것보다 훨씬 더 복잡한 시스템을 내포하고 있다.

**해설** STS '**통념 (Many people that they will be free of their anger if they express it, and that their tears will release their pain)에 대한 비판**'에 해당하는 문장 — But no psychologist has ever succeeded in proving the unburdening effects of the supposed safety valves of tears and anger.
+
STS '**연구의 결과를 나타내는 표현 — controlled studies showed that**'이 들어간 문장 — controlled studies showed that fits of anger are more likely to intensify anger, and that tears can drive us still deeper into depression.
이 두 문장이 답 도출 근거 문장이다.

**어휘** steam kettle 증기 주전자    unburdening 부담을 덜다    intensify 강하게 하다

**예제 2** 다음 글의 제목으로 가장 적절한 것은?　　　　정답 ③

Some people believe that when they are alone they are lonely. However, if we accept our aloneness, we can give ourselves to our projects and our relationships out of our freedom instead of running to them out of our fear. In writing about solitude, Father William McNamara says that it is a misunderstanding to equate solitude with isolation. In his view, the opposite is true. When we enter into genuine solitude, we then have the ability to enter into the center of our being and connect in a meaningful way with others. Silence and solitude provide a means for coming to know ourselves better, for becoming centered, and for forming meaningful relationships. The Dalai Lama stresses that to make changes in our lives we need solitude, by which he means "a mental state free of distractions, not simply time alone in a quiet place."

① Solitude: What Must Be Overcome
② Being Alone: The Grave of a Relationship
③ Positive Aspects of Solitude
④ Solitude vs Isolation: Which is worse?

**해석** 어떤 사람들은 혼자 있을 때 외롭다고 생각한다. 그러나 혼자인 것을 받아들이면, 우리는 두려움 때문에 일과 관계에 달려가는 것이 아니라 자유로운 선택에 따라 그것들에 전념할 수 있다. 고독에 관해 쓰면서 William McNamara 신부는 고독과 고립을 동일시하는 것은 오해라고 말한다. 그의 관점에서는 그 반대가 맞다. 진정한 고독에 들어갈 때, 우리는 그때 우리 존재 중심에 들어가서 다른 사람들과 의미 있는 방식으로 관계를 맺을 능력을 가진다. 침묵과 고독은 우리 자신을 더 잘 알게 되고, 집중하게 되고, 의미 있는 관계를 형성하기 위한 수단을 제공한다. Dalai Lama는 인생에서 변화를 일으키기 위해서는 우리가 고독을 필요로 한다는 것을 강조하는데, 여기에서 그가 의미하는 고독은 단지 "조용한 곳에 혼자 있는 시간이 아니라 산만함이 없는 정신 상태"이다.
① 고독: 극복해야만 하는 것
② 혼자 있는 것: 관계의 무덤
③ 고독의 긍정적인 측면들
④ 고독 vs 고립: 어떤 것이 더 나쁜 것인가?

**해설** STS '통념 (Some people believe that shen they are alone they are lonely)에 대한 비판'에 해당하는 문장 — However if we accept our aloneness, we can give ourselves to our projects and our relationships out of our freedom instead of running to them out of our fear.
이 문장이 답 도출 근거 문장이다.

**어휘** aloneness 외로움　solitude 고독　equate 같게 하다

**5  문제점 발생 — 해결책 제시**

**예제 1**  다음 글의 요지로 가장 적절한 것은?   **정답** ①

> Mass political opinion can be sort of like guessing the number of marbles in a glass jar. Most people's guesses will miss the mark, but the average guess of a large enough crowd is generally very accurate. The idea that the masses generally come up with good overall decisions is sometimes referred to as the "wisdom of crowds," and it really does work amazingly well for some things. The problem is that in politics we don't see the glass jar for ourselves — we view it through the lens of the media, and the media show us a distorted view of politics. Thus, we should be aware of such media biases in order to minimize the likelihood that they'll throw off our political judgment, even though there's no way to permanently "fix" them.

① 정치적 판단의 혼란을 최소화하려면 미디어의 편향을 의식해야 한다.
② 편향되지 않은 정보를 습득하기 위해서는 다양한 매체를 접해야 한다.
③ 정치적 견해는 소수보다 다수에서 더 정확할 수 있다.
④ 미디어의 발전으로 대중의 정치 참여가 확대되어 왔다.

**해석** 대중의 정치적 견해는 유리병에 담긴 구슬의 수를 짐작하는 것과 다소 비슷할 수 있다. 대부분 사람들의 짐작은 빗나가지만 충분히 많은 수의 사람들의 평균 짐작은 일반적으로 아주 정확하다. 일반적으로 대중이 훌륭한 종합적 결정을 내놓는다는 생각은 종종 '대중의 지혜'라고도 일컬어지며, 어떤 경우에는 정말로 놀랄 만큼 잘 맞는다. 문제는 정치에서는 우리가 유리병을 우리 스스로 보는 것이 아니라는 것이다. 즉 우리는 미디어의 렌즈를 통해서 그것을 보고, 미디어는 우리에게 정치에 대한 왜곡된 관점을 보여준다. 그러므로 우리는, 그러한 미디어의 편향을 영구적으로 '고칠'방법은 없을지라도, 그것이 우리의 정치적 판단을 혼란스럽게 할 가능성을 최소화하기 위해서는 그러한 미디어의 편향을 인식해야 한다.

**해설** STS '문제점에 대한 해결책 제시'에 해당하는 문장 — Thus we should be aware of such media biases in order to minimize the likelihood that they'll throw off our political judgement, even though there's no way to permanently "fix" them.
이 문장이 답 도출 근거 문장이다.

**어휘** mass 대중   likelihood 개연성   throw off 벗다

**예제 2** 다음 글의 제목으로 가장 적절한 것은?　　　　　정답 ②

> Most of the world does not have access to the education afforded to a small minority. For every Albert Einstein, Yo-Yo Ma, or Barack Obama who has the opportunity for education, there are uncountable others who never get the chance. This vast waste of talent translates directly into reduced economic output. In a world where economic ruin is often tied to collapse, societies are well advised to exploit all the human capital they have. The Internet opens the gates of education to anyone who can get her hands on a computer. This is not always a trivial task, but the mere feasibility redefines the playing field. A motivated teen anywhere on the planet can walk through the world's knowledge, from Wikipedia to the curricula of MIT's Open Course Ware.

① The Use of The Internet In A Variety of Fields
② The Internet Can Provide Equal Educational Opportunities
③ Internet: New Areas of Economic Activity
④ Internet: A luxury That Only Privileged People Can Enjoy

**해석** 세계의 대부분은 소수의 사람에게 제공되는 교육에 접근하지 못한다. 교육의 기회를 가진 모든 Albert Einstein, Yo-Yo Ma, 또는 Barack Obama와 같은 사람들에 비해, 결코 기회를 얻지 못하는 셀 수 없을 정도로 많은 다른 사람들이 있다. 이러한 재주 있는 사람들의 엄청난 낭비는 바로 경제 생산량의 감소로 바뀐다. 경제적 파멸이 흔히 (사회 전체의) 와해와 연관되는 세계에서, 사회는 그것이 가지고 있는 모든 인적 자본을 활용하는 것이 가장 현명하다. 인터넷은 컴퓨터에 접할 수 있는 어느 누구에게도 교육의 문을 열어 준다. 이것이 늘 작은 일은 아니지만, 실행 가능성만으로도 경기장(일련의 경쟁 여건)은 재정의 된다. 지구의 어디에서든지 동기 부여를 받은 십 대는 Wikipedia에서부터 MIT의 OpenCourseWare의 교육과정에 이르기까지 세계의 지식을 두루 섭렵할 수 있다.
① 다양한 분야에서의 인터넷 사용
② 인터넷이 평등한 교육적 기회를 제공할 수 있다
③ 인터넷: 경제활동의 새로운 분야들
④ 인터넷: 단지 특권층만 즐길 수 있는 사치

**해설** STS '문제점에 대한 해결책 제시'에 해당하는 부분 − The Internet opens the gates of education to anyone who can get her hands on a computer. This is not always a trivial task, but the mere feasibility redefines the playing field. A motivated teen anywhere on the planet can walk through the world's knowledge, from Wikipedia to the curricula of MIT's Open Course Ware. 이 부분이 답 도출 근거 문장이다.

**어휘** access 접근　uncountable 셀 수 없는　trivial 하찮은　feasibility 실행할 수 있는　curricula 커리큘럼(의 복수형)

## 6 시간상의 대조

**예제 1**  다음 글의 제목으로 가장 적절한 것은?  **정답** ③

> In the 20th century social scientists undertook serious studies of the phenomenon of leadership. It has only been over the past thirty years that researchers have made a lot of progress in determining how people become effective leaders. We used to think that leaders were born and not made. Back in the old days, when strong social class barriers made it next to impossible for anyone to become a leader, we were trained to think that leadership was inherited. If your name wasn't Rockefeller, Firestone, Rothschild, or some other famous family name, you were not destined to become a leader. As class barriers crumbled and leaders arose from all parts of society, it became clear that leadership required more than being born into the right family. We begin to realize that everybody has the potential of becoming a leader, if they're given the chance.

① Leadership: Ability to Solve Social Problems
② Requirements For a Great Leader
③ Leaders: Are They Born or Made?
④ Why Is It Difficult To Study Leadership?

**해석** 20세기에 사회과학자들은 지도자의 지위라는 현상에 대한 진지한 연구에 착수했다. 사람들이 어떻게 유능한 지도자가 되는지를 밝히는 데 연구자들에게 많은 진전이 있는 것은 불과 지난 30년 동안이었다. 우리는 지도자가 태어나는 것이지 만들어지는 것이 아니라고 생각해왔었다. 먼 옛날, 강력한 사회 계층의 장벽이 아무나 지도자가 되는 것을 거의 불가능하게 했을 때, 지도자의 지위는 물려받는 것이라고 생각하도록 교육받았다. 여러분의 이름이 Rockefeller, Firestone, Rothschild 또는 다른 유명한 가문의 이름이 아니었다면, 여러분은 지도자가 될 운명이 아니었던 것이다. 계층의 장벽이 허물어지고 지도자들이 사회의 곳곳에서 나오면서, 지도자의 지위는 제대로 된 가문에 태어나는 것 이상을 필요로 한다는 것이 분명해졌다. 사람들은 기회가 주어진다면 모든 이들이 지도자가 될 잠재력이 있다는 것을 깨닫기 시작했다.
① 지도력: 사회 문제를 해결하는 능력
② 위대한 지도자가 갖춰야 할 요구조건들
③ 지도력: 타고나는 것인가 아니면 만들어지는 것인가?
④ 왜 지도력을 공부하는 것이 어려울까?

**해설** STS '시간상의 대조 (과거 〈 현재)'에 해당하는 문장 — We begin to realize that everybody has the potential of becoming a leader, if they're given the chance.
이 문장이 답 도출 근거 문장이다.

**어휘** determining 결정   barrier 장벽   inherit 상속하다, 물려받다   crumble 무너지다

**예제 2**  다음 글의 주제로 가장 적절한 것은?

**정답** ④

> Within the societal cultures of the United States, subcultural differences once ignored by many managers now command significant attention and sensitivity. Historically, the U.S. workforce has consisted primarily of white males. Today, however, white males make up far less than 50 percent of business new hires in the United States, whereas women and African American, Hispanic, and Asian men account for increasingly large portions of the U.S. workforce. Moreover, in. the last ten years the number of women and minorities assuming managerial positions in the U.S. workforce has grown by over 25 percent. It is becoming-and will continue to become-even more important for managers to know about and be ready to respond to the challenges deriving from individual differences in abilities, personalities, and motives. Knowledge about the workplace consequences of these differences can provide managers with help in this regard.

① problems resulting from cultural diversity in the United States

② the abolition of racism in employment in the United States

③ conflicts between minority and majority in the U.S. society

④ a change in the perception of the diversity in the U.S. workforce

**해석** 미국의 사회 문화 내에서 한때 많은 관리자가 무시했던 하위문화의 차이점은 이제 상당한 관심과 세심한 배려를 받고 있다. 역사적으로 미국의 노동 인구는 주로 백인 남성으로 구성되어 왔다. 그러나 오늘날 백인 남성은 미국 내 회사의 신규 사원 비율에서 50퍼센트보다 훨씬 적은 비율을 형성하는 반면에, 여성, 아프리카계 미국인, 라틴 아메리카계 및 아시아 남성이 미국 노동 인구에서 점점 더 큰 부분을 차지하고 있다. 게다가, 지난 10년 사이에 미국 노동 인구에서 관리직을 맡은 여성과 소수 민족 출신의 사람들의 수가 25퍼센트 넘게 늘어났다. 관리자가 능력, 성격, 그리고 동기의 개인적인 차이에서 비롯되는 어려운 문제에 관해 알고 그에 대응할 준비를 갖추는 것이 훨씬 더 중요해지고 있고, 계속해서 중요해질 것이다. 이러한 차이들이 직장에 가져오는 결과에 대해 아는 것은 이런 점에서 관리자에게 도움을 줄 수 있다.
① 미국에서 문화적 다양성으로부터 나오는 문제점들
② 미국의 고용에서의 인종차별주의의 폐지
③ 미국 사회에서 소수 집단과 다수 집단 사이의 갈등들
④ 미국 노동력에서 다양성 인식의 변화

**해설** STS '시간상의 대조 (과거 〈 현재)'에 해당하는 문장 — Today, however, white males make up far less than 50 percent of business new hires in the United States, whereas women and African American, Hispanic, and Asian men account for increasingly large portions of the U.S. workforce.
이 문장이 답 도출 근거 문장이다.

**어휘**  consist 이루어져 있다  whereas 반면  managerial 관리의  deriving from ~에서 유래

## 7 예시

**예제 1**　다음 글의 주제로 가장 적절한 것은?　　　**정답** ①

> There are many aspects of sustainability and, even if you decide you want to address all of them, the problem is that buildings are complex assemblies of different elements. There will always be a series of factors to balance. For example, if you put a building in a business park in the middle of nowhere, it will be possible to align it perfectly to make the most of the sun and to have windows that open because there will be very little noise. It will not, however, be possible for most users of the building to reach it by public transport or to walk or cycle there. Almost everyone will have to drive. Studies show that the overall carbon footprint of a super-green building in such a location will be greater than that of a less-than-ideal building in a city center well served by public transport.

① things to consider when building eco-friendly buildings
② factors to check when starting up a new business
③ the way to select a profitable location for business
④ advantages and drawbacks of going to work by public transportation

**해석**　지속 가능성의 많은 측면이 있는데 여러분이 그것을 모두 다루겠다고 결정하더라도 문제는 빌딩이 여러 다양한 요소로 이루어진 복잡한 조립체라는 점이다. 항상 균형을 이뤄야 하는 일련의 요인들이 있다. 예를 들어 여러분이 멀리 외떨어진 상업구역에 빌딩을 세운다면 햇빛을 최대한 활용할 수 있도록 완벽하게 배치하고, 소음이 거의 없기 때문에 열리는 창문을 갖추는 것이 가능할 것이다. 그러나 그 빌딩의 대부분 사용자들이 대중교통을 이용해서 그곳에 가거나 걸어서, 또는 자전거를 타고 가는 것은 가능하지 않을 것이다. 거의 모든 사람이 운전을 해야 할 것이다. 연구에 의하면 그런 위치에 있는 매우 환경 친화적인 빌딩의 전체 탄소발자국이 대중교통이 잘되어 있는 도심에 위치한 결코 이상적이라고 할 수 없는 빌딩의 탄소발자국보다 더 많을 것이다.
① 친환경 건물을 세울 때 고려해야 할 것들
② 새로운 사업을 시작할 때 검토해야 할 요소들
③ 사업을 위한 수익성이 좋은 장소를 선택하는 방법
④ 대중교통으로 일하러 가는 장점들과 단점들

**해설**　STS '예시[For example]의 앞부분' – There are many aspects of sustainability and, even if you decide you want to address all of them, the problem is that buildings are complex assemblies of different elements. There will always be a series of factors to balance.
 +
STS '연구의 결과를 나타내는 표현 – Studies show that이 들어간 문장 – Studies show that the overall carbon footprint of a super-green building in such a location will
be greater than that of a less-than-ideal building in a city center well served by public transport.
이 문장들이 답 도출 근거 문장들이다.

**어휘**　sustainability 지속 가능성　address 착수하다, 다루다, 연설하다　assembly 집합, 집회　align 맞추다

**예제 2** **다음 글의 주제로 가장 적절한 것은?**    정답 ③

When people move from one country to another or from one area to another, their economic status may change. They will be introduced to new foods and new food customs. Although their original food customs may have been nutritionally adequate, their new environment may cause them to change their eating habits. For instance, if milk was a staple food in their diet before moving and is unusually expensive in the new environment, milk may be replaced by a cheaper, nutritionally inferior beverage such as soda, coffee, or tea. Candy, possibly a luxury in their former environment, may be inexpensive and popular in their new environment. As a result, a family might increase consumption of soda or candy and reduce purchases of more nutritious foods. Someone who is not familiar with the nutritive values of foods can easily make such mistakes in food selection.

① significance of a well-balanced diet
② negative effects of immigration on family budgets
③ influences of relocation on food habits
④ misunderstanding about the nutritional value of foods

**해석** 사람들이 한 나라에서 다른 나라로 혹은 한 지역에서 다른 지역으로 이주할 때 그들의 경제적 지위가 바뀔 수도 있다. 그들은 새로운 음식과 새로운 식생활 관습에 접하게 될 것이다. 그들의 원래 식생활 관습이 영양 면에서 적절했다고 하더라도 그들은 새로운 환경으로 인해 자신들의 식습관을 바꾸게 될 수도 있다. 예를 들어, 그들이 이주하기 전에 우유가 식단의 주식이었는데 새로운 환경에서 대단히 비싸다면 우유는 탄산음료, 커피, 혹은 차와 같이 더 싸고 영양 면에서 뒤지는 음료로 대체될 수 있다. 그들의 이전 환경에서 어쩌면 사치품이었을 수도 있는 캔디가 새로운 환경에서는 비싸지 않고 대중적인 것일 수도 있다. 결과적으로, 한 가족의 탄산음료나 캔디의 소비가 늘고 영양가가 더 많은 식품의 구입이 줄어들 수도 있다. 식품의 영양가를 잘 알지 못하는 사람은 식품을 선택할 때 쉽사리 그런 실수를 할 수 있다.
① 잘 균형 잡힌 식단의 중요성
② 이주가 가정 예산에 미치는 부정적인 영향들
③ 이전(이동)이 식습관에 미치는 영향들
④ 음식의 영양학적 가치에 관한 오해

**해설** STS '예시[For instance]의 앞부분' — When people move from one country to another or from one area to another, their economic status may change. They will be introduced to new foods and new food customs. Although their original food customs may have been nutritionally adequate, their new environment may cause them to change their eating habits. 이 문장들이 답 도출 근거 문장들이다.

**어휘** adequate 적절한   consumption 소비

**예제 3** 다음 글의 주제로 가장 적절한 것은?　　정답 ①



Some distinctions between good and bad are hardwired into our biology. Infants enter the world ready to respond to pain as bad and to sweet (up to a point) as good. In many situations, however, the boundary between good and bad is a reference point that changes over time and depends on the immediate circumstances. Imagine that you are out in the country on a cold night, inadequately dressed for the torrential rain, your clothes soaked. A stinging cold wind completes your misery. As you wander around, you find a large rock that provides some shelter from the fury of the elements. The biologist Michel Cabanac would call the experience of that moment intensely pleasurable because it functions, as pleasure normally does, to indicate the direction of a biologically significant improvement of circumstances. The pleasant relief will not last very long, of course, and you will soon be shivering behind the rock again, driven by your renewed suffering to seek better shelter.

① variability in what is considered good and bad
② human's inborn instinct for gratification
③ biology as a instructor for our action
④ individual ability to distinguish cold from warmth

**해석** 좋음과 나쁨 사이의 몇 가지 구별은 우리의 생명 활동 안에 타고난 속성이다. 유아는 고통은 나쁘다고 반응하고 (어느 정도까지의) 달콤함은 좋다고 반응할 준비가 된 채로 세상에 나온다. 하지만, 많은 경우에서 좋음과 나쁨의 경계는 시간에 따라 변하는 기준점이며 당면한 상황에 의해 결정된다. 추운 밤에 폭우에 부적절한 옷을 입고 옷이 흠뻑 젖은 채로 시골에서 바깥에 있다고 상상해 보라. 찌르는 듯한 차가운 바람으로 완전히 고통을 느낀다. 주변을 서성이다가 격렬한 악천후에 대한 어떤 피난처를 제공하는 커다란 바위를 발견한다. 생물학자인 Michel Cabanac은 그 순간에 대한 경험을 대단히 즐겁다고 보곤 했는데, 즐거움이 보통 그렇듯이 그것이 생물학적으로 상황에 대한 상당한 개선의 방향을 보여주는 기능을 하기 때문이다. 물론 그 즐거운 안도는 아주 오래 지속되지는 않을 것이고, 여러분은 곧 바위 뒤에서 다시 몸을 떨고 있게 될 것이며, 새로워진 고통에 의해 결국 더 좋은 피난처를 찾게 될 것이다.
① 좋고 나쁜 것이라고 생각되는 것에 대한 가변성
② 만족감에 대한 인간의 타고난 본능
③ 우리의 행동 지침으로서의 생물학적 요인
④ 차갑고 따뜻함을 구별하는 개인적 능력

**해설** STS '예시[Imagine]의 앞부분' — Some distinctions between good and bad are hardwired into our biology. Infants enter the world ready to respond to pain as bad and to sweet (up to a point) as good. In many situations, however, the boundary between good and bad is a reference point that changes over time and depends on the immediate circumstances. 이 문장들이 답 도출 근거 문장들이다.

**어휘** distinction 구별　hardwired 타고난　torrential 심한　misery 불행　variability 가변성

**예제 4** 다음 글의 주제로 가장 적절한 것은?  정답 ④

Suppose you wish to determine which brand of microwave popcorn leaves the fewest unpopped kernels. You will need a supply of various brands of microwave popcorn to test, and you will need a microwave oven. If you used different brands of microwave ovens with different brands of popcorn, the percentage of unpopped kernels could be caused by the different brands of popcorn or by the different brands of ovens. Under such circumstances, the experimenter would be unable to conclude confidently whether the popcorn or the oven caused the difference. To eliminate this problem, you must use the same microwave oven for every test. In order to reasonably conclude that the change in one variable was caused by the change in another specific variable, there must be no other variables in the experiment. By using the same microwave oven, you control the number of variables in the experiment.

① safety rules to be followed in an experiment
② benefits of using various experimental methods
③ impact of background knowledge on experiments
④ the need for controlling variables in experiments

**해석** 여러분이 어느 상표의 전자레인지용 팝콘이 덜 튀겨진 낱알을 가장 적게 남기는지를 알아내고 싶다고 가정해 보자. 여러분은 조사할 어느 정도 양의 다양한 상표의 전자레인지용 팝콘을 필요로 할 것이고, 전자레인지 한 대도 필요로 할 것이다. 만일 여러분이 여러 다른 상표의 전자레인지를 여러 다른 상표의 팝콘과 함께 사용한다면, 덜 튀겨진 낱알의 비율은 그 여러 상표의 팝콘 또는 그 여러 상표의 전자레인지가 원인일 수 있을 것이다. 그런 상황하에서는, 실험자가 그 차이를 야기한 것이 팝콘인지 또는 전자레인지를 자신 있게 결정할 수 없을 것이다. 이 문제를 제거하려면, 여러분은 모든 조사에서 반드시 동일한 전자레인지를 사용해야만 한다. 하나의 변수에서의 변화가 다른 하나의 특정 변수에서의 변화에 의해 야기되었다고 합리적으로 결론을 내리기 위해서는, 그 실험에 다른 변수들이 있으면 안 된다. 동일한 전자레인지를 사용함으로써, 여러분은 실험에서 변수의 개수를 통제하는 것이다.
① 실험에서 따라야 할 안전 규칙들
② 다양한 실험 방식을 사용하는 것의 장점들
③ 배경 지식이 실험에 미치는 영향
④ 실험에서 변수들을 통제할 필요성

**해설** 예시[Suppose]를 정리해 주는 부분이자, STS 'you must'가 들어간 문장 — To eliminate this problem, you must use the same microwave oven for every test.

+

STS 'must'가 들어간 문장 — In order to reasonably conclude that the change in one variable was caused by the change in another specific variable, there must be no other variables in the experiment.
이 두 문장이 답 도출 근거 문장들이다.

**어휘** kernel 핵심, 알맹이   variables 변수

**예제 5** 다음 글의 주제로 가장 적절한 것은? **정답** ③

---

**Radical developments in technology have revolutionized the way in which artists and entertainers tell their stories**. From live-streamed transmissions from London's Royal Opera House and the New York Met to the innovative use of sound, film and projection in plays such as the National Theater's The Waves, technology is constantly opening up staged entertainment to new formats and audiences. The British producing company Artichoke are masters of harnessing technology to tell a story: In May 2006 they brought French company Royal de Luxe's The Sultan's Elephant to the streets of London, fascinating audiences young and old with a 42-ton mechanical elephant and a 6-meter-tall princess, who traveled on a London bus and disappeared in a rocket.

① reasons some performances are thought of as valuable
② growing popularity of diverse performing arts
③ effect of technology on artistic expression
④ using artistic formats in selling goods and services

---

**해석** 기술의 엄청난 발달은 예술가들과 연예인들이 그들의 이야기를 전달하는 방식을 혁신해왔다. 런던의 Royal Opera House와 New York Met의 라이브 스트리밍에 의한 전송에서부터 National Theater의 The Waves와 같은 연극에서 소리, 필름, 프로젝션의 혁신적인 사용에 이르기까지, 기술은 무대에 올리는 오락을 새로운 형식과 관객에게 끊임없이 열어주고 있다. 영국의 공연 제작사 Artichoke는 이야기를 전달하기 위해 기술을 이용하는 데 대가들이다. 2006년 5월 그들은 프랑스 회사 Royal de Luxe의 The Sultan's Elephant를 런던의 거리에 가져다 놓았는데, 42톤의 기계로 된 코끼리와 키가 6미터인 공주로 노소를 불문한 모든 관객을 매료시켰으며, 그녀(공주)는 런던의 버스로 돌아다니다가 로켓을 타고 사라졌다.

① 몇 가지 공연이 가치 있다고 생각되어진 이유들
② 다양한 공연 예술들의 커지는 인기
③ 기술이 예술적 표현에 미치는 영향들
④ 재화와 용역을 판매할 때 예술적 구성 방식을 사용하기

**해설** STS '예시[고유명사]의 앞부분' — Radical developments in technology have revolutionized the way in which artists and entertainers tell their stories.
이 문장이 답 도출 근거 문장이다.

**어휘** radical development 급진적 발전   transmission 전송   projection 투사

**예제 6** 다음 글의 주제로 가장 적절한 것은?　　　　정답 ④

> As an advocate, mass media can promote the work of the nonprofit sector. Quite apart from sensational reports that amplify charity scandals, the media often does share on the positive aspects of the sector as well. The wide-ranging reach of nonprofit sector work has opened up new segments in the media industry. No longer confined to just the local news sections of the newspapers, there are magazines, such as Good and Ode to tell the stories of individuals, teams, and organizations that seek to do good in this world. There are also publications and websites that focus entirely on a growing nonprofit audience. Examples include The Chronicle of Philanthropy, Stanford Social Innovation Review, and Beyond Profit.

① 대중 매체가 비영리 부문의 사업의 폭을 넓혀주었다.
② 대중 매체의 선정적 보도는 비영리 부문의 긍정적인 측면을 가린다.
③ 다양한 분야의 보도가 미디어 산업의 진보를 가져왔다.
④ 비영리 부문을 홍보하는 대중 매체가 증가하고 있다.

**해석** 대중매체는 지지자로서 비영리 부문의 사업을 홍보하기도 한다. 자선 단체의 스캔들을 증폭시키는 선정적인 보도와는 완전히 별도로, 대중매체는 흔히 그 부문의 긍정적인 측면에 대해서도 실제로 말한다. 비영리 부문이 하는 사업의 폭넓은 도달 범위는 미디어 산업의 새로운 영역을 열었다. 더 이상 신문의 지역 소식란에만 한정되지 않고 이 세상에서 선행을 추구하는 사람들, 팀들, 단체들에 대한 이야기를 하는 'Good'과 'Ode'같은 잡지들이 있다. 또한 증가하는 비영리 부문 독자에 전적으로 초점을 맞춘 출판물이나 웹 사이트도 있다. 예로는 'The Chronicle of Philanthropy', 'Stanford Social Innovation Review', 및 'Beyond Profit'이 있다.

**해설** STS '예시[고유명사]의 앞부분' — As an advocate, mass media can promote the work of the nonprofit sector. Quite apart from sensational reports that amplify charity scandals, the media often does share on the positive aspects of the sector as well. 이 부분이 답 도출 근거 문장들이다.

**어휘** advocate 지지하다　sector 분야　sensational 선풍적인　amplify 더욱 상세히 하다　segment 부분

**예제 7** 다음 글의 요지로 가장 적절한 것은?  **정답** ②

In 1879 Thomas Edison announced that he would publicly display the electric lightbulb by December 31, even though all his experiments had, to that point, failed. He threw his knapsack over the brick wall — the numerous challenges that he still faced — and on the last day of that year, there was light. In 1962, when John F. Kennedy declared to the world that the United States was going to land a man on the moon by the end of the decade, some of the metals necessary for the journey had not yet been invented, and the technology required for completing the journey was not available. But he threw his and NASA's knapsack over the brick wall. Though making a verbal commitment, no matter how bold and how inspiring, does not ensure that we reach our destination, it does enhance the likelihood of success.

① 위대한 발명은 실현 불가능해 보이는 아이디어에서 비롯된다.
② 목표를 내세우고 이를 공표하는 것이 성공의 가능성을 높여준다.
③ 꿈을 이루려면 말만 하기보다 구체적인 행동을 해야 한다.
④ 여러 번의 실패와 끊임없는 재시도를 통해 과학의 발전이 이루어졌다.

**해석** 1879년에 Thomas Edison은 그때까지 그의 모든 실험이 실패했음에도 불구하고 12월 31일까지 백열전구를 공개적으로 내보이겠다고 발표하였다. 그는 그의 배낭을 벽돌담 – 그가 여전히 직면하고 있던 수많은 어려움 – 너머로 던졌고, 그해의 마지막 날 빛(전구)이 있었다. 1962년, John F. Kennedy가 미국이 60년대 말까지 인간을 달에 착륙시킬 것이라고 세계를 향해 공표했을 때, 그 우주여행에 반드시 필요한 일부 금속은 아직 발명되지 않았었고, 그 여행의 완수에 요구되는 기술도 없었다. 그러나 그는 자신의 그리고 NASA의 배낭을 벽돌담 너머로 던졌다. 말로 하는 약속이 아무리 대담하고 고무적일지라도 목표에 도달하는 것을 보장해 주지는 못하지만 분명히 성공의 가능성을 높여 준다.

**해설** 예시[人이름]를 정리해주는 부분이자, STS '양보절과 주절 / 강조의 do'가 들어간 문장 — Though making a verbal commitment, no matter how bold and how inspiring, does not ensure that we reach our destination, it does enhance the likelihood of success. 이 문장이 답 도출 근거 문장이다.

**어휘** knapsack 배낭

## 8 Story / 일화

**예제 1** 다음 글의 제목으로 가장 적절한 것은?　　　　　　　　　　　　　**정답** ①

It is said that a music student once approached Mozart and asked him for advice on what he should compose and how he should do it to create something really good. Mozart took a good look at him and said, "You are still young. I think you should start with composing a duet." This young man got upset and told Mozart that he too was still young, and that since he had composed more serious music than duets, why shouldn't he? Mozart replied, "That is true, but I did not go around asking people what to compose. I knew what to do." The point is that many have attempted to create great art, but only a very tiny percentage have become true masters.

① What Differentiates a Master from a Beginner
② Mozart's One and Only Mistake
③ Who laughs last : The Winner
④ Great Works Come From Endless Efforts

**해석** 음악을 공부하는 한 학생이 한번은 모차르트에게 다가가 자기가 무엇을 작곡해야 하고 정말로 좋은 작품을 창작하기 위해 어떻게 그것을 해야 하는지에 대한 조언을 요청했다고 한다. 모차르트는 그를 유심히 보고는 "당신은 아직 어립니다. 당신은 이중주곡 작곡부터 시작해야 할 것 같습니다."라고 말했다. 이 젊은이는 화가 나서 모차르트에게 그(모차르트) 역시 아직 어리다고 말하고는 그(모차르트)가 이중주곡보다 더 진지한 음악을 작곡했는데, 자기는 왜 하면 안 되느냐고 물었다. 모차르트는 "맞는 말입니다만, 저는 사람들에게 무엇을 작곡해야 하는지를 물으면서 돌아다니지는 않았습니다. 저는 무엇을 해야 할지를 알고 있었거든요."라고 대답했다. 요컨대 많은 사람이 위대한 예술을 창조하려고 노력해 왔지만, 단지 아주 적은 소수만이 진정한 대가가 되었다는 것이다.
① 달인과 초보자를 구별해 주는 것
② 모차르트의 한 가지 유일한 실수
③ 누가 마지막에 웃는가: (그가) 승자
④ 위대한 작품은 끊임없는 노력으로부터 나온다

**해설** 글의 종류가 Story이므로 전반적인 글의 흐름을 읽어 나가야 하지만, 이 글의 마지막 문장이자 STS 'The point is'가 들어간 문장 — The point is that many have attempted to create great art, but only a very tiny percentage have become true masters. 이 문장이 답 도출 근거 문장이다.

**어휘** attempt 시도

## 9 설명문

**예제 1** 다음 글의 주제로 가장 적절한 것은?　　　　　　　　　　　정답 ①

When scientists use a device called a calorimeter, the piece of food to be measured is placed inside the device, sealed, and then burned. The energy from the food heats the water surrounding the chamber. By weighing the amount of water heated, noting the increase in the water temperature, and multiplying the two, the energy capacity of the food can be measured. For example, if 10 liters of water surrounding the chamber is 20 degrees centigrade before combustion and then is measured at 25 degrees after combustion, the difference in temperature (5 degrees) is multiplied by the volume of water (10 liters) to arrive at the caloric value (50 calories of energy).

① the way to calculate the caloric value of food
② importance of water and temperature in food conservation
③ how to measure water content in a food
④ limitations of calorie measurements using a calorimeter

**해석** 과학자들이 칼로리미터라는 기구를 이용할 때, 측정하려는 음식물 조각을 이 기구 안에 넣고, 뚜껑을 닫은 후 태운다. 그 음식물로부터의 에너지가 주변공간에 있는 물을 데운다. 데워진 물의 양을 재고, 물의 온도의 상승량을 측정하고, 이 두 수치를 곱함으로써 그 음식의 에너지량을 측정할 수 있다. 예를 들어, 주변공간의 물 10리터가 연소 전과 후에 각각 화씨 20도와 25도였다면, 그 차이(5도)와 물의 부피(10리터)를 곱하면 칼로리(50칼로리의 에너지)를 계산할 수 있다.
① 음식의 칼로리 수치를 계산하는 방법
② 음식 보존에서 물과 온도의 중요성
③ 음식에서 수분 함유량을 측정하는 방법
④ 칼로리 측정기를 사용한 칼로리 측정의 한계점들

**해설** 순수 설명문으로 특정 문장이 답 도출 근거로 활용되는 글은 아니다. 전반적으로 '음식의 칼로리 수치를 계산하는 방법'에 대해서 설명하고 이에 대한 예시가 나온 글이다.

**어휘** measure 측정하다　chamber 방　centigrade 섭씨　combustion 연소

**예제 2** 다음 글의 요지로 가장 적절한 것은?　　　　　　　　　　　　　　　　　　　　　　　정답 ②

Unlike oil, we can't mine hydrogen gas from the Earth. The hydrogen that is present has all already "burned" — that is, combined with oxygen to make water ($H_2$ O), or with carbon to make sugars, starches, and hydrocarbons (including plant matter, wood, oil, and natural gas). To use hydrogen we have to separate the hydrogen from the other atoms. We can remove the hydrogen from water by running electric current through it — a process called electrolysis. But that process takes energy, and when we use the released hydrogen as fuel, we get back only 30% to 40% of the energy that we put in; the rest is wasted as heat. Beware of inventions that claim to use ordinary water as fuel; these usually obtain the hydrogen by using other energy to separate it from water, by electrolysis or use of another fuel such as a purified metal.

① 수소는 에너지 낭비 없이 연료로 사용할 수 있는 자원이다.

② 전기나 다른 연료를 이용하여 수소 연료를 얻는 것은 효율성이 떨어진다.

③ 대부분의 물질에 수소가 포함되어 있으므로 수소연료의 사용은 효율적이다.

④ 수소 연료의 효율성을 높이려면 수소 분리 과정의 개선이 필요하다.

**해석** 석유와 달리, 우리는 수소 가스를 지구에서 채굴할 수 없다. 존재하는 수소는 모두 이미 '연소'되었다. 즉 산소와 결합하여 물(H2O)을 만들거나 탄소와 결합하여 당, 전분, 그리고 (식물질(植物質), 나무, 석유, 그리고 천연가스를 포함하는) 탄화수소를 만들었다. 수소를 사용하기 위해 우리는 다른 원자들로부터 수소를 분리해야 한다. 우리는 물에 전류를 흐르게 하여 물로부터 수소를 추출할 수 있는데, 그것은 '전기 분해'라고 불리는 과정이다. 그러나 그 과정은 에너지를 필요로 하고, 우리가 방출된 수소를 연료로 사용할 때, 우리는 들인 에너지의 겨우 30퍼센트에서 40퍼센트만을 돌려받고, 나머지는 열로 낭비된다. 보통의 물을 연료로 사용한다고 주장하는 발명품을 조심하라. 이것들은 보통 물로부터 그것(수소)을 분리하기 위해 다른 에너지를 사용함으로써, 즉 전기 분해나 정제된 금속과 같은 다른 연료의 사용에 의해 수소를 얻는다.

**해설** 글의 전반부는 설명문의 분위기로 이끌어 가다가, 이 내용을 바탕으로 후반부에 필자의 생각을 드러내는 형태의 글이다.

STS 'But'이 들어간 문장 — But that process takes energy, and when we use the released hydrogen as fuel, we get back only 30% to 40% of the energy that we put in; the rest is wasted as heat.

+

STS '명령문'이 들어간 문장 — Beware of invention that claim to use ordinary water as fuel; these usually obtain the hydrogen by using other energy to separate it from water, by electrolysis or use of another fuel such as a purified metal.

이 두 문장이 답 도출 근거 문장들이다.

**어휘** hydrogen 수소　　hydrocarbon 탄화수소　　electrolysis 전기분해　　purify 정화하다

## 10 열거

**예제 1** 다음 글의 주제로 가장 적절한 것은?  정답 ③

> The public and donors expect charities to be "run by highly motivated but relatively modestly paid people." And charity workers have come to accept this. There are two reasons for this state of affairs. The first is that in meeting the goal of operating at minimum costs, staff costs also have to be kept low. The second is that charity workers are asked to be aligned, and show their alignment, with the charitable nature of the organization they are working for by taking a wage less than what they might have been offered elsewhere. The wage subsidy is thus a partial donation to the cause. Interestingly, this moral argument of contributing to the cause ignores the morality of paying a man less than he is worth; even if, at times, he is paid below-subsistence rates.

① the financial crisis of international charities
② the way to increase public donation
③ the reason charity workers are poorly paid
④ the influence of charity on society

**해석** 대중 기부자들은 자선단체가 '대단히 의욕적이지만 비교적 그다지 많지 않게 보수를 받는 사람들에 의해 운영'되기를 바란다. 그리고 자선단체 직원들은 이를 수용하게 되었다. 이런 상황에는 두 가지 원인이 있다. 첫째는 최소 비용으로 운용하려는 목표를 충족시킬 때 직원 비용 또한 낮게 유지되어야 한다는 것이다. 둘째는 자선단체 직원들이 다른 곳에서라면 제공받았을지도 모르는 것보다 더 적은 봉급을 가져감으로써 그들이 근무하고 있는 단체의 자선을 베푸는 본질에 동조할 것을 요구받고 동조를 보인다는 것이다. 임금 보조금은 그러므로 대의명분에 대한 일부 기부가 되는 셈이다. 흥미롭게도, 대의명분에 기여하는 것이라는 이러한 도덕과 관련된 주장은 어떤 사람에게 그가 가진 가치보다 임금을 덜 지불하는 것의 도덕성 문제를 모른 체하는 것이다. 심지어 때로는 그가 최저 생활수준에 못 미치는 임금을 받더라도 말이다.
① 국제 자선 단체의 재정적 위기
② 대중의 기부를 증가시키는 방법
③ 자선 단체 노동자들이 급여를 적게 받는 이유
④ 자선 단체가 사회에 미치는 영향

**해설** STS '**열거의 앞부분**' — The public and donors expect charities to be "run by highly motivated but relatively modestly paid people." And charity workers have come to accept this. There are two reasons for this state of affairs.
이 문장들이 답 도출 근거 문장들이다.

**어휘** motivate 동기를 부여하다   modestly 겸손하게   operating 운영   alignment 조정   charitable 자비로운   wage 임금

**예제 2** 이 글의 제목으로 가장 적절한 것은?   정답 ①

Farming began about 12,000 years ago and it has developed very quickly in the last 300 years. There are no signs that the speed of development will slow down. Agriculture will continue to develop in several ways. First, farming will become even more efficient by using new types of technology. Many processes will be controlled by computers. Second, new ways of growing, storing, and selling crops will be developed which can be used by poor people as well as rich people. Third, agricultural products will be used in many different ways.

① The Development of Agriculture
② The Progress of Agriculture Technology
③ An Increase in Crop Yields
④ The Limitations of Agricultural Technology

**해석** 농업은 약 12,000년 전에 시작되었고, 또한 그것은 지난 300년 사이에 빠르게 발전하였다. 발전의 속도가 지체되리라는 징후는 보이지 않았다. 농업은 여러 가지 면에서 앞으로도 발전할 것이다. 첫째, 농업은 새로운 유형의 기술을 이용함으로써 훨씬 더 능률적이게 될 것이다. 많은 과정들이 컴퓨터에 의해서 통제받게 될 것이다. 둘째로, 새로운 곡물의 재배법, 저장법, 그리고 판매 기법이 개발되고, 그것이 부자는 물론이고 가난한 사람들도 이용하게 될 것이다. 셋째로, 농업 생산물이 서로 다른 많은 방식으로 활용되게 될 것이다.
① 농업의 발달
② 농업 기술의 진보
③ 농작물 수확량의 증가
④ 농업 기술의 제한점들

**해설** STS '열거의 앞부분' – Agriculture will continue to develop in several ways.
이 문장이 답 도출 근거 문장이다.

**어휘** agriculture 농업

## 11  나열식 구조

### 예제 1  이 글의 제목으로 가장 적절한 것은?

정답 ④

Some people find that exercising when they have a mild cold makes them feel better. Illnesses vary in severity and people react differently to them, so listen to your body. If you have a minor problem, such as a cough or a tight muscle, and otherwise feel fine, it is probably acceptable to work out. Avoid exercise to the point of exhaustion. Avoid exercise if you have the flu, have a fever, have a body ache, feel extremely tired, have a breathing problem, or have swollen glands. Exercise does not cure illness. The old saying that "you can sweat out a cold" with exercise is untrue. When you recover from illness, do not start exercising at the same level as before. Give yourself a few days to build back to normal levels.

① Dangers of Living an Inactive Life
② How Does Your Body Respond To Illness?
③ Exercise: Medicine to Cure All Diseases
④ Exercising When Sick: A Good Move?

**해석**  일부 사람들은 가벼운 감기에 걸렸을 때 운동을 하는 것이 그들이 더 건강해졌다고 느끼게 만든다고 알고 있다. 질병은 심한 정도가 다양하고 사람들은 질병에 서로 다르게 반응하므로, 자신의 몸에 귀를 기울여라. 기침이나 뭉친 근육과 같은 심각하지 않은 문제만 있고 다른 모든 점에서는 몸 상태가 괜찮다고 느껴지면, 운동을 하는 것은 아마도 용인될 수 있을 것이다. 기진맥진할 정도까지 운동하는 것은 피해라. 독감에 걸렸거나 열이 나거나 몸이 쑤시거나 극도로 피로를 느끼거나 호흡에 문제가 있거나 혹은 내분비선이 부었다면 운동하는 것을 피해라. 운동이 질병을 치료하지는 않는다. 운동을 하며 "땀을 내서 감기를 낫게 할 수 있다"는 옛 격언은 사실이 아니다. 질병으로부터 회복될 때는 이전과 똑같은 수준으로 운동을 시작하지 말아라. 자신에게 며칠 시간을 할애하여 정상 수준으로 다시 몸을 만들도록 해라.
① 활동성이 없는 삶의 위험
② 당신의 신체는 질병에 어떻게 반응을 하는가?
③ 운동: 모든 질병을 치료하는 약
④ 아플 때 운동: 좋은 움직임인가?

**해설**  **같은 모양(명령문 + 같은 단어 [의미])이 들어간 문장** – Avoid exercise to the point of exhaustion.
+
Avoid exercise if you have the flu, have a fever, have a body ache, feel extremely tired, have a breathing problem, or have swollen glands.
+
do not start exercising at the same level as before.
이 세 문장이 답 도출 근거 문장들이다.

**어휘**  severity 심각성   exhaustion 피로   glands 땀샘

**예제 2** 다음 빈칸에 들어갈 말로 가장 적절한 것은?

정답 ② 

> Do you know people who have plenty of ideas but don't follow through? These people need collaborators to help them implement. What about artists who paint masterpieces that nobody sees? They need a collaborator to help them promote themselves. Then there are inventors who need help protecting their ideas, entrepreneurs who need help gaining capital, or composers who need help with lyrics. Working together allows for different points of view and sparks new ideas. It's not enough to be a lone innovator. Good ideas can be made into great ideas when we utilize each other's specialized expertise. In fact, venture capitalists say the most important quality they look for in businesses isn't the ideas but the ___________ . Look for partners who don't duplicate your skills but complement them.

① gifts

② teams

③ incentives

④ endeavors

**해석** 많은 아이디어를 갖고 있지만 (그 아이디어를) 끝까지 발전시키지 못하는 사람들을 여러분은 알고 있는가? 이러한 사람들은 그들이 실행하도록 도울 협력자들이 필요하다. 아무도 보지 않는 걸작을 그리는 화가들은 어떤가? 그들은 그들이 판촉을 할 수 있도록 도울 협력자가 필요하다. 그리고 또 자신들의 아이디어를 보호하는 데 도움을 필요로 하는 발명가들, 자본을 얻는 데 도움이 필요한 기업가들, 또는 가사(를 쓰는 것)에 도움이 필요한 작곡가들이 있다. 함께 일한다는 것은 다양한 관점을 허용하고 새로운 아이디어를 촉발한다. 혁신가 혼자서는 충분하지 않다. 우리가 서로의 전문 지식을 이용할 때 좋은 아이디어가 위대한 아이디어로 바뀔 수 있다. 실제로, 벤처 투자가는 사업체에서 그들이 찾는 가장 중요한 자질이 아이디어가 아니라 (일을 함께 하는) 팀이라고 말한다. 여러분의 기술을 복제하는 것이 아니라 그것을 보완해 주는 동업자를 찾아라.
① 재능
② 팀
③ 동기 부여
④ 노력

**해설** **공통인 사례에 해당하는 내용이 들어간 문장**
What about artists who paint masterpieces that nobody sees?
+
Then there are inventors who need help protecting their ideas, entrepreneurs who need help gaining capital, or composers who need help with lyrics.
이 두 문장이 답 도출 근거 문장들이다.

**어휘** implement 구현하다    entrepreneurs 기업가    spark 불꽃    lone 고독한    utilize 활용하다    expertise 전문적 지식
duplicate 복제하다

**예제 3** 다음 글의 제목으로 가장 적절한 것은?　　　　　　　　　**정답** ②

> You may not always be aware of them, but you are continually making pictures in your mind. These pictures have a favourable effect if they are positive (and, in contrast, a harmful effect if they are negative). A writer said, "What the mind can conceive, the will can achieve." That's why top sportsmen and women use creative imagery and autosuggestion to help them win trophies and break world records; business executives use them to help make better sales presentations and gain promotion; leading doctors teach patients to relieve painful symptoms and even rid themselves of serious diseases, using these techniques; and psychotherapists help their clients overcome a wide range of emotional problems using them, including fears and panic attacks, eliminating unwanted habits, stress and lack of confidence.

① Making Desirable Conditions for Psychological Stability
② Powers of Positive Imagery for Better Achievement
③ Ways to Avoid a Negative Picture of Yourself
④ Mental Capacity for Creative Thinking

**해석** 항상 의식하고 있지 않을 수도 있지만, 사람은 자신의 정신 속에 심상을 끊임없이 만들어 내고 있다. 이러한 심상은 긍정적인 것이라면 유리한 효과를 가진다.(그에 반해서 부정적이라면 해로운 효과를 가진다.) 어떤 작가는 "정신이 상상할 수 있는 것을 의지가 성취해 낼 수 있다"라고 말했다. 그런 이유로 최고의 남녀 운동선수들은 자기들이 우승컵을 차지하고 세계기록을 깨뜨리는 데 도움이 되도록 창의적인 심상과 자기 암시를 사용한다. 회사의 경영 간부들은 제품 소개를 더 잘하여 승진을 하는 데 도움이 되도록 그것을 사용한다. 선구적인 의사들은 이러한 기법을 사용하여 환자들이 고통스러운 증상을 덜고 심지어는 심각한 질병에서 벗어나도록 가르친다. 그리고 정신 요법 의사들은 그것을 사용하여 그들의 고객들이 원하지 않는 습관과 스트레스와 자신감 부족을 없애고, 공포와 공황 발작을 포함한 광범위한 정서적 문제를 극복하도록 돕는다.
① 심리적 안정감을 위한 바람직한 조건을 만들기
② 더 나은 성취를 위한 긍정적인 이미지의 힘
③ 너 자신에 대한 부정적인 장면을 피하는 방법들
④ 창의적인 사고를 위한 정신적 능력

**해설** **공통인 사례에 해당하는 내용이 들어간 문장**
That's why top sportsmen and women use creative imagery and autosuggestion to help them win trophies and break world records; business executives use them to help make better sales presentations and gain promotion; leading doctors teach patients to relieve painful symptoms and even rid themselves of serious diseases, using these techniques; and psychotherapists help their clients overcome a wide range of emotional problems using them, including fears and panic attacks, eliminating unwanted habits, stress and lack of confidence.
이 문장이 답 도출 근거 문장이다.

**어휘** favourable 유리한　conceive 배다, 상상하다　autosuggestion 자기 암시　psychotherapist 심리치료사

## 12 인과관계

**예제 1** 다음 빈칸에 들어갈 말로 가장 적절한 것은?   **정답** ①

> The obvious role of sugar in ice cream is to sweeten the product. However, sugar also plays a role in determining the ________________ of the frozen ice cream, because sugar causes the freezing temperature of the mixture to drop. In fact, a cup of sugar in a quart of the ice cream mixture will decrease the freezing point approximately 2°F. This means that the ice cream must be chilled below the normal freezing temperature of water if ice crystals are to form. The greater the content of sugar in an ice cream, the lower the freezing point. This delayed freezing temperature helps to keep the size of crystals in the ice cream very small because a reasonable amount of stirring can be done during the freezing process to help break up any ice crystal aggregates as they slowly form.

① textural characteristics
② nutritive value
③ expiration date
④ sweet flavor

**해석** 아이스크림에서 설탕의 명백한 역할은 그 상품을 달게 만드는 것이다. 그러나 설탕은 혼합물의 결빙 온도를 떨어뜨리기 때문에, 냉동 아이스크림의 조직상의 특징을 결정하는 역할도 한다. 사실, 1쿼트의 아이스크림 혼합물에서 한 컵의 설탕은 빙점을 약 화씨 2도 정도 떨어뜨릴 것이다. 이것은 얼음 결정이 형성되려면, 그 아이스크림이 통상적인 물의 결빙 온도 밑으로 냉각되어야 한다는 것을 의미한다. 아이스크림 안에 설탕의 함유량이 더 많을수록, 빙점은 더 낮아진다. 얼음 결정 집합체가 천천히 형성되므로, 이것을 분쇄하는 것을 돕기 위해서 상당한 양의 휘젓기를 결빙 과정 동안 할 수 있기 때문에, 이렇게 지연된 결빙 온도는 아이스크림 안에서의 결정의 크기를 매우 작게 유지시키는 데 도움을 준다.
① 질감(조직)의 특징들
② 영양학적 가치
③ 유효기간
④ 달콤한 맛

**해설** 글의 종류는 순수 설명문이고, 전반적으로 인과관계의 연속으로 글이 구성되어 있다.
　　'설탕 → 혼합물의 어는 점↓ → 아이스크림의 결정체의 크기↓ → 아이스크림의 질감의 특징을 결정'이 핵심 인과관계의 흐름이다.

**어휘** quart 쿼트 (부피를 재는 단위)　aggregate 집계, 집합체, 총합(의)　textural 질감의　nutritive 영양가 있는　expiration date 유통기한

# 03 CLUES(문장 간의 연결 관계)



## CHAPTER 03

## 1 연결사

**예제 1** 다음 (A), (B)에 들어갈 말로 가장 적절한 것은?　　　정답 ④

> Culture is the primary factor affecting the way in which man responds to the environment, and since there is a wide variety of cultures, there is a wide variety of cultural responses, even to the same environment. _______(A)_______, in the Fijian Islands of the Pacific, two distinct cultures can be identified, each with a different relationship with the environment. On the one hand, there is the old Melanesian culture whose members utilise the environment to grow a small range of subsistence crops and whose wants are very limited. _______(B)_______, there are the new Melanesians, largely Indian immigrants, who have a much more Westernised view of the environment, growing cash crops such as sugar cane for export. Similar contrasts can be found throughout the world, between Chinese and Malay in Malaysia, African and European in Kenya, and Indian and Latino in Mexico.

|     | (A)          | (B)          |
| --- | ------------ | ------------ |
| ①   | However      | In fact      |
| ②   | However      | In addition  |
| ③   | For example  | In fact      |
| ④   | For example  | In contrast  |

**해석** 문화는 사람이 환경에 반응하는 방식에 영향을 주는 주된 요소이며 매우 다양한 문화가 있기에 심지어 같은 환경에 대해서도 매우 다양한 문화적 반응이 존재한다. 예를 들면 태평양의 피지 제도에서는 두 개의 뚜렷이 다른 문화가 확인될 수 있는데 각각은 환경에 대한 서로 다른 관계를 가진다. 한편으로는 부족들이 환경을 활용하여 작은 범위의 자급용 (농)작물을 재배하며 필요한 것이 매우 한정된 옛 멜라네시아 문화가 있다. 그에 반해서 주로 인도인 이주민들인 신 멜라네시아 사람들이 있는데, 이들은 환경에 대해 훨씬 더 서구화된 관점을 가지며 수출을 위해 사탕수수와 같은 환금 작물을 재배한다. 비슷한 차이는 말레이시아의 중국인과 말레이 사람 간에, 케냐의 아프리카인과 유럽인 간에, 멕시코의 인디오(족)과 라틴 아메리카인 간에, 세계 전역에 걸쳐 발견될 수 있다.

**해설** (A) – (A)의 앞부분의 상위개념에 해당하는 the same environment / a wide variety of responses와 (A)의 뒷부분의 하위개념에 해당하는 in the Fijian Islands / two different cultures, each with a different relationship with the environment를 연결시켜 주는 'For example'이 적절하다.

(B) – (B)의 앞부분의 '먹고 살기 위해 농작물을 재배하는 old Melanesian culture'와 이와 대조를 이루는 (B)의 뒷부분의 '환금작물을 재재하는 new Melanesian culture'을 연결시켜 주는 'In contrast'가 적절하다.

**어휘** utilise 활용하다　　subsistence 생활　　cash crop 환금작물

**예제 2** 다음 (A), (B)에 들어갈 말로 가장 적절한 것은? **정답** ②

Destination choice is an important attribute that significantly differentiates between inbound and outbound tourism. Typically mature age customers have more time at hand with greater disposable incomes. Therefore mature age customers would prefer to go on a real holiday and tend to be more inclined towards selecting an international destination. _____(A)_____, mature age customers may try alternative modes of travel such as cruises, trains etc., as time is not a factor that blocks them from selecting these options. However, younger customers have many limitations in comparison to mature age customers in terms of time, money, and career. _____(B)_____, outbound tourism is a preferred destination choice for younger customers only when it is linked to business or personal purposes. Also in comparison to mature age customers, younger customers would spend less time in a single destination and may tend to travel to a greater number of destinations in a year.

|     | (A)         | (B)           |
| --- | ----------- | ------------- |
| ①   | Similarly   | Nevertheless  |
| ②   | Similarly   | Therefore     |
| ③   | In contrast | Moreover      |
| ④   | For example | Therefore     |

**해석** 목적지 선택은 국내와 해외로 가는 관광을 크게 구별하는 중요한 특성이다. 대개 원숙한 나이의 소비자들은 사용할 수 있는 시간이 더 많고 더 많은 실소득이 있다. 그러므로 원숙한 나이의 소비자들은 진정한 휴가를 가기를 좋아하고 외국의 여행지를 더욱 선택하고 싶어 하는 경향이 있다. 마찬가지로 원숙한 나이의 소비자들은 시간이 이런 선택을 하는 것을 가로막는 요인이 되지 않기 때문에 유람선, 기차 등과 같은 대안의 여행 방식을 시도할 수 있다. 그렇지만 더 젊은 소비자들은 원숙한 나이의 소비자들에 비해 시간, 돈, 경력 면에서 많은 제약이 있다. 그러므로 해외로 가는 관광은 그것이 사업이나 개인적인 목적과 관련이 있을 때만 젊은 소비자들이 선호하는 목적지의 선택이다. 또한 원숙한 나이의 소비자에 비해, 더 젊은 소비자들은 한곳의 여행지에서 더 적은 시간을 보내려 하고 한 해에 더 많은 여행지를 여행하는 경향이 있을 수 있다.

**해설** (A) − (A)를 중심으로 앞뒤에서 'mature age customers'의 여행에 대한 비슷한 성향을 나열하고 있으므로, 'Similarly'가 적절하다.
(B) − (B)의 앞부분의 'younger customers는 시간이나 경비에 있어서 많은 한계점을 가지고 있다'라는 '원인'과 (B)의 뒷부분의 'younger customer는 특별한 경우(일이나 개인적 목적)을 제외하고는 해외여행이 어렵다'라는 '결과'를 연결시켜 주는 'Therefore'가 적절하다.

**어휘** attribute 속성, 자질　inbound 국내여행의　outbound 해외여행의

**예제 3** 다음 (A), (B)에 들어갈 말로 가장 적절한 것은?   **정답** ④

Names are an important guide to the social significance of pets. Like pet food during the 1960s, pets themselves were frequently given dog-specific names such as Rex, Fido and Rover; or cat-specific names such as Kitty, Tibby or Sooty. ______(A)______, in Australia, the UK and USA companion animals are now more likely to be given human names. In Britain, for example, the 1980s marked a turning point away from the use of 'traditional canine' names, especially Shep, Brandy, Whisky, Rex, Lassie and Rover. By 1995 the National Canine Defence League's survey found that the ten most popular dog names were all human. ______(B)______, many of them, such as Ben, Lucy, Sam, Sophie and Charlie, were also currently among the most popular names given to babies. In 1996 the most common name given to a dog by Australians was Sam, whereas in the past Dog was the most common name.

|  | (A) | (B) |
|---|---|---|
| ① | Therefore | In contrast |
| ② | However | Instead |
| ③ | Therefore | Moreover |
| ④ | However | Moreover |

**해석** 이름은 애완동물의 사회적 중요성에 대해 중요한 지침이 된다. 1960년대의 애완동물 사료와 마찬가지로 애완동물에게도 흔히 Rex, Fido, 그리고 Rover와 같이 개에 특유한 이름과 Kitty, Tibby 혹은 Sooty와 같이 고양이에 특유한 이름이 주어졌다. 하지만 호주, 영국, 미국에서는 이제 반려동물에게 인간의 이름이 주어질 가능성이 더 크다. 예를 들어 영국에서는 1980년대가 '전통적인 개의' 이름, 특히 Shep, Brandy, Whisky, Rex, Lassie 그리고 Rover의 사용에서 벗어나는 전환점이 되었다. 1955년 무렵에는, National Canine Defence League의 조사가 가장 인기 있는 개 이름 10개가 모두 인간의 이름이라는 것을 밝혀냈다. 더구나 Ben, Lucy, Sam, Sophie 그리고 Charlie와 같은, 그들 이름 중 많은 이름들은 또한 그 당시 아기에게 주어지는 가장 인기 있는 이름에 속했다. 1996년에 호주 사람들이 개에게 지어 주는 가장 흔한 이름은 Sam이었지만, 과거에는 Dog이 가장 흔한 이름이었다.

**해설** (A) − (A)의 앞부분에서 '애완동물에만 나타나는 이름'과 대조를 이루는 (A)의 뒷부분의 '애완동물에게 인간의 이름을 부여'를 연결시켜 주는 'However'가 적절하다.
(B) − (B)를 중심으로 앞뒤에서 '유명한 개의 이름이 인간의 이름과 동일하다'라는 비슷한 내용이 나오고 있으므로, 'Moreover'가 적절하다.

**어휘** significance 중요성   companion 동반자   canine 개과의

**예제 4** 다음 (A), (B)에 들어갈 말로 가장 적절한 것은?   정답 ①

Even if the individual activities in which we engage in our life have the potential to make us feel satisfied, we can still feel unhappy or frustrated with the final result. The most delicious food in the world — be it chocolate, lasagna, or a hamburger — cannot be enjoyed if consumed in large quantities. _______(A)_______, we cannot enjoy activities if we have too much of them, no matter how potentially "delicious" they are. Quantity affects quality; there can be too much of a good thing. A wine connoisseur does not swallow the entire glass of wine in one gulp. _______(B)_______, to fully enjoy the richness of the drink, she smells, she tastes, she savors, and she takes her time. To become a life connoisseur, to enjoy the richness that life offers, we, too, need to take our time.

| | (A) | (B) |
|---|---|---|
| ① | Likewise | Instead |
| ② | Likewise | Moreover |
| ③ | Nevertheless | Instead |
| ④ | Nevertheless | Therefore |

**해석** 우리가 생활하면서 참여하는 개별적인 활동들이 우리에게 만족감을 느끼게 할 가능성이 있다 하더라도, 우리는 최종적 결과로 불행함과 좌절감을 느낄 수 있다. 그것이 초콜릿이건 라자냐이건 또는 햄버거이건 간에 세상에서 가장 맛있는 음식은 너무 지나친 양으로 소비된다면 즐거움을 줄 수 없다. <u>마찬가지로</u> 활동들이 아무리 "맛있을" 가능성이 있을지라도 그것들의 너무 많은 것을 취하게 되면 그 활동들을 즐길 수 없다. 양은 질에 영향을 주어서 좋은 것도 지나치게 많을 수 있다. 와인 감식가는 와인 한 잔을 한 번에 꿀꺽 모두 삼키지는 않는다. <u>대신에</u> 한잔의 풍요로움을 최대한 즐기기 위해 그 사람은 향을 맡고, 맛을 보고, 맛을 감상하며, 시간 여유를 갖는다. 인생의 감식가가 되기 위해서, 그리고 인생이 제공할 것으로 갖는 풍요로움을 즐기기 위해서 우리도 또한 시간적 여유를 가질 필요가 있다.

**해설** (A) − (A)를 중심으로 (A)의 앞부분에서는 '맛있는 음식도 너무 많이 먹으면 먹는 즐거움이 줄어든다'의 내용이 그리고 (A)의 뒷부분에서는 '활동도 너무 많이 하면 그 활동의 즐거움이 줄어든다'의 내용이 나오고 있는데, 비슷한 성향의 내용이므로, 'Likewise'가 적절하다.
(B) − (B)의 앞부분에서 '와인 감식가가 와인을 한꺼번에 들이키지 않는다'라는 내용이 나오고, (B)의 뒷부분에서 앞에서 나온 내용의 '대안'에 해당하는 내용으로 '와인 감식가는 와인을 마실 때, 냄새를 맡고, 음미하고, 천천히 즐긴다'가 나왔으므로, 'Instead'가 적절하다.

**어휘** engage in ~에 관여하다, 참여하다   frustrate ~에게 좌절감을 일으키게 하다   lasagna 라자냐   quantity 수량
connoisseur 감정가   gulp 꿀떡꿀떡 마시다

**예제 5** 다음 (A), (B)에 들어갈 말로 가장 적절한 것은?   **정답** ②

> Shakespeare said, "Make use of time, let advantage not slip." This applies in every field of our activity today. There is a time and place for everything. No idleness and no laziness are allowed. You may know the true value of time: notice, seize, and enjoy every minute of it. Never put off until tomorrow what you can do today. If work is done now, it'll save a lot of labor later on. ______(A)______, you notice that the button on your shirt is hanging loose. It would be better to sew it on tightly before you lose the button. This also applies to studying. If you keep studying daily and don't put it off to a later time, examination time would not be one of tension and worry. ______(B)______ you would cram and try to learn too much at the last minute.

|   | (A) | (B) |
|---|---|---|
| ① | For example | Therefore |
| ② | For example | Otherwise |
| ③ | First of all | Otherwise |
| ④ | Nevertheless | Therefore |

**해석** "장점을 놓치지 않도록 시간을 활용하라"라고 셰익스피어가 말했다. 이는 오늘날 우리의 활동의 모든 분야에 적용된다. 모든 것에는 시간과 장소가 있다. 빈둥거리며 게으름을 피우는 것은 어떤 것도 허락되지 않는다. 당신은 시간의 진정한 가치 — 시간의 매 1분을 주목하고 꽉 쥐고 즐겨라 — 를 알고 있을 것이다 당신이 오늘 할 수 있는 일을 내일로 결코 미루지 마라. 만약 일이 지금 마무리 된다면 나중에 많은 번거로움을 덜 것이다. 예를 들면 당신은 셔츠의 단추가 헐렁하게 달려 있는 것을 발견한다. 당신이 단추를 잃어버리기 전에 그것을 팽팽하게 꿰매는 것이 더 나을 것이다 이것은 또한 공부하는 것에도 적용된다. 만약 당신이 매일 계속 공부 하고 그것을 이후의 시간으로 미루지 않는다면 시험시간이 긴장과 걱정의 시간이 되지는 않을 것이다. 그렇지 않으면 당신은 마지막 순간에 벼락치기를 해서 너무 많이 익히려고 할 것이다.

**해설** (A) – (A)의 앞부분에 '지금 행동에 옮겨지면, 나중에 많은 노동이 줄어들 것이다'라는 상위개념의 내용이 나오고, (A)의 뒷부분에 '옷에 단추가 느슨해질 때, 지금 바느질을 하면, 나중에 단추를 잃어버리지 않을 것이다'라는 하위개념의 내용이 나오므로, (A)에는 'For example'이 적절하다.

(B) – (B)의 앞부분에 '미리 공부하면, 시험시간이 긴장과 걱정의 시간이 아닐 것이다'라는 내용이 나오고, (B)의 뒷부분에 앞에서 말한 내용(미리 공부한다는 내용)을 하지 않으면 나오게 되는 결과인 '시험 기간에 벼락치기를 할 것이다'라는 내용이 나오고 있으므로, (B)에는 'Otherwise'가 적절하다.

**어휘** idleness 게으름   put off 연기하다   cram 벼락치기

**예제 6** 다음 (A), (B)에 들어갈 말로 가장 적절한 것은?   정답 ③

Thanks to the introduction of numerous politically correct words, we have become more sensitive in our speech. Instead of using 'disabled' or 'handicapped,' we use a more encouraging expression such as 'physically challenged.' ________(A)________, 'stewardess' is now referred to as 'flight attendant' and 'garbage man' as 'sanitation officer.' It is undeniable that most politically correct terms are positive and encouraging. Some of them, however, are much too radical. For example, substituting 'gasoline transfer technician' for 'gas station attendant' is going much too far. Another extreme would be calling 'hunter' 'animal assassin.' There is nothing wrong with using indirect expressions and sensitive terms. ______(B)______, we should not push such endeavors to the extreme, because as Leslie Fiedler puts it, 'The middle against both ends' is the best rule of thumb.

|  | (A) | (B) |
|---|---|---|
| ① | In spite of that | Similarly |
| ② | In spite of that | Conversely |
| ③ | For the same reason | Nevertheless |
| ④ | For the same reason | Therefore |

**해석** Politically correct words(정치적으로 올바른 단어들)가 많이 소개되어서, 우리는 말할 때 좀 더 신경을 쓰게 되었다. 우리는 '불구가 된', '장애가 있는'이라는 말을 사용하는 대신에 '신체적으로 노력을 요하는'이라는 좀 더 고무적인 표현을 사용한다. <u>같은 이유로</u> '여승무원'은 이제 '비행기 승무원'으로, '쓰레기 청소부'는 '환경미화원'으로 불린다. 대부분의 정치적으로 옳은 표현들이 긍정적이고 고무적이라는 것은 부정할 수 없다. 하지만, 그 중 몇몇은 너무나 극단적이다. 예를 들어, '주유소 종업원'을 '휘발유 전송 기술자'로 대체하는 것은 너무 지나치다. '사냥꾼'을 '동물 암살자'로 부르는 것은 또 다른 극단적인 예이다. 우회적이고 조심스러운 용어를 사용하는 것에는 문제가 없다. <u>그럼에도 불구하고</u>, 우리는 그러한 노력을 극단으로 몰아가서는 안 된다. Leslie Fiedler가 말했듯이, 중도를 지키는 것이야말로 경험에서 얻은 최고의 지식이기 때문이다.

**해설** (A) − (A)의 앞부분에 장애인을 가리키는 용어가 'disabled나 handicapped'에서 'physically challenged'라는 더 격려할 수 있는 단어로 바뀌었다는 내용과 (A)의 뒷부분에 여승무원을 가리키는 용어가 'stewardess'에서 'flight attendant'로, 환경미화원을 가리키는 용어가 'garbage man'에서 'sanitation officer'라는 더 격려할 수 있는 단어로 바뀌었다는 내용이 비슷한 내용이므로 'For the same reason'이 적절하다.

(B) − (B)의 앞에서 '간접적인 표현과 예민한 용어를 사용하는 것이 잘못된 것이 없다'라는 것을 '인정'하고 있고, (B)의 뒤에서 '우리는 간접적인 표현과 예민한 용어를 극단적으로 사용해서는 안 된다'라는 내용을 '더 인정'하고 있으므로, (B)에는 'Nevertheless'가 적절하다.

**어휘** stewardess 스튜어디스    sanitation 위생    substitute 대리, 대용품    assassin 암살자    endeavor 노력

**예제 7** 다음 (A), (B)에 들어갈 말로 가장 적절한 것은?   **정답** ①

Dave Dobbs, a sociologist, introduces the idea of two types of people, 'dandelions' and 'orchids.' Dandelions can thrive anywhere, despite their environment. _______(A)_______, orchids are more sensitive and require a stable environment to survive. They are likely to be affected by mood disorders and psychological disease. The astonishing part of Dobbs' report is that given the right care, or environment, the orchids do not just do OK, but far surpass the dandelions in performance. _______(B)_______, given the right training, orchids may in fact be destined for greatness. This finding redefines conditions we typically may have classified as undesirable. Depression and generalized anxiety disorder are no longer conditions to dread, because given the right training, people with these conditions may in fact be the true 'movers and shakers' in the world.

|  | (A) | (B) |
|---|---|---|
| ① | However | In other words |
| ② | However | On the contrary |
| ③ | Similarly | In conclusion |
| ④ | Similarly | In other words |

**해석** 사회학자인 Dave Dobbs는 두 가지 유형의 인간으로 '민들레형'과 '난초형'을 소개했다. 민들레형의 인간들은 그들의 환경과 상관없이 어디에서든 성공할 수 있다. 그러나 난초형의 인간들은 더 민감하고 생존하는 데 안정적인 환경을 필요로 한다. 그들은 기분 장애와 심리적인 질병에 영향을 받기 쉽다. Dobbs 연구의 놀라운 점은 적절한 보살핌이나 환경이 주어진다면, 난초형 인간들은 단지 양호한 정도가 아니라, 민들레형 인간들보다 더 월등한 성취능력을 보인다는 것이다. 다시 말해서, 적절한 훈련이 주어진다면, 난초형 인간은 사실상 더 탁월할지도 모른다. 이러한 발견은 우리가 통상적으로 바람직하지 못하다고 분류해왔던 증세들을 재정의한다. 우울증과 일반화된 불안장애는 더 이상 두려워할 증세가 아니다. 왜냐하면, 적절한 훈련이 주어진다면 이러한 증세가 있는 사람들은 사실 세상에서 '세상을 이끌고 움직이는 사람들'일지도 모른다.

**해설** (A) – (A)의 앞부분에 '환경과 관계없이 어느 곳에서도 번성할 수 있는 Dandelions'와 (A)의 뒷부분에 '안정적인 환경에서만 생존할 수 있는 예민한 orchids'가 대조를 이루고 있으므로, 'However'가 적절하다.
(B) – (B)를 중심으로 (B)의 앞부분과 (B)의 뒷부분이 '적절한 관심과 환경이 주어 지면 orchids가 dandelions보다 뛰어나게 된다'는 거의 같은 내용이 나오고 있으므로, 'In other words'가 적절하다.

**어휘** dandelions 민들레   orchids 난초   surpass 능가하다, 뛰어넘다   dread 공포

**예제 8** 다음 (A), (B)에 들어갈 말로 가장 적절한 것은?

정답 ② 

---

Most people are slightly nervous about flying. According to several recent reports, "economy-class syndrome" has captured as much public attention as concerns about high levels of cosmic radiation and the questionable quality of the air we breathe in cabins. ______(A)______, it is believed that the cramped sitting leads some passengers to develop the blood clots, causing sharp pain and swelling in the lower leg. Then, more seriously, part of the clot may travel through bloodstream to the lungs. The airlines, ______(B)______, maintain there is no conclusive evidence so far that suggests the cramped aircraft cabin might be more dangerous than sitting still on a crowded train, bus, or car. They say it's basically a matter of self-care.

---

|   | (A) | (B) |
|---|---|---|
| ① | In fact | therefore |
| ② | In fact | however |
| ③ | In contrast | besides |
| ④ | On the other hand | therefore |

**해석** 사람들 대부분은 비행하는 것을 다소 불안해한다. 최근의 몇몇 보고서에 따르면, "비행기 일반석 신드롬"은 높은 수준의 우주 방사선과 우리가 기내에서 마시는 공기의 의문스러운 품질에 대한 염려만큼이나 대중적 관심을 끌었다. 실제로, 비좁은 좌석에 앉게 되면 일부 승객은 혈액응고물이 생겨 종아리가 심한 통증과 함께 부어오르게 된다고 본다. 그러면 더 심각하게 그 혈액응고물 중 일부는 혈류를 통해 폐로 이동할 수도 있다. 그러나 항공회사들은 비좁은 비행기 선실이 혼잡한 기차나 버스, 또는 자동차에서 가만히 앉아있는 것보다 더 위험하다고 암시하는 어떤 결정적인 증거도 지금까지 없었다고 주장한다. 그들은 그것이 본질적으로 자기 관리의 문제라고 말한다.

**해설** (A) − (A)를 중심으로 (A)의 앞뒤가 '대조'를 이루고 있지는 않으므로, 'In contrast'나 'On the other hand'보다는 'In fact'가 자연스럽다.
(B) − (B)의 앞부분은 'economy-class syndrome'의 부작용에 대한 내용이 나오고, (B)의 뒷부분은 이 내용을 부인하는 항공사의 입장이 나오고 있으므로, (B)에는 'however'가 적절하다.

**어휘** cosmic radiation 우주 방사선　cabins 선실　cramp 경련　blood clot 혈전　conclusive 단호한　aircraft 항공기

## 3  지시사

**예제 1** 글의 흐름으로 보아, 주어진 문장이 들어가기에 가장 적절한 곳은?　　**정답** ③

> This cooperation can only be secured by allowing every level of employee to suggest ideas, express their views, and share their experiences.

To a large extent, the success of an organization requires an atmosphere in which there is a free flow of information — upward, downward, and horizontally. At the workplace, the primary goal is getting things done. ( ① ) For this, instructions, guidelines, supervision, monitoring, and periodic reporting are usually considered enough. ( ② ) But if the company wishes to achieve more than the set task, a real involvement of all employees, from the highest to the lowest levels, is required. ( ③ ) Such a system of communication can only be established within the organization by the manager. ( ④ ) In fact, the manager functions as the point of intersection for all communication channels. One of the most important concerns of the manager is to organize and ensure an effective information system across the organization.

**해석** 상당한 정도로 한 조직의 성공은 위로, 아래로, 그리고 수평으로 자유롭게 정보가 흐르는 분위기를 필요로 한다. 직장에서 주요 목표는 일이 처리되도록 하는 것이다. 이를 위해서라면 지시, 지침, 관리, 감시, 그리고 주기적인 보고면 충분한 것으로 여겨진다. 하지만 회사가 정해진 과업 그 이상을 달성하기를 소망한다면, 최상층으로부터 최하층에 이르기까지의 모든 직원들의 실질적인 참여가 요구된다. (이러한 협력은 모든 직위의 직원이 아이디어를 제안하고, 자신의 견해를 표현하며, 그리고 자신의 경험을 공유하도록 허용하는 것에 의해서만 확보될 수 있다.) 그런 의사소통 체계는 조직 내에서 관리자에 의해서만 확립될 수 있다. 사실 관리자는 모든 의사소통 통로를 위한 교차점으로서 기능한다. 관리자의 가장 중요한 일 중 하나는 조직 전체에 걸쳐 효과적인 정보 체계를 세워서 그것을 공고히 하는 것이다.

**해설** Clue 'This + N' – 주어진 문장에 있는 'This cooperation'
+ Clue⁻¹ 'Such + N' – (③) 뒤에 있는 'Such a system of communication'
을 이용하면 주어진 문장의 위치는 ③번이다.

**어휘** cooperation 협력　periodic 주기적　intersection 교차로

**예제 2** 주어진 글 다음에 이어질 글의 순서로 가장 적절한 것은?  정답 ②

---

Someone hands you a piece of paper bearing a fine grid — as in a school exercise book. The person tells you that he is thinking of just one of the small squares.

---

(A) If the answer is 'no' then the box must be in B — there is nowhere else it could be. So you now forget about A and proceed to divide B in half, lettering each half as before.

(B) He wants you to locate that square by asking questions which will only get a 'yes' or 'no' answer. So you divide the sheet in half with a line and call one half A and the other half B. You ask: 'Is the desired box in A?'

(C) Again you ask the question. In the end you must come to the chosen box. The point about this simple strategy is that at every moment the desired box must lie in A or not-A (which is B). There is nowhere else. Nor can the box lie in both A and B.

---

① (C) − (B) − (A)          ✓ (B) − (A) − (C)

③ (B) − (C) − (A)          ④ (C) − (A) − (B)

---

**해석** 누군가가 당신에게 학교 연습장처럼 미세한 격자무늬가 있는 종이 한 장을 건네준다. 그 사람은 당신에게 그가 그 (격자무늬에 있는) 작은 정사각형중 하나를 생각하고 있다고 말해준다.

(B) 그는 당신이 단지 'yes'아니면 'no'로 대답할 수 있는 질문을 던짐으로써 그 정사각형의 위치를 맞춰보기를 원한다. 그래서 당신은 그 종이를 줄을 그어서 반으로 나누고 한 쪽은 A라고, 나머지 한쪽은 B라고 부른다. 당신은 질문을 한다.: '그 원하는(생각하는) box(정사각형)가 A에 있나요?'

(A) 그 대답이 그때 'no'이면 그 box는 B에 있음에 틀림없다. − 그것이 있을 수 있는 다른 곳이 없다. 그래서 당신은 A는 이제 잊어버리고 B를 다시 반으로 나누기를 진행해서 전처럼 각각에 명칭을 붙인다.

(C) 다시 당신은 그 질문을 한다. 결국 당신은 그 선택한 box에 도달하게 된다. 이 간단한 전략의 포인트는 모든 순간 그 원하던 box가 A에 있거나 A가 아닌 곳(즉 B)에 있어야 한다는 점이다. 다른 곳에 있을 수는 없다. 그 box는 A와 B둘 다에 있을 수는 없다.

**해설** [          ]

(A) the answer를 근거로 (A) (×) / Again you ask the question을 근거로 (C) (×)

He와 that square를 근거로 (B) !

(B)

the answer로 근거로 (A) !

(A)

Again you ask the question을 근거로 (C) !

(C)

**어휘**  bear 지니다    proceed 진행하다

### 1 -2 주제/제목/요지/주장 Application

**예제 1** 다음 글의 요지로 가장 적절한 것은?　　　　　　　　　　　　**정답** ②

> What most parents do is stop sharing books as soon as a child can read alone. That makes reading a solitary happening, with no chance to talk about a book or discuss what it is saying. Read aloud together. Read alone yourself, then say, "Have you read this book? I really liked it." Once you begin to be book-sharers you will have no end of delight in sharing. Our son brought us a copy of Brian Jacques' Redwall and said, "I think you'll like this. It's a good book." We respect each other's opinions because we have read aloud together and talked about books. That son is in college now and recently visited us. He left a book behind, saying, "I'd like you to read this. It tells you some of my thinking about relationships." Sharing a book makes for a delightful companionship. It is sharing yourself.

① 부모는 자녀와 함께 독서를 할 때 그들의 이해를 돕기 위해 설명을 해주어야 한다.
② 부모와 자녀가 함께 책 읽기를 하면 행복한 동반자 관계를 형성할 수 있게 된다.
③ 아이들에게는 부모가 없이 혼자 힘으로 자발적인 독서를 할 수 있는 환경이 필요하다.
④ 부모는 자녀에게 책을 읽어 줄 때 그들의 눈높이에 맞는 적정 수준의 책을 선택해야 한다.

**해석** 대부분의 부모들이 하는 것은 자녀가 혼자 책을 읽을 수 있게 되자마자 책을 함께 읽는 것을 중단하는 것이다. 그렇게 할 경우 책에 대해 이야기하거나 책이 말하고 있는 바에 대해 논의할 기회가 전혀 없기 때문에, 책 읽기는 고독한 일이 되고 만다. 소리 내어 함께 읽어라. 여러분 혼자서 읽고 나서, "이 책 읽어 봤어? 나는 정말 좋았는데."라고 말해라. 일단 책을 함께 읽기 시작하면, 여러분은 함께 읽는 데서 무한한 기쁨을 맛볼 것이다. 우리 아들이 우리에게 BrianJacques의 'Redwall'이란 책 한 권을 가져와서, "이 책을 좋아하실 것 같아요. 좋은 책이거든요."라고 말했다. 우리는 책을 소리 내어 함께 읽고 책에 대해서 이야기를 해 왔기 때문에 서로의 의견을 존중한다. 그 아들이 지금 대학에 다니고 있고 최근에 우리를 방문했다. 그는 "이것을 읽어 보셨으면 해요. 그 속에 관계에 대한 제 생각이 좀 드러나 있어요."라고 말하면서 책 한 권을 남겨 두고 갔다. 책을 함께 읽는 것은 즐거운 동반자 관계에 도움이 된다. 그것은 여러분 자신을 함께 나누는 것이다.

**해설** STS '강조의 do'가 들어간 문장 — What most parents do is stop sharing books as soon as a child can read alone.
+
STS '명령문'이 들어간 문장 — Read aloud together.
+
STS '필자의 주관 단어 delightful'이 들어간 문장 — Sharing a book makes for a delightful companionship.
이 세 문장이 답 도출 근거 문장들이다.

**어휘** solitary 외로운

**예제 2** 다음 글의 요지로 가장 적절한 것은?     **정답** ④

> **Having a business card is an obvious, but very important**, everyday method to get your name, your artwork, and your message out. It's also an easy way for people to access your name at some later date. **Amazingly enough, though, most artists don't use them**. It's surprising but true that many fine artists are inept at designing anything with type and small graphic elements, especially for themselves. Maybe you think business cards are too businesslike. Try thinking of them as calling cards or, with your artwork on them, as art cards — little gifts you give away. **Business cards are too important to your success to avoid**. Imagine if you, with your business cards, and another artist, without business cards, meet a dealer or collector at the same time. Which one of you is more likely to be contacted later? It won't matter who's the better artist.

① 명함 디자인이 더 특이할수록 그 판매량이 증가하게 된다.
② 인맥 관리를 위해서 받은 명함을 잘 분류해서 관리하는 것이 좋다.
③ 명함 디자인에는 반드시 필요한 내용만 간단명료하게 적어 넣어야 한다.
④ 명함의 사용은 미술가의 성공에 있어서도 매우 중요한 필수 요소이다.

**해석** 명함을 갖는 것은 여러분의 이름, 여러분의 미술 작품, 그리고 여러분의 메시지를 알리는 뻔하지만 매우 중요한 일상적인 수단이다. 그것은 또한 이후에 사람들이 여러분의 이름에 접근하기 쉬운 방법이기도 하다. 하지만 매우 놀랍게도 대부분의 미술가들은 그것을 사용하지 않는다. 많은 순수 미술가들이 특히 자신을 위해서 활자와 작은 그래픽 요소를 가지고 어떤 것을 디자인하는 데 서툴다는 것은 놀랍지만 사실이다. 아마도 여러분은 명함이 너무 사무적이라고 생각할지도 모른다. 그것들을 전화 카드라고 생각하거나, 여러분의 미술 작품이 거기에 있다면 미술 카드, 즉 여러분이 나누어 주는 작은 선물이라고 생각해 보아라. 명함은 여러분의 성공에 매우 중요하므로 회피할 수 없다. 명함을 갖고 있는 여러분과 명함을 갖고 있지 않은 다른 미술가가 동시에 판매상이나 수집가를 만난다고 상상해 보아라. 여러분들 중 누가 나중에 연락을 받을 가능성이 더 클까? 누가 더 나은 미술가인지는 중요하지 않을 것이다.

**해설** STS 'but / important'가 들어간 문장의 부분 – Having a business card is an obvious, but very important
　+
STS '필자의 주관 단어 Amazingly / though'가 들어간 문장 – Amazingly enough, though, most artists don't use them.
　+
STS 'important'가 들어간 문장 – Business cards are too important to your success to avoid.
이 세 문장이 답 도출 근거 문장들이다.

**어휘** inept 서투른

**예제 3** 다음 글에서 필자가 주장하는 바로 가장 적절한 것은?   **정답** ③

> Active, energetic, rambunctious boys are not bad boys and should not be made to feel so. Boys are naturally active. They have energy to burn. That's why they need avenues where they can be active, burn up that energy, and test their strength. Boys need exercise. It is not a luxury, it is a necessity. Video games don't provide exercise. And neither do television or computers. All boys need to romp and learn that even in rambunctious play, there are rules and order. Through sports and exercise, they learn to control their muscles, control their bodies, and even control their emotions and their minds. As a boy grows older, he can transfer these skills he learns into other areas of his life. He can never learn to control his energy if he is not allowed to experience the fullness of its power.

① 부모는 자녀가 원하는 것을 파악해 이를 충족시켜 주어야 한다.
② 부모는 어린 자녀들이 지나친 경쟁에 빠지지 않게 해야 한다.
③ 남자아이들에게는 충분한 운동의 기회가 제공되어야 한다.
④ 아동 비만 예방을 위해서 체육 수업을 확대해야 한다.

**해석** 활동적이고, 힘이 넘치며, 미친 듯이 날뛰는 남자아이들은 나쁜 아이들이 아니며 그렇게 느끼도록 만들어서는 안 된다. 남자아이들은 선천적으로 활발하다. 그들에게는 태워야 할 에너지가 있다. 바로 그런 이유로 그들에게는 활동하고, 그 에너지를 태우며, 자신의 힘을 시험해 볼 수 있는 통로가 필요한 것이다. 남자아이들은 운동을 필요로 한다. 그것은 사치가 아니라 필수이다. 비디오 게임은 운동을 제공하지 않는다. 텔레비전이나 컴퓨터도 또한 그러하다. 모든 남자아이들은 까불면서 뛰놀아야 하고 미친 듯이 날뛰는 놀이에도 규칙과 질서가 있음을 배워야 한다. 스포츠와 운동을 통해서, 그들은 자신의 근육을 통제하고, 자신의 몸을 통제하며, 심지어 자신의 감정과 마음을 통제하는 법을 배운다. 남자아이는 나이가 들어갈수록, 자신이 배우는 이러한 기술들을 자기 삶의 다른 영역으로 옮길 수 있다. 만약 그 힘의 충만함을 경험하는 것이 허락되지 않으면, 그는 결코 자신의 에너지를 통제하는 것을 배울 수 없다.

**해설** STS 'should'가 들어간 문장 — Active, energetic, rambunctious boys are not bad boys and should not be made to feel so.
\+
STS 'need'가 들어간 문장 — Boys need exercise.
\+
STS 'need to'가 들어간 문장 — All boys need to romp and learn that even in rambunctious play, there are rules and order.
이 세 문장이 답 도출 근거 문장들이다.

**어휘** rambunctious 사나운   romp 말괄량이, 뛰놀다

**예제 4** 다음 글에서 필자가 주장하는 바로 가장 적절한 것은?   정답 ①

Suppose that you and I are discussing the current president of the United States. I feel that he is the best president we have ever had. You totally disagree and feel that he is the worst one we have ever had. In the discussion that follows, you ask, "Why do you think he is the most important or best president?" I then give you a list of reasons, as well as some of the important things that he has done. Rather than trying to explain how I'm wrong or thinking up arguments about what I've said, you should try to listen to me and try to understand my position. In other words, the listener should try to hear and understand where the other person is coming from, and not prepare arguments or retaliations. The individual who is really listening tends not to interrupt and give her own point of view, but rather will ask additional questions in order to clarify and understand the other person's position.

① 상대방의 의견을 무조건 반박하기보단 경청하고 이해해야 한다.
② 주장을 제시할 때 해당 논점을 벗어나는 주장인지 주의해야 한다.
③ 상대방이 반박할 수 있는 여지를 남기는 표현의 사용은 지양해야 한다.
④ 상대방에게 자신의 주장을 간단명료하고 모호하지 않게 전달해야 한다.

**해석** 여러분과 내가 현재의 미국 대통령에 대해 토론하고 있다고 가정해 보자. 나는 그가 지금까지의 대통령 중 가장 훌륭하다고 생각한다. 여러분은 완전히 의견이 다르고 그가 지금까지의 대통령 중 최악이라고 생각한다. 이어지는 토론에서, 여러분은 "당신은 왜 그가 가장 중요한 혹은 가장 훌륭한 대통령이라고 생각하나요?" 라고 묻는다. 이에 나는 여러분에게 그가 했던 중요한 일들 중 일부는 물론 조목조목 이유까지 제시한다. 내가 어째서 틀렸는지를 설명하려고 하거나 내가 이야기한 것에 대한 반대 의견을 생각해 내기보다는 오히려, 여러분은 내 말을 듣고 내 입장을 이해하려고 노력해야 한다. 다시 말해서, 듣는 사람은 상대방의 입장의 근거가 무엇인지를 듣고 이해하려 해야지, 반대 의견이나 보복을 준비해서는 안 된다. 정말로 듣고 있는 사람은 이야기를 중단시켜 자신의 관점을 제시하려는 경향이 있기보다는 오히려 상대방의 입장을 명확히 하고 이해하기 위해 추가적인 질문을 할 것이다.

**해설** STS 'you should'가 들어간 문장의 부분 – you should try to listen to me and try to understand my position.
+
STS 'should'가 들어간 문장 – In other words, the listener should try to hear and understand where the other person is coming from, and not prepare arguments or retaliations.
이 두 문장이 답 도출 근거 문장들이다.

**어휘** retaliation 보복   interrupt 방해하다   clarify 밝히다

**예제 5** 다음 글의 주제로 가장 적절한 것은?  정답 ②

The massive tombs and ceremonial structures built from huge stones in the Neolithic period are known as megalithic architecture, from the Greek words for "large" (megas) and "stone" (lithos). Archaeologists disagree about the nature of the societies that created them. Some believe megalithic monuments reflect complex, stratified societies in which powerful religious or political leaders dictated their design and commanded the large workforce necessary to accomplish these ambitious engineering projects. Other interpreters argue that these massive undertakings are clear evidence for cooperative collaboration within and among social groups, coalescing around a common project that fueled social cohesion without the controlling power of a ruling elite. Many megalithic structures are associated with death, and recent interpretations stress the fundamental role of death and burial as public theatrical performances in which individual and group identity, cohesion, and disputes were played out.

① megalithic architecture as emblematic reflection of the natural scenery
② various ideas about the nature of societies that built megalithic architecture
③ the importance of megalithic memorials in archaeological investigation
④ the defining requirements of civilization in the Neolithic Era

**해석** 신석기 시대의 커다란 돌로 만든 거대 무덤과 의례를 위한 구조물은 그리스어 단어 '커다란(megas)'과 '돌(lithos)'에서 유래된 말인 거석 건축물로 알려져 있다. 고고학자들은 그것들을 만든 사회의 성격에 대해 의견이 분분하다. 일부는 거석 기념물이 강력한 종교 혹은 정치 지도자가 그것들의 설계를 지시하고 이런 의욕적인 토목 계획을 완수하는 데 필요한 대규모 노동력을 지휘했던 복잡하고 계층화된 사회를 나타낸다고 믿는다. 다른 해석자들은 이런 대규모 사업이 지배층의 통제력 없이 사회적 결속을 강화한 공동의 계획을 중심으로 하나가 되는, 사회 집단 내부와 사회 집단 간의 협조적 공동 작업의 명백한 증거라고 주장한다. 많은 거석 구조물은 죽음과 연관되어 있는데, 최근의 해석은 개인 및 집단의 정체성, 결속, 그리고 분쟁이 펼쳐졌던 대중적 연극 공연으로서의 죽음과 매장 의식의 근본적인 역할을 강조한다.
① 자연의 경치에 대한 상징적 반영으로서의 거석 구조물
② 거석 구조물을 세운 사회의 본질에 대한 다양한 생각들
③ 고고학 조사에서의 거석 기념물의 중요성
④ 신석기 문명을 정의 내리는 요구조건들

**해설** STS '열거의 앞부분'에 해당하는 문장 — The massive tombs and ceremonial structures built from huge stones in the neolithic period are known as megalithic architecture, from the Greek words for "large" (megas) and "stone" (lithos). Archaeologists disagree about the nature of the societies that created them.
이 문장이 답 도출 근거 문장들이다.

**어휘** massive 엄청난  tomb 무덤  ceremonial 의식  neolithic 신석기 시대  megalithic 거석  monument 기념물  stratify 계층화  dictacte 명령하다  undertaking 일, 프로젝트  cohesion 응집력  interpretation 해석  theatrical 연극의  dispute 분쟁

## 예제 6  다음 글의 주제로 가장 적절한 것은?

정답 ③

The domestication of animals occurred some 10,000 years ago and represented a milestone for the history of human civilization. The origin and sequence of domestication is a hotly debated topic among anthropologists and historians. Richard Bulliet, professor of history at Columbia University, argues that animals were probably first kept in captivity for use in sacrificial rites. This practice allowed ancient civilizations to observe which species were tame enough for use as work animals. Animals, notably cattle, provided labor and locomotion when they were harnessed to plows, sledges, and wagons beginning in about 4000 BC. Thus, animal agriculture was indispensable to accelerating the development of crop agriculture. The flesh and hides of sacrificial animals were routinely consumed by those in the royal house or the priesthood. Eventually, the habit of having the animals under human control at all times provided a constant and consistent food supply ready at hand. It also thereby created the leisure time necessary to societal progress.

① different forms of sacrificial rites in diverse cultures
② significance of animal's labor in production of food
③ origin and usefulness of the domestication of animals
④ limitations on the further growth of crop agriculture

**해석** 동물의 가축화는 약 10,000년 전에 일어났으며, 인류 문명사에서의 획기적 사건에 해당했다. 가축화의 기원과 후속된 결과는 인류학자와 역사가들 사이에서 뜨거운 논쟁거리이다. Columbia 대학교의 역사학 교수 Richard Bulliet은 동물은 아마도 처음에는 제물로 바치는 의식에 사용할 목적으로 가두어 길러졌을 것이라고 주장한다. 이런 관행을 통해 고대의 문명사회는 어떤 종이 노동 동물로 사용할 수 있을 만큼 유순한지 관찰할 수 있었다. 기원전 4,000년경부터 동물들, 특히 소에게 쟁기, 썰매, 그리고 마차를 매자, 그것들은 노동과 이동을 제공했다. 따라서, 동물을 이용한 농업은 작물 농업의 발전을 가속화하는 데 없어서는 안 되는 것이었다. 제물로 바치는 동물의 살과 가죽은 관례적으로 왕가나 성직에 있는 사람들이 소비하였다. 결국, 동물을 항상 인간의 통제하에 두었던 관습을 통해 바로 쓸 수 있도록 준비된 지속적이고 일관된 식량 공급을 받았다. 그렇게 함으로써 그것은 사회 발전에 필요한 여가 시간도 만들어 냈다.
① 다양한 문화에서 희생제의 다른 형태들
② 식량 생산에서 동물 노동의 중요성
③ 동물 가축화의 기원과 유용함
④ 농작물 생산의 더 깊은 성장의 한계점들

**해설** 일반 type에 해당하는 '순수 설명문'으로, 전체 내용을 파악해야 하는 글이다. 결과론적인 답 도출 근거 문장들은 다음과 같다.
The origin and sequence of domestication is a hotly debated topic among anthropologists and historians.
+
Eventually, the habit of having the animals under human control at all times provided a constant and consistent food supply ready at hand. It also therby created the leisure time necessary to societal progress.
이 두 부분이 답 도출 근거 문장들이다.

**어휘** domestication 길들임, 가축사육   milestone 중요한 단계, 획기적 사건   anthropologist 인류학자   captivity 포로, 감금   sacrificial 희생의   rite 의식   tame 길들인, 길들이다   notably 특히   cattle 가축   locomotion 운동   sledge 썰매   wagon 마차   indispensable 없어서는 안될   flesh and hides 살과 가죽   priesthood 사제직

**예제 7** 다음 글의 주제로 가장 적절한 것은?  **정답** ①

---

Recent measurements using radiometers on satellites suggest that solar energy, which is an input to our climate system, can vary considerably. Changes of the order of 0.1% of the total solar energy reaching the Earth have already been measured, within a period of less than 20 months. This kind of change could be linked to sunspot activity, which has a periodicity of 11 years. Sunspots are magnetic storms giving (or showing) cooler regions on the Sun's surface. Thus a sunspot maximum corresponds to a minimum of received solar energy. According to measurements during the period 1976 to 1980, the Sun's surface cooled by about 6°C corresponding to an increase in the number and the size of sunspots. These changes may alter the Earth's climate since, according to numerical climate models, a 0.5% change in solar output could be enough to change the climate. In addition, a decrease in solar energy of the order of 1% could lead to a decrease in the Earth's average temperature by 1.0°C.

① potential effects of solar output variations on global climate change
② common factors of the global greenhouse effect in modern society
③ general definition of the Earth's mean temperature
④ great accuracy of measurements derived from satellite

**해석** 위성에 달린 복사량 측정기를 이용한 최근의 측정치는 우리의 기후 시스템에 입사되는 태양 (복사) 에너지가 크게 다를 수 있다는 것을 보여준다. 지구에 도달하는 태양 에너지의 총량이 20개월 미만의 주기 안에서 대략 0.1퍼센트 정도 변화된 것이 이미 측정되었다. 이런 종류의 변화는 11년의 주기성을 가진 태양 흑점 활동과 관계가 있을 수 있다. 흑점은 태양 표면에 온도가 더 낮은 지역을 제공하는 (혹은 보여 주는) 자기 폭풍이다. 따라서 흑점량의 최대 시기는 지구에 도달하는 태양 에너지양이 최소가 되는 시기에 해당한다. 1976년에서 1980년에 이르는 기간 동안의 측정치에 따르면, 태양 표면은 흑점의 수와 크기의 증가에 상응하여 섭씨 약 6도 온도가 낮아졌다. 이런 변화가 지구 기후를 바꿀 수 있는데, 수치로 표시되는 기후 모델에 따르면, 태양에서 방출되는 (복사) 에너지양이 0.5퍼센트만 변해도 기후를 바꾸기에 충분할 수 있기 때문이다. 게다가, 대략 1퍼센트 정도의 태양 에너지 감소가 섭씨 1도의 지구 평균 온도 하락으로 이어질 수 있다.
① 태양 에너지의 생산량 변화가 지구 기후변화에 미치는 잠재적인 영향들
② 현대 사회에서 지구의 온실효과의 공통적인 요소들
③ 지구의 평균 온도에 일반적인 정의
④ 위성에서 나온 측정의 큰 정확성

**해설** STS '연구의 결과를 보여주는 표현 Recent measurements ~ suggest that'이 들어간 문장이자, '수치 나열 예시'의 앞부분에 해당하는 문장 — Recent measurements using radiometers on satellites suggest that solar energy, which is an input to our climate system, can vary considerably.
+
결과를 보여주는 문장의 부분 — These changes may alter the Earth's climate
이 두 부분이 답 도출 근거들이다.

**어휘** radiometer 복사계  sunspot 흑점  periodicity 주기성  numerical 수치의

**예제 8**  다음 글의 제목으로 가장 적절한 것은?  정답 ④

The innovativeness of cities is related directly to the quality of human talent. China's coastal cities have been quicker off the mark because they have been more successful in nurturing quality, retaining the most talented knowledge workers, and attracting the cream of the knowledge workers from other parts of the country. The coastal cities are also more open and accessible to outsiders and have integrated with global knowledge networks. For smaller inland cities to become innovative smart cities, they will need to specialize and pull in some of the best brains in their fields of specialization from across the country. Any serious attempt to become an innovative city built on the quality of talent, which after all is the life blood of innovation, will have to combine urban design and renewal with a focus on developing a few core areas of world-class expertise.

① Risky Chances for China's Coastal City to Grow
② Innovation : An Element of Organizational Sustainability
③ What Can We Do to Motivate Knowledge Workers?
④ What Makes a City More Innovative?

**해석** 도시의 혁신성은 인간 재능의 우수성과 직접적인 관계가 있다. 중국의 해안 도시들은 우수성을 양성하고, 가장 재능이 있는 지식 근로자를 보유하고, 국내의 다른 지역 출신의 지식 근로자 중 최고를 끌어들이는 데 더 성공적이었기 때문에 상황 대처가 더 빨랐다. 그 해안 도시들은 또한 외부인에게 더 개방적이고 접근성이 있으며 전 세계의 지식 네트워크와 통합되었다. 더 작은 내륙 도시가 혁신적인 스마트 도시가 되기 위해서는 전문화하고 전국에서 전문 분야에 있는 최고의 두뇌 중 일부를 견인할 필요가 있을 것이다. 결국, 혁신의 생명선인 재능의 우수성을 기반으로 하여 구축되는 혁신적인 도시가 되기 위한 모든 진지한 시도는 도시 설계와 재개발을 세계 정상급의 전문 기술을 갖춘 일부 핵심 분야의 개발에 대한 집중과 결합해야 할 것이다.
① 중국의 해안 도시가 성장했을 때 위험한 가능성
② 혁신: 조직의 지속 가능성의 요소
③ 우리는 지식 노동자들에게 무엇으로 동기 부여를 할 수 있을까?
④ 무엇이 도시를 혁신적으로 만드는 것일까?

**해설** STS '예시(고유명사)의 앞부분'에 해당하는 문장 — The innovativeness of cities is related directly to the quality of human talent.
+
STS 'need to'가 들어간 문장 — For smaller inland cities to become innovative smart cities, they will need to specialize and pull in some of the best brains in their fields of specialization from across the country.
이 두 문장이 답 도출 근거 문장들이다.

**어휘** innovativeness 혁신성   quicker of 더 빠른   nurture 양육하다   retain 유지하다   integrated with ~와 통합된   renewal 갱신

**예제 9** 다음 글의 제목으로 가장 적절한 것은?   정답 ①

> U.S. manufacturing companies discovered the bright side of decision problems when they were forced by law to eliminate environmentally harmful materials from their operating processes. At first, the companies saw only the negatives — disruptions, higher costs, more paperwork. But then some of them began to see opportunities. Instead of viewing the problem in its narrow and obvious form — How can we get rid of the harmful materials? — they redefined it more broadly: How can we produce our product in the best and most efficient way? As a result, they made breakthroughs in their operations that have actually enabled them to have lower production costs without toxic materials than with them. By changing a problem into an opportunity, they gained an important advantage over their less savvy competitors.

① Reframe a Problem: Turn Crisis into Opportunity
② Making a Problem Clear Before Seeking a Solution
③ Cost Efficiency: A Significant Factor in Decision-making
④ Green Technology: Is it Truly Beneficial?

**해석** 미국 제조사들은 법에 따라 어쩔 수 없이 작업 공정에서 환경에 해로운 물질을 제거해야 했을 때 결정 문제의 긍정적 측면을 발견했다. 처음에 그 회사들은 (가동) 중단, 더 높은 비용, 더 많은 서류 작업 같은 부정적 측면만 보았다. 그러나 그런 다음 몇몇 회사들은 기회를 포착하기 시작했다. '어떻게 그 해로운 물질을 없앨 수 있을까?'라는 편협하고 뻔한 방식으로 문제를 바라보는 대신에, 그들은 '어떻게 최선의 그리고 가장 효율적인 방식으로 제품을 생산할 수 있을까?'라고 문제를 더 폭넓게 재정의했다. 결과적으로 그들은 실제로 유독성 물질을 포함했을 때보다 없는 경우에 자신들에게 더 낮은 생산 비용이 들 수 있게 하는 공정에서의 비약적인 발전을 이룩했다. 문제를 기회로 바꿈으로써 그들은 전문 지식이 더 적은 경쟁사들보다 중요한 우위를 점했다.
① 문제를 재구조화하기: 위기를 기회로 만들라
② 해결책을 찾기 전에 문제점을 분명하게 하기
③ 비용 효율성: 의사 결정에 있어서 중요한 요소
④ 친환경 기술: 이것이 진정으로 이로울까?

**해설** STS '**important / 필자의 주관 단어 advantage**'가 들어간 문장 — By changing a problem into an opportunity, they gained an important advantage over their less savvy competitors.
이 문장이 답 도출 근거 문장이다.

**어휘** disruption 방해   breakthrough 돌파구

**예제 10** 다음 글의 제목으로 가장 적절한 것은?  정답 ②

> Minorities tend not to have much power or status and may even be dismissed as troublemakers, extremists or simply 'weirdos'. How, then, do they ever have any influence over the majority? The social psychologist Serge Moscovici claims that the answer lies in their behavioural style, i.e. the way the minority gets its point across. The crucial factor in the success of the suffragette movement was that its proponents were consistent in their views, and this created a considerable degree of social influence. Minorities that are active and organised, who advocate and defend their position consistently, can create social conflict, doubt and uncertainty among members of the majority, and ultimately this may lead to social change. Such change has often occurred because a minority has converted others to its point of view. Without the influence of minorities, we would have no innovation, no social change. Many of what we now regard as 'major' social movements (e.g. Christianity, trade unionism or feminism) were originally due to the influence of an outspoken minority.

① Why Consistency Matters in Public Relations
② How Does the Minority Bring Change to Society?
③ Minority Rights: the Secret of Conflict Prevention
④ What Encourages People to Accept Common Rules?

**해석** 소수 집단은 많은 힘이나 지위를 가지고 있지 않은 경향이 있고 심지어 말썽꾼, 극단주의자, 또는 단순히 '별난 사람'으로 일축될 수도 있다. 그렇다면 대체 그들은 어떻게 다수 집단에 대한 영향력을 행사하는가? 사회 심리학자 Serge Moscovici는 그 답은 그들의 행동 양식, 즉 소수 집단이 자기네 의견을 이해시키는 방식에 있다고 주장한다. 여성 참정권 운동이 성공을 거둔 중대한 요인은 지지자들이 자신들의 관점에서 일관적이었다는 것이었는데, 이것이 상당한 정도의 사회적 영향력을 행사하였다. 자신들의 입장을 일관되게 옹호하고 방어하는 활동적이고 조직적인 소수 집단이 다수 집단의 구성원 사이에 사회적 갈등, 의심, 그리고 불확실을 만들어 낼 수 있고, 궁극적으로 이것이 사회 변화를 가져올 수도 있다. 그러한 변화가 흔히 일어난 까닭은 소수 집단이 다른 사람들을 자신의 관점으로 바꿔 놓았기 때문이다. 소수 집단의 영향 없이는 우리는 어떤 혁신, 어떤 사회 변화도 일으킬 수 없을 것이다. 우리가 현재 '주요' 사회 운동(예를 들어, 기독교 사상, 노동조합 운동, 또는 남녀평등주의)으로 여기는 많은 것이 원래 거침없이 말하는 소수 집단의 영향력 때문에 생겨났다.
① 홍보에 있어서 일관성이 중요한 이유
② 소수 집단이 어떻게 사회에 변화를 가져다주는 것일까?
③ 소수 집단의 권리: 갈등 예방의 비결
④ 무엇이 사람들이 공공의 규칙을 받아들게 하는 것일까?

**해설** STS '의문문 (How, then, do they ever have any influence over the majority?)에 대한 답변'에 해당하는 문장 — The social psychologist Serge Moscovici claims that the answer lies in their behavioural style, i.e. the way the minority gets its point across.
+
**이중부정으로 강한 긍정을 나타내는 문장** — Without the influence of minorities, we would have no innovation, no social change. 이 두 문장이 답 도출 근거 문장들이다.

**어휘** **dismiss** 해고하다　**extremist** 극단주의자　**suffragette** 참정권 운동을 벌인 여성들　**proponents** 지지자들　**convert** 변환하다

## 2 빈칸

### 1 Types

**예제 1** 다음 빈칸에 들어갈 말로 가장 적절한 것은?   **정답** ①

---

The opposite of talking is knowing when to stop. Speakers often have a problem with that. They're afraid that stopping might look like they forgot or lost what to say next. It's difficult to realize that as eloquent as well-chosen words are, ______________ is equally, and often more, eloquent. Eloquent not because it gives the audience a chance to stop and think but because it compels them to do so. When you're hot on the trail of delivering a message, the audience is busy absorbing it, and you're both moving at quite a pace. It is therefore invaluable for them to be given a pause in which to consider what you have just said. Not only for relief from the one-way charge but to be able to think on their own instead of running with you.

---

① silence
② refusal
③ sound
④ action

**해석** 말하기의 반대는 언제 멈출지를 아는 것이다. 연사들은 흔히 그 점에 문제가 있다. 그들은 말을 멈추면 자기들이 다음에 무슨 말을 해야 할지 잊어버렸거나 놓쳐버린 것으로 보일까봐 두려워한다. 정선된 말이 설득력 있기는 하지만 침묵도 그와 동일하게, 그리고 흔히 더 설득력 있다는 것을 깨닫기는 어렵다. (이는) 청중에게 멈춰서 생각할 기회를 주기 때문이 아니라 청중이 그렇게 할 수밖에 없게 만들기 때문에 설득력 있다. 여러분이 메시지 전달에 치열하게 매진하고 있을 때, 청중은 그것을 흡수하느라 바쁘고, 여러분은 양측 모두 상당한 속도로 나아가고 있다. 그러므로 그들에게 여러분이 방금 말한 것에 대해 생각해 볼 수 있는 휴지기가 주어지는 것은 매우 유용하다. (이는) 일방적인 돌진(강연)으로부터 한숨 돌릴 수 있게 하기 위한 것일 뿐 아니라 여러분과 함께 달리는 대신 그들 스스로 생각할 수 있게 하기 위해서이다.
① 침묵
② 거절
③ 소리
④ 행동

**해설** STS type으로 STS 'therefore / invaluable'이 들어간 문장 — It is therefore invaluable for them to be given a pause in which to consider what you have just said.
+
STS 'Not only A but B'가 들어간 문장 — Not only for relief from the one-way charge but to be able to think on their own instead of running with you.
이 두 문장이 답 도출 근거 문장들이다.

**어휘** eloquent 웅변의, 설득력 있는   compel 강요하다   trail 자취

## 예제 2 · 다음 빈칸에 들어갈 말로 가장 적절한 것은?   정답 ③

We often forget that the main purpose of criticizing is not to be negative but to be constructive: to fix something. But general criticism is destructive. It doesn't lead anyone to know how to fix things; it just makes people feel bad. We all have different verbal and visual styles and conceive different ways to say the same thing. But, unless you can explain ________________, you haven't started fixing anything. To help the criticized person know how to fix what you object to, define exactly what went wrong and why it is unsatisfactory. Most people are generally so sensitive to criticism that they'll say, "Yes, I understand," when they actually don't, just to get the criticism to end. Specific examples for improvement as well as specific descriptions of exactly what you mean are a must.

① typically
② respectfully
③ specifically
④ originally

**해석** 우리는 비판의 주된 목적이 반대하는 것이 아니라 건설적인 것, 즉 무엇인가를 바로잡는 것이라는 점을 종종 잊어버린다. 그러나 일반적인 비판은 파괴적이다. 그것은 어떤 사람에게 고치는 방법을 알게 이끌지 못한다; 그것은 단지 사람들을 기분 나쁘게 만들 뿐이다. 우리 모두에게는 각기 다른 언어적 스타일과 시각적 스타일이 있으며 같은 것을 말하는 데 다른 방법을 생각한다. 그러나 구체적으로 설명할 수 없다면, 어떤 것도 바로잡기를 시작하지 않은 것이다. 비판을 받는 사람이 여러분이 반대하는 것을 바로잡는 방법을 알도록 도우려면 정확히 무엇이 잘못되었고 왜 그것이 불만족스러운지 명확히 해라. 대다수 사람들은 일반적으로 비판에 너무 민감하여 실제로는 알지도 못하면서 단지 비판을 끝내기 위해서 '네, 알아요.' 하고 말할 것이다. 정확히 무슨 뜻인지에 대한 구체적인 기술뿐 아니라 개선을 위한 구체적인 예도 필수적인 것이다.
① 전형적으로
② 공손하게
③ 구체적으로
④ 독창적으로

**해설** middle type으로 글의 중반부에 있는 빈칸 문장의 뒷부분이 답 도출 근거 문장들이다. 그 중에서도 STS '명령문'이 들어간 문장 — To help the criticized person know how to fix what you object to, define exactly what went wrong and why it is unsatisfactory.
+
STS 'must'가 들어간 문장 — Specific examples for improvement as well as specific descriptions of exactly what you mean are a must.
이 두 문장이 답 도출 근거 문장들이다.

**어휘** constructive 건설적인   destructive 파괴적인

**예제 3** 다음 빈칸에 들어갈 말로 가장 적절한 것은?    정답 ①

A small business owner could never afford to offer his employees healthcare benefits. It was not typically a problem because most of the employees accessed healthcare through their working spouses. However, tragedy struck one year when two of his most productive employees were stricken with life-threatening illnesses. One had a heart attack, and the other had lung cancer. They each, obviously, had to miss work. With productivity gone and the business hurting, he chose to give the employees the only portion of their salary he could afford. The business operated at a loss that year, but when the two individuals overcame their life-threatening illnesses, he found that their new-found loyalty reaped a new set of rewards as they told their stories of a business owner who ________________________.

① cares about much more than a profit
② be able to maximize productivity
③ doesn't take care of employee benefits
④ responds sensitively to the voices of the employees

**해석** 어떤 소규모 사업주가 자기 직원들에게 의료보험 급부금을 제공해 줄 능력이 전혀 없었다. 대부분의 직원들은 직업을 갖고 있는 자신의 배우자를 통해 의료보험 급부금을 받을 수 있었으므로, 일반적으로 그것은 문제가 되지 않았다. 그렇지만, 어느 해에 그의 가장 생산적인 직원들 중 두 사람이 생명을 위협하는 질병에 걸렸을 때 비극적인 상황이 발생했다. 한 사람은 심장 마비를 일으켰고, 다른 한 사람은 폐암에 걸렸다. 분명히, 그들 각 사람은 일을 중단해야만 했다. 업무의 생산성이 사라지고 사업이 타격을 입는 상황에서, 그는 그 직원들의 월급 중에서 자신이 감당할 수 있는 만큼의 액수만을 그들에게 지급하기로 결정했다. 그 해에 사업은 손실을 보는 상태로 운영되었지만, 그 두 명의 사람들이 생명을 위협하는 질병을 이겨냈을 때, 이익보다 더 많은 것을 신경써 주는 사업주의 이야기를 그들이 했을 때에 새롭게 생겨난 그들의 충성심이 일련의 새로운 보상을 가져왔다는 것을 그는 알게 되었다.
① 이익보다 더 많은 것을 신경쓰다
② 생산성을 극대화 시킬 수 있다
③ 직원의 이익을 돌보지 않는다
④ 직원들의 목소리에 민감하게 반응하지 않는다

**해설** 일반 type에 해당하는 'Story'글로, 주인공이 작은 영세업체를 운영하는 사장님이고, 회사의 수익보다는 직원들에게 많은 신경을 쓰고 있다는 줄거리를 잡으면 되는 문제이다.

**어휘** spouse 배우자

**예제 4** 다음 빈칸에 들어갈 말로 가장 적절한 것은?  **정답** ③

A new study suggests that children who often get serious ear infections are twice as likely to ________________________ than kids with healthier ears. To explain the findings, lead researcher Linda Bartoshuk from the University of Florida says repeated ear infections might permanently damage a nerve called the chorda tympani. This nerve starts at the front of the tongue, where it pick up taste sensations. From there, where it delivers messages about what the tongue just tasted. When the nerve is damaged, she says, people become extra sensitive to the feel or texture of fatty foods, such as butter, which tend to be creamy and slippery. The food doesn't taste different, but feeling fatty sensations more than usual. That drives them to eat even more fatty foods.

① get nervous easily
② be mentally challenged
③ become obese later in life
④ damage their sense of taste

**해석** 귀에 심각한 감염이 자주 발생하는 아이들이 건강한 귀를 가진 아이들보다 <u>살아가면서 나중에 비만이 될</u> 가능성이 두 배나 높다는 새로운 연구결과가 있다. 그 결과를 설명하기 위하여 Florida 대학의 수석 연구자 Linda Bartoshuk는 반복되는 귀 감염이 chorda tympani라고 불리는 신경을 영구적으로 손상시킨다고 말한다. 이 신경은 미각을 감지하는 혀의 앞부분에서 시작한다. 거기로부터, 그 신경은 혀가 방금 맛 본 것에 대한 메시지를 전달한다. 그 신경이 손상될 때, 사람들은 크림 성분이 있고 미끄러운 경향이 있는 버터와 같은 지방이 있는 음식에 대한 질감에 매우 민감해진다고 그녀는 말한다. 음식은 다른 맛이 나지 않지만, 평소보다 지방에 대한 감각을 느낀다. 이것이 그들이 훨씬 더 지방이 많은 음식을 먹게 만든다.
① 쉽게 긴장한다
② 정신적으로 힘들어한다
③ 살아가면서 나중에 비만이 된다
④ 그들의 미각에 손상을 입힌다

**해설** 일반 type에 해당하는 글의 종류는 순수 설명문이고, 전반적으로 인과관계의 연속으로 글이 구성되어 있다. '중이염 → chordra tympani라는 신경을 손상 → 지방이 있는 음식에 sensitive → <u>지방이 있는 음식을 더 많이 섭취</u>'가 핵심 인과관계의 흐름이다. 그래서 중이염에 걸리면 (지방이 있는 음식을 더 많이 섭취하게 되어) 나중에 비만이 된다는 흐름의 글이다.

**어휘** infection 감염   nerve 신경

## <sup>2</sup> 활용

**예제 1** 다음 빈칸에 들어갈 말로 가장 적절한 것은?          정답 ④

In the classical notion of pleasure and pain, an organism strives to maintain equilibrium with its environment. Pain occurs as it deviates from equilibrium and pleasure occurs as it returns. For instance, when cold threatens body temperature, it registers as unpleasantness that can become intense pain if carried to an extreme. Conversely, we feel immediate pleasure in warming up from being cold. Pleasure results not from the warmth in itself, but from the approach to ideal body temperature. Too much warmth can also upset equilibrium, and a different kind of discomfort or outright pain will set in. So pleasures are not absolute but rather are _________________________ . The same taste or feeling or sight or sound that is pleasurable in one context can become painful in another.

① permanent in the overall scheme of things
② often relative to the individual's feelings
③ generally dependent upon different stimuli
④ always relative to an equilibrium point

**해석** 기쁨과 고통이라는 고전적인 개념에서 유기체는 자기의 환경과 균형 상태를 유지하려고 애쓴다. 유기체가 균형 상태에서 벗어날 때 고통이 발생하고 균형 상태로 돌아가면 기쁨이 발생한다. 예를 들어, 추위가 체온을 위협할 때, 추위는 그것이 극단으로 가게 되면 극심한 고통이 될 수 있는 불쾌감으로 인식된다. 반대로 추위로부터 따뜻해질 때 우리는 즉각적인 기쁨을 느낀다. 기쁨은 따뜻함 그 자체로부터 기인하는 것이 아니라 이상적인 체온에 가까워지는 데 있다. 지나친 따뜻함 역시 균형 상태를 깰 수 있고 다른 종류의 불편함과 명백한 고통이 오게 된다. 그래서 기쁨은 절대적인 것이 아니라 오히려 항상 균형점에 상대적인 것이다. 어떤 상황에서 기쁨을 줄 수 있는 동일한 맛과 느낌과 보이는 것과 들리는 것이 다른 상황에서는 고통스러울 수 있다.
① 상황에 대한 전반적인 계획에 있어서 영구적인
② 종종 개인의 감정에 상대적인
③ 일반적으로 다른 자극들에 의존하는
④ 항상 균형점에 상대적인

**해설** **For example의 활용으로 예시 (For instance)에 해당하는 부분** – For instance, when cold threatens body temperature, it registers as unpleasantness that can become intense pain if carried to an extreme. Conversely, we feel immediate pleasure in warming up from being cold.
이 부분이 답 도출 근거 부분이다.

**어휘** equilibrium 평형   deviate 일탈하다   outright 노골적인

**예제 2** 다음 빈칸에 들어갈 말로 가장 적절한 것은?　　　　　정답 ②

---

Contemporary artists have presented their views in lectures, interviews, essays, and a variety of novel formats. E-mails, text and voice messages, and other virtual public forums have all but replaced letters and journals. Many artists have sophisticated websites with blogs, chats and, nowdays, some social media accounts. These new possibilities allow the audience, not just specialists, to be informed and to engage in meaningful dialogues, with these exciting electronic platforms. Unlike tangible documents, e-mails and other electronic textual, visual, and audio materials may be, and often are deleted. Every when they are saved, digital media's endurance over time is still unknown. This raises important questions about ________________________ .

---

① whether a change in the way artists express their views is desirable
② how many contemporary art records might be available in the future
③ what will make it easier to express emotions in the future
④ how artists express their views using social network services

**해석** 현대의 예술가들은 강의, 인터뷰, 에세이, 그리고 다양한 새로운 형식으로 자신들의 견해를 제시해 왔다. 이메일, 문자와 음성 메시지, 그리고 다른 가상의 공개 토론장이 편지와 일지를 거의 대체해 버렸다. 많은 예술가들이 블로그, 채팅, 그리고 요즘에는 몇몇 소셜미디어 계정을 가진 세련된 웹사이트를 가지고 있다. 이런 새로운 가능성들은 전문가들만이 아니라 청중들도 정보를 제공받고 예술가들과의 의미 있는 대화에 참여할 수 있게 해준다. 그러나 이런 흥미로운 전자 플랫폼에는 잠재적인 문제가 있다. 유형의 문서와는 달리, 이메일과 다른 전자적 문자, 시각, 그리고 청각 자료는 삭제될 수도 있고, 자주 삭제가 된다. 심지어 그것들이 저장되어 있을 때도, 시간이 경과한 이후의 디지털 매체의 내구성은 여전히 알려져 있지 않다. 이것은 얼마나 많은 현대 예술 기록들이 미래에 이용 가능할지에 관한 중요한 의문을 제기한다.
① 예술가들이 자신의 견해를 표현하는 방식서의 변화가 바람직한지
② 얼마나 많은 현대 예술 기록들이 미래에 이용 가능할지
③ 무엇이 미래에 감정을 표현하는 것이 더 쉽게 만들 것인지
④ 예술가들이 소셜 네트워크 서비스를 사용하여 자신의 견해를 표현하는 방식

**해설** 빈칸 앞뒤의 활용으로 빈칸 문장의 앞부분 'This'라는 대명사를 clue로 사용하면, 빈칸 문장의 앞부분 — Unlike tangible documents, e-mails and other electronic textual, visual, and audio materials may be, and often are deleted. Every when they are saved, digital media's endurance over time is still unknown.
이 부분이 답 도출 근거 부분이다.

**어휘** tangible 명백한　　endurance 지구력

**예제 3**　다음 빈칸에 들어갈 말로 가장 적절한 것은?　　**정답** ③

The ability to detect danger in the posture of others has been studied by neuroscientist Beatrice Gelder. Her research has demonstrated that the brain of an observer reacts more powerfully to the body language of a person in a posture indicating fear than it does even to a fearful facial expression. Looks of fear can paralyze or, at least, evoke our own potent fear-based reactions. Yet as powerful as facial expressions are in conveying danger, a person's uptight posture and furtive movements make us even more uncomfortable. Wouldn't you, too, be startled by the sudden recoiling of the hiker in front of a coiled snake? This type of _______________ behavior occurs throughout the animal world. If, for example, one bird in a flock on the ground suddenly takes off, all the other birds will follow immediately after, they do not need to know why.

① calculative

② redundant

③ imitative

④ scaring

**해석**　타인의 자세에서 위험을 감지하는 능력은 신경 과학자 Beatrice Gelder에 의해 연구되어 왔다. 그녀의 연구는 관찰자의 뇌가 심지어 두려워하는 얼굴 표정보다 두려움을 나타내는 자세를 취하는 사람의 신체언어에 더 강하게 반응한다는 것을 보여주었다. 두려워하는 표정은 두려움에 근거한 우리 자신의 강력한 반응을 마비시키거나, 혹은 적어도 생기게 할 수는 있다. 하지만, 얼굴 표정이 위험을 전달함에 있어서 강력하다 하더라도, 한 사람의 긴장한 자세와 수상한 움직임이 우리를 훨씬 더 불편하게 만든다. 당신도 몸을 휘감고 있는 뱀의 쉿쉿 하는 소리를 듣기 아주 짧은 시간 전에 당신 앞에 있는 등산객이 갑자기 움찔하는 것에 당신도 깜짝 놀라지 않겠는가? 이러한 종류의 <u>모방하는</u> 행동은 동물 세계 전반에서 나타난다. 예를 들어, 만약 땅 위에 있는 세때 중 한 마리가 갑자기 날아오르면, 모든 다른 새들은 그 후 즉시 따라갈 것 이다. 그들은 그 이유를 알 필요도 없다.
① 계산적인
② 불필요한
③ 모방하는
④ 무섭게 하는

**해설**　빈칸 앞뒤의 활용으로 빈칸 문장의 뒤 문장의 앞부분 'for example'이라는 연결사를 clue로 사용하면, 빈칸 문장의 뒷부분 − If, for example, one bird in a flock on the ground suddenly takes off, all the other birds will follow immediately after, they do not need to know why.
이 문장이 답 도출 근거 문장이다.

**어휘**　neuroscientist 신경과학자　posture 자세　evoke 일깨우다　furtive 몰래 하는　recoil 움찔하다　calculative 계산적인
redundant 불필요한　imitative 모방

**예제 4** 다음 빈칸에 들어갈 말로 가장 적절한 것은?　　　　　　　　　　　　　정답 ①

> There is no doubt that mountainous areas with low valleys among them tend to have higher species richness than surrounding areas of flat land. This is partly because there are more different environments, each with its own characteristic set of species. For one thing there are different climate zones on a mountain, but only one climate in a flat lowland area. For example, in the Santa Catalina Mountains of Arizona, many different plant species occur in the same mountains but at distinct altitudes, each species at its own climatic optimum. A similar ____________ of species composition with elevation is found in the Siskiyou Mountains of Oregon, and in fact on almost any set of high mountains, simply because there is a wide range of climates there. Even on a very local scale, a varied landscape can have micro climatic differences adding to species richness.

① diversity

② activity

③ competition

④ extinction

**해석** 사이에 낮은 계곡이 있는 산악 지역은 주변의 평평한 지역보다 더 많은 종의 풍요로움을 가지고 있는 경향이 있다는 것은 의심의 여지가 없다. 이것은 부분적으로 더 다양한 환경이 있고, 각각의 환경에 그 자체의 특징을 가진 종의 집단이 있기 때문이다. 우선 산에 다양한 기후대가 있는데, 평평한 저지대 지역에는 오직 한 가지 기후만 있다. 예를 들어, Arizona 주의 Santa Catalina 산맥에는 많은 다양한 식물 종이 똑같은 산에서도 별개의 고도에 존재하지만, 각각의 종은 그 나름의 기후 최적 조건에 있다. 고도에 따른 종 구성의 비슷한 <u>다양성</u>은 Oregon 주의 Siskiyou 산맥과 사실상 거의 모든 높은 산에서 발견되는데, 그것은 단지 거기에 광범위한 기후가 있기 때문이다. 매우 국지적인 규모에서도, 다양한 지형은 종의 풍요로움을 증가시키는 미세 기후의 차이를 가지고 있을 수 있다.

① 다양성

② 활동성

③ 경쟁

④ 멸종

**해설** 빈칸 앞뒤의 활용으로 빈칸 문장의 앞부분 'similar'라는 형용사를 clue로 사용하면, 빈칸 문장의 앞 문장 — For example, in the Santa Catalina Mountains of Arizona, many different plant species occur in the same mountains but at distinct altitudes, each species at its own climatic optimum.

이 문장이 답 도출 근거 문장이다.

**어휘** optimum 최적의　　elevation 높이

**예제 5** 다음 빈칸에 들어갈 말로 가장 적절한 것은?   정답 ④

Pet food used to be about selecting a small, medium, or large bag of whatever your local feed of grocery store stocked. Today, choosing pet food from among the hundreds of varieties in the $17 billion United States market can be a complicated task. Beef, duck, vegetables, and salmon are part of today's pet diets. Once created to profit from human food manufacturing waste, the pet food industry now makes products with human-grade ingredients that sell well because people want something better for their beloved animal companions. The number of people purchasing pet food with human-grade ingredients is on increase. As a result, pets truly do increase the burden on agriculture, because ___________________________.

① it is difficult for farmers to choose crops for them

② there is no standard for classifying animals' edible food

③ there is a limit to the amount of crops farmers can harvest

④ they are no longer eating the "leftover" products

**해석** 애완동물 먹이는 과거에는 동네 사료 가게나 식료품 가게에 있는 모든 것들 중에서 작은 봉지, 중간 봉지, 또는 큰 봉지를 선택하는 것에 관한 것이었다. 오늘날에는, 170억 달러 규모의 미국 시장에 있는 수백 가지의 다양한 먹이 가운데 애완동물 먹이를 고르는 것은 복잡한 일이 될 수 있다. 소고기, 오리고기, 야채, 그리고 연어가 오늘날 애완동물 식단의 일부이다. 한때 인간의 식품 제조 중에 버려지는 것에서 이득을 얻기 위해 만들어졌지만, 애완동물 먹이 산업은 이제 사람이 먹는 수준의 재료를 가진 잘 팔리는 제품을 만드는데, 그 이유는 사람들이 자신이 아끼는 반려동물을 위해 더 좋은 것을 원하기 때문이다. 인간이 먹는 수준의 재료로 만든 애완동물 먹이를 구매하는 사람들의 수는 계속 증가하고 있다. 그 결과, 애완동물은 정말로 농업계에 대한 부담을 증가시키고 있는데, 그 이유는 <u>그들이 더 이상 '먹다 남은 것으로 만든' 제품을 먹고 있지 않기 때문이다.</u>

① 농부가 자신의 농작물을 선택하는 것은 어렵다

② 동물이 먹을 수 있는 식품을 분류하는 기준은 없다

③ 농부들이 수확할 수 있는 농작물의 양에 한계점이 있다

④ 그들은 더 이상 '먹다 남은 것으로 만든' 제품을 먹지 않는다

**해설** 빈칸 앞뒤의 활용으로 빈칸 문장의 앞부분 'As a result'라는 연결사를 clue로 사용하면, 빈칸 문장의 앞 문장 − The number of people purchasing pet food with human-grade ingredients is on increase.
이 문장이 답 도출 근거 문장이다.

**어휘** edible 먹을 수 있는   leftover 남은 음식

**예제 6** 다음 빈칸에 들어갈 말로 가장 적절한 것은?  정답 ②

Modern psychological theory states that the process of understanding is a matter of construction, not reproduction, which means that the process of understanding takes the form of the interpretation of data coming from the outside and generated by our mind. For example, the perception of a moving object as a car is based on an interpretation of incoming data within the framework of our knowledge of the world. While the interpretation of simple objects is usually an uncontrolled process, the interpretation of more complex phenomena, such as interpersonal situations, usually requires active attention and thought. Psychological studies indicate that it is knowledge possessed by the individual that determines which stimuli become the focus of that individual's attention, what significance he or she assigns to these stimuli, and how they are combined into a larger whole. This subjective world, interpreted in a particular way, is for us the "objective" world; we cannot know any world other than _________________.

① the reality placed upon us through social conventions
② the one we know as a result of our own interpretations
③ the world of images not filtered by our perceptual frame
④ the external world independent of our own interpretations

**해석** 현대의 심리학 이론은 이해의 과정은 재생이 아니라 구성의 문제라고 말하는데, 그것은 이해의 과정이 외부로부터 들어오고, 우리 마음에 의해 생성되는 정보의 해석이라는 모습을 취한다는 말이다. 예를 들어 움직이는 물체를 차라고 인식하는 것은 세상에 대한 우리의 지식이라는 틀 안에서, 들어오는 정보를 해석하는 것에 근거한다. 간단한 물체의 해석은 대개 통제되지 않는 과정이지만, 대인 관계의 상황 같은 더 복잡한 현상에 대한 해석은 대개 적극적인 주의집중과 사고를 필요로 한다. 심리학 연구는 어떤 자극이 그 개인의 주의에 초점이 되는지, 그 사람이 이 자극에 어떤 의미를 부여하는지, 그리고 그 자극들이 어떻게 결합되어 더 커다란 전체를 이루는지를 결정하는 것은 바로 그 개인이 소유하고 있는 지식이라는 점을 보여준다. 특정한 방식으로 해석되는 이 주관적 세계는 우리에게 있어 '객관적인' 세계인데, 우리는 우리 자신의 해석의 결과로 알고 있는 세계 외에는 그 어떤 세계도 알 수 없다.
① 사회적 관습을 통해 우리에게 놓인 현실
② 우리 자신의 해석의 결과로 우리가 알고 있는 것
③ 우리의 인식체계로 여과되지 않은 이미지의 세상
④ 우리의 해석과 관계없는 외부적인 세계

**해설** STS '연구의 결과에 해당하는 modern psychological theory states that / 예시 (For example)의 앞부분'이 들어간 문장 — Modern psychological theory states that the process of understanding is a matter of construction, not reproduction, which means that the process of understanding takes the form of the interpretation of data coming from the outside and generated by our mind.
+
STS '연구의 결과를 보여주는 표현 Psychological studies indicate that / it-that강조'가 들어간 문장 — Psychological studies indicate that it is knowledge possessed by the individual that determines which stimuli become the focus of that individual's attention, what significance he or she assignes to these stimuli, and how they are combined into a larger whole.
이 두 문장이 답 도출 근거 문장들이다.
다만, 빈칸 문장에 있는 부정어 'not'과 'other than'을 잘 이용해서 선지 선택을 해야 한다.

**어휘** framework 뼈대    interpersonal 대인 관계의

**예제 7** 다음 빈칸에 들어갈 말로 가장 적절한 것은?　　　　　　　　정답 ③

> To say that we need to curb anger and our negative thoughts and emotions does not mean that we should deny our feelings. There is an important distinction to be made between denial and restraint. The latter constitutes a deliberate and voluntarily adopted discipline based on an appreciation of the benefits of doing so. This is very different from the case of someone who suppresses emotions such as anger out of a feeling that they need to present a facade of self-control, or out of fear of what others may think. Such behaviour is like closing a wound which is still infected. We are not talking about rule-following. Where denial and suppression occur, there comes the danger that in doing so the individual ___________ anger and resentment. The trouble here is that at some future point they may find they cannot contain these feelings any longer.

① fades out

② copes with

③ stores up

④ soothes

**해석** 우리가 분노와 우리의 부정적인 생각과 감정을 억제할 필요가 있다고 말하는 것은 우리의 감정을 부정해야 함을 의미하지는 않는다. 부인과 자제 사이에는 구분해 두어야 할 중요한 차이점이 있다. 후자는 그렇게 하는 것이 가져오는 이점들을 이해하는 바탕에서 의도적이고 자발적으로 취해진 규율로 여겨진다. 이는 겉으로는 자기 통제를 보일 필요가 있다고 느껴서, 혹은 다른 이들이 어떻게 생각할지에 대한 두려움에서 분노와 같은 감정을 억제하는 사람의 경우와는 매우 다르다. 그러한 행동은 여전히 감염된 상처를 덮어두는 것과 같다. 우리는 규율 준수에 대해서 이야기하고 있는 것이 아니다. 부인과 억압이 일어나는 곳에서, 그렇게 함으로써 그 사람이 분노와 분한 마음을 <u>쌓아 놓는</u>다는 위험성이 오기 마련이다. 여기서 문제는 미래의 어느 시점에 이르게 되면 그들이 더는 이러한 감정을 억누르고 있을 수 없다는 것을 알 수 있다는 것이다.

① 사라지다

② 대처하다

③ 쌓아놓다

④ 위로하다, 달래다

**해설** '＋ vs － pattern '의 활용으로 빈칸의 위치가 문장 내의 동격의 that 뒤에 있다는 점과 이 that 앞의 내용이 ' － '의 흐름이므로 that 절의 내용도 ' － '의 흐름이 나와야 한다는 점에서, 빈칸에 들어갈 말로, 선지에 있는 stores up이 가장 적절하다. 다른 선지에 있는 'fades out / copes with / soothes'는 모두 동격의 that 절의 내용을 ' ＋ '의 흐름으로 바꾸어 주므로, 오답을 만드는 단어들이다.

**어휘** curb 억제하다　restraint 제지　deliberate 고의의　adopt 입양하다, 채택하다, 받아들이다　discipline 규율　appreciation 감사　facade 정면　resentment 원한　copes with 대처하다　stores up 저장하다　soothe 달래다

**예제 8**  다음 빈칸에 들어갈 말로 가장 적절한 것은?                정답 ③

Recent evidence suggests that the common ancestor of Neanderthals and modern people, living about 400,000 years ago, may have already been using pretty sophisticated language. If language is based on genes and is the key to cultural evolution, and Neanderthals had language, then why did the Neanderthal toolkit show so little cultural change? Moreover, genes would undoubtedly have changed during the human revolution after 200,000 years ago, but more in response to new habits than as causes of them. At an earlier date, cooking selected mutations for smaller guts and mouths, rather than vice versa. At a later date, milk drinking selected for mutations for retaining lactose digestion into adulthood in people of western European and East African descent. ________________________________. The appeal to a genetic change driving evolution gets gene-culture co-evolution backwards: it is a top-down explanation for a bottom-up process.

① Genetic evolution is the mother of new habits

② The linguistic shovel paves the way for a cultural road

③ The cultural horse comes before the genetic cart

④ When the cultural cat is away, the genetic mice will play

**해석** 최근의 증거는 약 400,000년 전에 살았던 네안데르탈인과 현대인의 공통 조상이 아주 세련된 언어를 이미 사용하고 있었을지도 모른다는 점을 시사한다. 만약 언어가 유전자에 기반을 두며 문화적인 진화로 가는 열쇠라면, 그리고 네안데르탈인이 언어가 있었다면, 왜 네안데르탈인의 도구세트는 문화적인 변화를 거의 보여주지 않았을까? 게다가 유전자는 200,000년 전 이후의 인간의 혁명 동안에 의심할 여지없이 변해왔을 것이지만, 새로운 습관의 원인으로서라기보다는 새로운 습관에 대한 반응으로서 변해왔을 것이다. 초기에는, 요리는 그 반대의 경우보다는 더 작은 창자와 입을 위한 변화를 선택했다. 나중에는, 우유 섭취가 서구 유럽인들과 동아프리카계 사람들에게서 락토오스 소화를 성인기까지 유지하기 위한 변화를 선택했다. 문화적인 말이 유전자라는 수레 앞에 온다. 진화를 이끄는 유전적인 변화에의 호소는 유전과 문화의 공동 진화를 역행한다. 그것은 상향식 과정에 대한 하향식 설명이다.

① 유전자 진화가 새로운 습관의 어머니이다

② 언어라는 삽이 문화 도로를 포장한다

③ 문화적인 말이 유전자라는 수레 앞에 온다

④ 문화라는 고양이가 사라질 때, 유전자라는 쥐가 활동할 것이다

**해설** 인과관계의 활용으로 글의 종류는 순수 설명문이고, 전반적으로 인과관계의 연속으로 글이 구성되어 있다. '새로운 습관 (문화) → 유전자'가 핵심 인과관계의 흐름이다. 글의 앞부분에 언급한 '유전자 → 언어 → 문화'라는 순서는 잘못되었음을 입증하고 있는 내용도 있다. 따라서 선지에 있는 'The cultural horse comes before the genetic cart. (문화적인 말이 유전자라는 수레 앞에 온다.)'라는 비유가 가장 적절하다.

**어휘** mutation 돌연변이   vice versa 그 반대도 마찬가지   lactose 락토스

**예제 9** 다음 빈칸에 들어갈 말로 가장 적절한 것은?  **정답** ①

Human are predisposed to ________________________________________ . We have all seen the shape of the Big Dipper among the stars  at night, even though the only thing we have really seen are seven points of light. Humans infer meanings not only with visual perceptions but other information as well. Errors in logic are committed by drawing conclusions from  a few facts when no such conclusion is warranted by the available evidence. Retailers know this when they announce low prices on a few very visible items, leading to the inference that overall prices are lower at that store. If one person wins the lottery with a ticket purchased at the local mini-mart, that becomes the lucky location to purchase tickets.

① see whole patterns from partial or random evidence
② prefer simple answers that can be readily comprehended
③ understand the new by a closer study of the world
④ assume that two events which occur together must be related

**해석** 인간은 부분적이거나 무작위적인 증거로부터 전체적인 패턴을 보는 경향이 있다. 비록 우리가 실제로 보는 것은 단지 일곱 개의 빛의 점일 뿐이지만, 우리는 모두 밤하늘의 별들 속에서 북두칠성을 본다. 인간은 시각적인 인식뿐만 아니라 다른 정보를 가지고서도 역시 의미를 추론한다. 이용 가능한 증거에 의해서 그런 결론이 보장되지 않을 때조차도, 몇 가지 사실로부터 결론을 도출함으로써 논리에서의 오류가 저질러진다. 소매업자들은 눈에 아주 잘 띄는 물건에 낮은 가격을 표시할 때 이러한 사실을 알고 있는데, 이는 그 가게에서는 전체적인 가격이 낮다는 추론을 하도록 한다. 어떤 사람이 동네 구멍가게에서 산 복권이 당첨이 되면, 그곳이 복권을 구입하는 행운의 장소가 되는 것이다.

**해설** 나열식 구조의 활용으로 총 3가지 case가 나온다.
case 1 – 인간은 밤하늘의 7개의 점을 보고 북두칠성의 형태를 본다.
case 2 – 인간은 가게에서 전략적으로 내놓은 미끼상품의 가격을 보고 이 가게의 모든 물건은 싸다고 느낀다.
case 3 – 인간은 복권 1등 당첨점을 운이 좋은 장소라고 인지한다.
이 세 가지 case의 공통점으로 빈칸에 들어갈 말은 'see whole patterns from partial or random evidence'이 가장 적절하다.

**어휘** predispose 영향을 미치다, ~하게 만들다    be warranted by ~에 의해 보증되다

## 3 -1  순서배열 Warmming Up!

**예제 1** 주어진 글 다음에 이어질 글의 순서로 가장 적절한 것은?    정답 ③

If you were trying to fall asleep, would a quiet room be the best place to go?

(A) In this experiment, people who experienced the tiresome repeating of a sound fell asleep more easily than people in a quiet room.

(B) An experiment has shown that a repeating sound brings on sleep better than silence.

(C) Next time you want to sleep, therefore, listen to the monotonous sound.

① (A) − (B) − (C)

② (A) − (C) − (B)

③ (B) − (A) − (C)

④ (B) − (C) − (A)

**해석** 만약에 당신이 잠들고자 노력하다면,  조용한 방이 자러가기에 최고의 장소인가?
(B) 한 실험에서 반복되는 소리가 침묵보다 잠을 더 잘 유도한다는 것을 보여줬다.
(A) 이 실험에서 지루하게 반복되는 소리를 경험했던 사람들이 조용한 방에 있는 사람들보다 더 쉽게 잠들었다.
(C) 그러므로, 다음번에 잠들기를 원한다면, 단조로운 소리를 들어라.

**해설** [          ]
(A) (×) / (B) 〉(C)
(B)
this N
(A)
therefore
(C)

**어휘** tiresome 귀찮은   monotonous 단조로운

**예제 2**  주어진 글 다음에 이어질 글의 순서로 가장 적절한 것은?   정답 ②

---

Most diamonds were formed billions of years ago in an inner layer of the earth called mantle.

---

(A) About 100 miles underground, the mantle puts extreme pressures on carbon.

(B) As the crystal grows, it may trap other chemicals inside, creating what we call "a space  capsule from the inner earth."

(C) These forces turn black carbon into clear diamond crystal.

---

① (A) − (B) − (C)

② (A) − (C) − (B)

③ (B) − (C) − (A)

④ (C) − (A) − (B)

---

**해석**  대부분의 다이아몬드는 맨틀이라고 불리는 지구 내면의 층에서 수십 억 년 전에 형성되었다.
(A) 대략 지하 100마일 정도에서, 그 맨틀은 탄소에 굉장한 압력들을 가한다.
(C) 이러한 힘들은 탄소를 투명한 다이아몬드 결정체로 바꾼다.
(B) 그 결정체가 커지면서, 그것은 다른 화학물질들을 내부에 가두게 되어 소위 "지구 내부로부터 온 우주 캡슐"이라는 것을 만들어 낸다.

**해설**

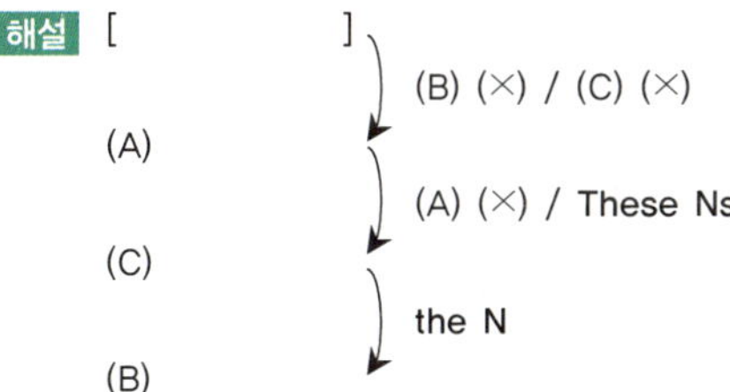


**어휘**  mantle 맨틀(지구의 층상 구조 속에서 지각과 핵 사이에 있는 부분)   carbon 탄소

**예제 3** 주어진 글 다음에 이어질 글의 순서로 가장 적절한 것은?  정답 ②

---

Footwear has a history which goes back thousands of years, and it has long been an article of necessity.

---

(A) The earliest footwear was undoubtedly born of the necessity to provide some protection when moving over rough ground in varying weather conditions. In ancient times, as today, the basic type of shoes worn depended on the climate.

(B) Shoes have not always served such a purely functional purpose, however, and the requirements of fashion have dictated some curious designs, not all of which made walking easy.

(C) For instance, in warmer areas the sandal was, and still is, the most popular form of footwear, whereas the modern moccasin derives from the original shoes adopted in cold climates by races such as Eskimos and Siberians.

---

① (A) − (B) − (C)

② (A) − (C) − (B)

③ (B) − (C) − (A)

④ (C) − (A) − (B)

**해석** 신발은 수천 년을 거슬러 올라가는 역사를 가지고 있고, 그것은 오랜 시간동안 필수품이어 왔다.

(A) 초기의 신발은 의심할 여지없이 변화하는 날씨 상황 속에서 거친 땅을 이동할 때 발을 보호해주는 필요성으로 탄생했다.

(C) 예를 들어, 따뜻한 지역에서는 샌들이 가장 인기 있는 형태의 신발이었고, 지금도 그렇다. 반면에 현대의 모카신은 Eskimos인들이나 Siberian들과 같은 인종들이 추운 기후에서 채택한 신발의 형태에서 유래되었다.

(B) 그러나, 신발이 그러한 순수 기능적인 목적만을 제공한 것은 아니었다. 패션의 요구사항이 약간 호기심에 찬 디자인을 만들게 하였다. 그러나 모든 것들이 걷는 것을 쉽게 만들지는 않았다.

**해설**

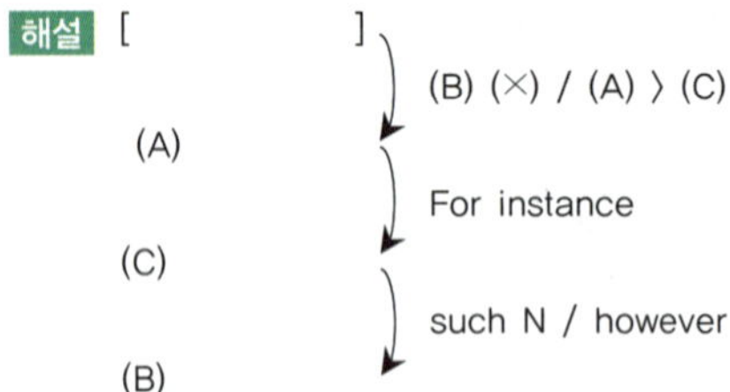


**어휘** race 인종

## 3 -2  순서배열 Application

**예제 1  주어진 글 다음에 이어질 글의 순서로 가장 적절한 것은?**  정답 ②

Most consumer magazines depend on subscriptions and advertising. Subscriptions account for almost 90 percent of total magazine circulation. Single-copy, or newsstand, sales account for the rest.

(A) For example, the Columbia Journalism Review is marketed toward professional journalists and its few advertisements are news organizations, book publishers, and others. A few magazines, like Consumer Reports, work toward objectivity and therefore contain no advertising.

(B) However, single-copy sales are important: they bring in more revenue per magazine, because subscription prices are typically at least 50 percent less than the price of buying single issues.

(C) Further, potential readers explore a new magazine by buying a single issue; all those insert cards with subscription offers are included in magazines to encourage you to subscribe. Some magazines are distributed only by subscription.

Professional or trade magazines are specialized magazines and are often published by professional associations. They usually feature highly targeted advertising.

① (B) − (A) − (C)
② (B) − (C) − (A)
③ (C) − (A) − (B)
④ (C) − (B) − (A)

**해석** 대부분의 소비자 잡지는 구독과 광고에 의존한다. 구독은 전체 잡지 판매 부수의 거의 90퍼센트를 차지한다. 낱권, 다시 말해 가판대 판매가 나머지를 차지한다.

(B) 하지만, 낱권 판매가 중요한데, 왜냐하면 구독 가격이 보통 낱권을 살 때의 가격보다 최소 50퍼센트는 더 싸서, 낱권 판매가 잡지 한 권당 더 많은 수익을 가져오기 때문이다.

(C) 게다가, 잠재적 독자들은 낱권의 잡지를 구매함으로써 새로운 잡지를 탐색한다. 구독 안내가 있는 그 모든 삽입 광고 카드는 여러분의 구독을 독려하기 위해 잡지에 들어가 있다. 어떤 잡지는 오로지 구독에 의해서만 유통된다. 전문가용 잡지, 다시 말해 업계지는 특성화된 잡지이며 흔히 전문가 협회에 의해 출판된다. 그것들은 보통 매우 표적화된 광고를 특징으로 한다.

(A) 예를 들어, Columbia Journalism Review는 전문 언론인들을 대상으로 마케팅을 하며 그 잡지의 몇 안 되는 광고는 뉴스 기관, 출판사 등이다. Consumer Reports와 같은 몇몇 잡지는 객관성을 지향하고 따라서 광고를 싣지 않는다.

**해설**  [        ]

(B) → However
/ 앞 단락 뒷부분 + 뒷 단락 앞부분(single-copy → single copy)

(C) → Further
/ 앞 단락 뒷부분 + 뒷 단락 앞부분 (single issues → a single issue)

(A) → For example

**어휘**  subscription 구독   circulation 순환   distribute 분배하다

## 예제 2 주어진 글 다음에 이어질 글의 순서로 가장 적절한 것은?  정답 ②

It takes time to develop and launch products. Consequently, many companies know 6−12 months ahead of time that they will be launching a new product.

(A) This marketing technique is called demand creation. It involves creating a buzz about a new potentially revolutionary nutrient or training technique through publishing articles and/or books that stimulate the reader' interest. Once this is done, a new product is launched.

(B) In order to create interest in the product, companies will often launch pre-market advertising campaigns. In the nutrition industry, articles are often written discussing a new nutrient under investigation.

(C) Over a series of issues, you begin to see more articles discussing this new nutrient and potential to enhance training and/or performance. Then, after 4−6 months, a new product is coincidentally launched that contains the ingredient that has been discussed in previous issues. Books and supplement reviews have also been used as vehicles to promote the sale of fitness and nutrition products.

① (B) − (A) − (C)
② (B) − (C) − (A)
③ (C) − (A) − (B)
④ (C) − (B) − (A)

**해석** 제품을 개발하고 출시하는 것은 시간이 걸린다. 결과적으로, 많은 회사들은 자신들이 신제품을 출시할 것을 6~12개월 먼저 안다.

(B) 그 제품에 대한 관심을 창출하기 위해 회사들은 흔히 출시 전 광고 캠페인에 착수하곤 한다. 영양제 업계에서는 연구 중인 새로운 영양분에 대해 논의하는 기사가 흔히 작성된다.

(C) 일련의 간행물에 걸쳐 이 새로운 영양분과 훈련 그리고/또는 경기력을 향상시킬 수 있는 잠재력에 대해 논의하는 더 많은 기사를 보기 시작한다. 그런 다음 4~6개월 후에, 이전의 간행물에서 논의되었던 성분을 함유한 신제품이 우연의 일치처럼 출시된다. 책과 보충 자료도 건강 및 영양 제품의 판매를 촉진하기 위한 도구로 이용되어 왔다.

(A) 이런 마케팅 기술을 수요 창출이라고 부른다. 그것은 독자의 관심을 자극하는 기사 그리고/또는 책의 출간을 통해, 어쩌면 혁명적일 수도 있는 새로운 영양분이나 훈련 기법에 관한 소문을 만들어 내는 것을 포함한다. 일단 이것이 이루어지고 나면 신제품이 출시된다.

**해설** [          ]

(A) (×) / (C) (×)
앞 단락 뒷부분 + 뒷 단락 앞부분 (many companies → companies)

(B)

this N

(C)

this N

(A)

**어휘** launch 출시하다

**예제 3** 주어진 글 다음에 이어질 글의 순서로 가장 적절한 것은?   **정답** ①

Psychologists Dember and Earl suggested that the motivation for exploration had its roots in a curiosity drive.

(A) This is very important for understanding why people will often return to explore things that they explored before or do things they have done before. In our daily lives, for example, we might decide to listen to a piece of music that we have listened to many times.

(B) They suggested that curiosity is stimulated by novelty and argued that novelty is in the eye of the beholder. We could have seen something many times before, but as the result of having new skills or competence, we discover new or different aspects of that object.

(C) By returning to that music with a new or fresh perspective, perhaps as a result of listening to other music, we find something new and interesting. One reason that people can play a card game such as bridge over and over is that no matter how many times you have played the game, it will be different in some way.

① (B) − (A) − (C)
② (B) − (C) − (A)
③ (C) − (A) − (B)
④ (C) − (B) − (A)

**해석** 심리학자 Dember와 Earl은 탐구의 동기는 호기심의 욕구에 뿌리를 두고 있다고 말했다.
(B) 그들은 호기심이 신기함에 의해 자극을 받는다고 말하며, 신기함은 보는 사람의 눈에 따라 다르다고 주장했다. 우리는 전에 어떤 것을 여러 번 보았을 수도 있겠지만, 새로운 기술이나 능력을 갖추게 되었으므로 그 물건의 새롭거나 다른 측면을 발견한다.
(A) 이것은 왜 사람들이 이전에 탐구했던 것들을 탐구하기 위해서, 또는 이전에 했던 것들을 하기 위해서 자주 돌아가곤 하는지를 이해하는 데 매우 중요하다. 예를 들어, 우리는 일상생활에서 여러 번 들었던 음악 작품을 듣기로 할 수도 있을 것이다.
(C) 아마도 다른 음악을 들은 것으로부터 생긴, 새롭거나 신선한 관점을 가지고 그 음악으로 돌아감으로써, 우리는 새롭고 흥미로운 어떤 것을 발견한다. 사람들이 브리지와 같은 카드 게임을 반복해서 할 수 있는 이유는, 그 게임을 아무리 여러 번 했을지라도, 그것이 어떤 면에서는 다를 터이기 때문이다.

**해설**

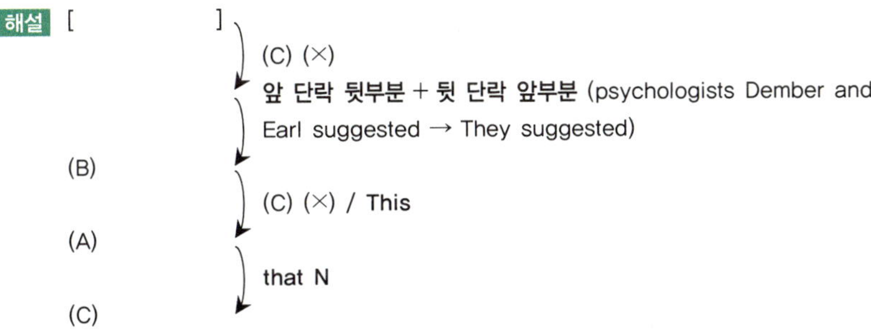


**어휘** motivation 동기 부여   exploration 탐구   beholder 구경꾼

**예제 4** 주어진 글 다음에 이어질 글의 순서로 가장 적절한 것은?   **정답** ②

---

The ancient Greeks sought to improve memory through brain training methods such as memory palaces and the method of loci. At the same time, they and the Egyptians became experts at externalizing information, inventing the modern library, a grand storehouse for externalized knowledge.

---

(A) We don't know why these simultaneous explosions of intellectual activity occurred when they did (perhaps daily human experience had hit a certain level of complexity). But the human need to organize our lives, our environment, even our thoughts, remains strong.

(B) Dogs have been known to collect their toys and put them in baskets; ants carry off dead members of the colony to burial grounds; certain birds and rodents create barriers around their nests in order to more easily detect invaders.

(C) This need isn't simply learned; it is a biological imperative — animals organize their environments instinctively. Most mammals are biologically programmed to put their digestive waste away from where they eat and sleep.

① (A) − (B) − (C)
② (A) − (C) − (B)
③ (B) − (A) − (C)
④ (B) − (C) − (A)

**해석** 고대 그리스인들은 기억의 궁전과 장소를 활용한 기억법과 같은 두뇌 훈련 방법을 통해 기억을 개선하려고 노력했다. 동시에 그들과 이집트인들은 외면화된(형체로 나타난) 지식의 웅대한 저장소인 현대적인 도서관을 처음으로 만들면서 정보를 외면화하는 일에 전문가들이 되었다.
(A) 지적 활동이 이렇게 동시에 급증하는 일이 왜 하필 그때(그렇게 일어났을 때) 일어났는지 우리는 알지 못한다. (아마 인간의 일상적인 경험이 어느 정도 복잡한 수준에 이르렀을 것이다). 하지만 우리의 삶과 우리의 환경과 우리의 사고까지도 정리하려는 인간의 욕구는 여전히 강력하다.
(C) 이런 욕구는 단순히 학습되는 것이 아니라 생물학적인 명령이다. 즉, 동물은 본능적으로 자기 환경을 정리한다. 대부분 포유동물은 자신의 소화 배설물을 자신이 먹고 자는 곳으로부터 치우는 생물학적 성향을 타고났다.
(B) 개는 자신의 장난감을 모아서 바구니에 넣는다고 알려져 왔고, 개미는 집단의 죽은 구성원을 매장지로 끌고 가고, 특정한 새와 설치류 동물은 침입자를 더 쉽게 발견하기 위하여 자기 보금자리 주변에 장애물을 만든다.

**해설** [          ]
(A)
    (C) (×) / these Ns

    this N
(C)

    예시 (上 − 下 관계)
(B)

**어휘** loci locus(장소)의 복수형   externalize 외부화하다   imperative 피할 수 없는

## 4 문장삽입

## 4 -1 문장삽입 Warming Up!

**예제 1** 글의 흐름으로 보아, 주어진 글이 들어가기에 가장 적절한 곳은?　　정답 ④

> The army gave up on camels, but not everyone did.

Camels are often called ships of the desert. They can carry heavy loads for many days without drinking water. ( ① ) Their broad feet don't sink in the sand and long eyelashes protect their eyes during sandstorms. ( ② ) In 1856, the U.S. Army imported camels for desert duty. ( ③ ) American solders never learned to manage the stubborn animals, though. ( ④ ) Today, over a century later, an American farmer raises fine racing camels in Arizona.

**해석** 낙타는 사막의 배라고 종종 불린다. 그것들은 물이 없이도 며칠 동안 무거운 짐들을 나를 수 있다. 낙타들의 넓은 발은 모래에서 가라앉지 않고 긴 속눈썹은 모래 폭풍우가 치는 동안 그들의 눈을 보호해준다. 1856년, 미국 군대는 사막 근무를 위해 낙타를 수입했다. 그러나 미국 군인들은 그 고집 센 동물을 다루는 법을 배우지 않았다. (그 군대는 낙타를 포기했다. 그러나 모두가 다 포기한 것은 아니다.) 1세기가 지나서, 오늘날 미국 농부가 Arizona에서 경주용 낙타를 기르고 있다.

**해설** Clue 'The + N' − 주어진 문장에 있는 'The army'
　　+ Context − (④) 뒤에 있는 문맥을 이용하면 주어진 문장의 위치는 ④번이다.

**어휘** camel 낙타

## 예제 2 글의 흐름으로 보아, 주어진 글이 들어가기에 가장 적절한 곳은?

> However, sometimes our facial expressions do not match our words.

We often express our feelings by doing things like smiling or frowning. ( ① ) Sometimes we use facial expressions to add information to something we are saying. ( ② ) Think about your classmate. ( ③ ) As she raised her eyebrows, she probably said, "Oh, what a surprise to see you here!" Both her face and words expressed her feeling. ( ④ ) If someone says to you, "I'm fine," but he is looking down and frowning, how do you think he really feels? You can easily know he is trying to hide his feeling.

**해석** 우리는 미소 짓기 또는 인상 쓰기와 같은 것을 하면서 우리의 감정을 자주 표현한다. 가끔씩 우리는 우리가 말하고 있는 것에 정보를 더하기 위해 얼굴표정을 사용한다. 당신의 반 친구를 생각해 보아라. 그 친구가 그녀의 눈썹을 올리면서, "오, 너를 여기서 만나다니 진짜 깜짝 놀랐어."라고 말했다. 그녀의 얼굴과 말 둘 다 그녀의 감정을 표현했다. (그러나, 가끔씩 우리의 얼굴표정이 우리가 하는 말과 일치하지 않는다.) 만약 누군가가 "난 괜찮아"라고 말하지만 그의 시선이 아래로 향해있고, 인상을 쓴다면, 그가 어떤 감정이라고 생각하겠는가? 당신은 쉽게 그가 자신의 감정을 숨기는 중이라는 것을 알 수 있다.

**해설** Clue '연결사' — 주어진 문장에 있는 'However'
+ Context — (④)를 기점으로 반대의 문맥을 이용하면 주어진 문장의 위치는 ④번이다.

**어휘** frown 인상을 찌푸리다

**예제 3** 글의 흐름으로 보아, 주어진 글이 들어가기에 가장 적절한 곳은?   **정답** ③

From there they were taken to Arizona and were reassembled by workers in the Arizona desert.

In the early 1960s, London Bridge was in trouble. Cars, trucks, and buses were too heavy for it, and the bridge was sinking into the Thames river. ( ① ) London city officials wanted to build a new bridge, and a businessman named Robert McCulloch decided to buy the old bridge and move it to Arizona. ( ② ) Workers disassembled the bridge in 1968, numbering the bricks, and sent them to Los Angeles. ( ③ ) The bridge was finally completed in 1971. ( ④ ) However, McCulloch knew he needed more than a famous bridge to attract people to Lake Havasu City, so he created an English village with typical English shops and restaurants. Today, London Bridge is one of Arizona's biggest attractions.

**해석** 1960년대 초에, London Bridge는 곤란함에 빠졌다. 자동차들, 트럭들, 그리고 버스들을 그 다리가 감당하기에 너무 무거워서 그 다리가 Thames강으로 가라앉고 있는 중이었다. 런던시 공무원들은 새로운 다리를 만들기를 원했다. 그리고 Robert McCulloch라는 한 사업가가 그 오래된 다리를 사서 Arizona로 옮기기로 결정했다. 노동자들이 1968년에 그 다리를 분해해서, 벽돌에 번호를 붙여 그것들을 Los Angeles로 보냈다. (그곳으로부터 그것들이 Arizona로 가져와져서 Arizona 사막에서 노동자들이 재조립하였다.) 그 다리는 마침내 1971년에 완공되었다. 그러나 MacCulloch는 그가 Lake Havasu City로 사람들을 끌어 모으기 위해, 유명한 다리 그 이상의 것이 필요하다는 것을 알았다. 그래서 그는 전형적인 영국의 가게들과 식당들이 있는 영국 마을을 만들었다. 오늘날, London Bridge는 Arizona의 가장 큰 명소 중 하나이다.

**해설** Clue '지시사' − 주어진 문장에 있는 'there / they'
+ Context − (③) 뒤에 있는 문맥을 이용하면 주어진 문장의 위치는 ③번이다.

**어휘** be reassembled by ~에 의해 재조립되다    disassemble 분해하다

## 4 -2  문장삽입 Application

**예제 1** 글의 흐름으로 보아, 주어진 글이 들어가기에 적절한 곳은?          정답 ③

---

Experiments show that rats display an immediate liking for salt the first time they experience a salt deficiency.

---

Both humans and rats have evolved taste preferences for sweet foods, which provide rich sources of calories. A study of food preferences among the Hadza hunter-gatherers of Tanzania found that honey was the most highly preferred food item, an item that has the highest caloric value. Human newborn infants also show a strong preference for sweet liquids. ( ① ) Both humans and rats dislike bitter and sour foods, which tend to contain toxins. ( ② ) They also adaptively adjust their eating behavior in response to deficits in water, calories, and salt. ( ③ ) They likewise increase their intake of sweets and water when their energy and fluids become depleted. ( ④ ) These appear to be specific evolved mechanisms, designed to deal with the adaptive problem of food selection, and coordinate consumption patterns with physical needs.

---

**해석** 사람과 쥐 모두 단 음식에 대한 맛의 선호를 진화시켜 왔는데, 이것(단 음식)은 풍부한 열량의 원천을 제공한다. 탄자니아의 Hadza 수렵 채집인 사이의 음식 선호에 관한 연구는 가장 높은 열량 값을 가진 식품인 꿀이 가장 많이 선호되는 식품이었음을 발견했다. 인간의 갓난아기 또한 단 음료에 대한 강한 선호를 보인다. 사람과 쥐 모두 쓰고 신 음식을 싫어하는데, 이것(쓰고 신 음식)은 독소를 포함하는 경향이 있다. 그들은 또한 자신의 섭식 행동을 물, 열량, 소금의 부족에 대응하여 적절히 조정한다. (실험에서는 쥐가 소금 결핍을 처음 경험할 때 소금에 대한 즉각적인 선호를 보이는 것으로 나타난다.) 그것들은 마찬가지로 에너지와 체액이 고갈되면 단것과 물 섭취를 늘린다. 이것들은 음식 선택의 적응적 문제를 다루고 음식 섭취 방식을 신체적 욕구와 조화시키도록 고안된, 특정한 진화된 기제처럼 보인다.

**해설** Clue⁻¹ '지시사' − (③) 뒤에 있는 They + Clue⁻¹ '연결사' − (③) 뒤에 있는 likewise
+ 2문장 간의 연결을 이용하면 주어진 문장의 위치는 ③번이다.

**어휘** deficiency 부족   preference 선호   adaptively 적응적으로   deficit 적자

 **예제 2** 글의 흐름으로 보아, 주어진 글이 들어가기에 적절한 곳은?  **정답** ②

> But the examination of the accuracy of information obtained in this manner is not a simple matter.

The one area in which the Internet could be considered an aid to thinking is the rapid acquisition of new information. But this is more fictional than real. ( ① ) Yes, the simple act of typing a few words into a search engine will virtually instantaneously produce links related to the topic at hand. ( ② ) What one often gets is no more than abstract summaries of lengthy articles. ( ③ ) As a consequence, I suspect that the number of downloads of any given scientific paper has little relevance to the number of times the entire article has been read from beginning to end. ( ④ ) My advice is that if you want to do some serious thinking, then you' better disconnect the Internet, phone, and television set and try spending twenty-four hours in absolute solitude.

**해석** 인터넷이 사고(思考)의 보조물[보조재료]로 여겨질 수 있는 단 하나의 영역은 새로운 정보의 신속한 습득이다. 그러나 이것은 실제적이기보다는 허구에 가깝다. 정말이지, 몇 개의 단어를 검색 엔진에 쳐 넣는 간단한 행위만으로도 다루고 있는 주제와 관련이 있는 링크가 거의 즉각적으로 바로 나타나게 된다. (그렇지만 이런 식으로 얻은 정보의 정확성을 검사하는 것은 간단한 문제가 아니다.) 우리가 흔히 얻게 되는 것은 긴 글을 추상적으로 요약해 놓은 것에 지나지 않는다. 그렇기에, 나는 어떤 특정한 과학 논문을 다운로드한 횟수가 전체 논문이 처음부터 끝까지 읽힌 횟수와 거의 관련이 없는 것이 아닌가 하고 생각한다. 내가 권하는 것은 만약 여러분이 어떤 진지한 생각을 하고자 한다면 인터넷, 전화, 텔레비전의 연결을 모두 끊고 24시간 동안 절대적인 고독 속에서 한 번 지내보라는 것이다.

**해설** Clue '연결사' — But + Clue '지시사' — this N
+ 2문장 간의 연결을 이용하면 주어진 문장의 위치는 ②번이다.

**어휘** acquisition 인수, 습득   instantaneously 순간적으로

**예제 3** 글의 흐름으로 보아, 주어진 글이 들어가기에 적절한 곳은?  정답 ③

Human beings discovered this art thousands of years ago, and they have invented several devices to make it easier and faster.

In fiber processing the word 'spinning' means two quite different things. One is the formation of individual fibers by squeezing a liquid through one or more small openings in a nozzle called a spinneret and letting it harden. ( ① ) Spiders and silkworms have been spinning fibers in this way for millions of years, but chemists and engineers learned the procedure from them only about a century ago. ( ② ) In the other kind of spinning — sometimes called throwing to prevent confusion with the first kind — two or more fibers are twisted together to form a thread. ( ③ ) The ancient distaff and spindle are examples that were replaced by the spinning wheel in the Middle Ages. ( ④ ) Later came the spinning jenny, the water frame, and Crompton' mule - spinning machines that became symbols of the Industrial Revolution.

**해석** 섬유 가공에 있어서 'spinning(방적)'은 두 가지 아주 다른 것을 의미한다. 한 가지 의미는 방사 노즐이라고 불리는 노즐의 하나 혹은 그 이상의 작은 구멍들을 통해 액체를 짜내어 그것을 굳어지게 함으로써 개개의 섬유를 형성하는 것이다. 거미와 누에가 수백만 년 동안 이런 방식으로 섬유를 뽑아내 왔으나 화학자들과 엔지니어들은 겨우 백 년 전쯤에 이런 방법을 그들로부터 배웠다. 다른 종류의 spinning(방적)에서는 — 첫째 종류와의 혼동을 막기 위하여 가끔 throwing(꼬기)이라고 불리는데 — 두 개 혹은 그 이상의 섬유들이 함께 꼬여서 섬유 하나를 형성한다. (인류는 수천 년 전에 이 기술을 발견했으며 그들은 그것을 더 쉽고 더 빠르게 하기 위해 몇 가지 장치들을 발명했다.) 고대의 실을 감는 막대와 추가 중세에 물레로 대치된 예이다. 그 후에 다축 방적기, 수력 방적기, Crompton의 뮬 정방기(精紡機)가 출현했는데, 이것들은 산업혁명 시대의 상징이 된 방적기들이었다.

**해설** Clue '지시사' — this N
  + '열거'를 시사하는 — several Ns을 이용하면 주어진 문장의 위치는 ③번이다.

**어휘** nozzle 노즐   spinneret 방적 돌기   procedure 절차

 **예제 4** 글의 흐름으로 보아, 주어진 글이 들어가기에 적절한 곳은?　　　　정답 ①

---

Even so, research confirms the finding that nonverbal cues are more credible than verbal cues, especially when verbal and nonverbal cues conflict.

---

Researchers have reported various nonverbal features of sarcasm. Most disagree as to whether nonverbal cues are essential to the perception of sarcasm or the emotion that prompts it. ( ① ) Also, nonverbal cues are better indicators of speaker intent. ( ② ) As the nature of sarcasm implies a contradiction between intent and message, nonverbal cues may "leak" and reveal the speaker's true mood as they do in deception. ( ③ ) Ostensibly, sarcasm is the opposite of deception in that a sarcastic speaker typically intends the receiver to recognize the sarcastic intent; whereas, in deception the speaker typically intends that the receiver not recognize the deceptive intent. ( ④ ) Thus, when communicators are attempting to determine if a speaker is sarcastic, they compare the verbal and nonverbal message and if the two are in opposition, communicators may conclude that the speaker is being sarcastic.

---

**해석** 연구자들은 빈정거림의 다양한 비언어적 특성들을 보고했다. 대부분의 연구자들은 비언어적 신호가 빈정거림 또는 그것을 촉발하는 감정을 인지하는 데 필수적인 것인지에 대해 의견이 다르다. (그렇다 하더라도 연구는 특히 언어적 신호와 비언어적 신호가 상충할 때에는 비언어적 신호가 언어적 신호보다 더 신빙성이 있다는 연구 결과를 확증해 준다.) 또한, 비언어적 신호가 화자의 의도를 더 잘 보여 준다. 빈정거림의 본질이 의도와 메시지 사이의 모순을 암시하므로, 속임수를 쓸 때 그러는 것처럼 비언어적 신호가 '새어 나와' 말하는 사람의 진정한 기분 상태를 드러낼지도 모른다. 일반적으로 빈정대는 말을 하는 사람은 받아들이는 사람이 그 빈정대는 의도를 알아차리기를 바라지만, 반면에 속임수를 쓸 때는 일반적으로 화자가 듣는 사람이 그 속이려는 의도를 알아차리지 못했으면 하고 바란다는 점에서 표면상으로 빈정거림은 속임과 반대되는 것이다. 따라서 의사 전달자들은 어떤 화자가 빈정대는 것인지 판단하려고 할 때, 언어적 메시지와 비언어적 메시지를 비교하며 두 개가 서로 반대이면 그 화자가 빈정대고 있다는 결론을 내릴 수 있다.

**해설** Clue '연결사 기능' – Even so
　+ 2문장 간의 연결을 이용하면 주어진 문장의 위치는 ①번이다.

**어휘** sarcasm 풍자　prompt 촉발하다　intent 의지, 의도　deceptive 속이는

## 5  문장 제거

### 5-1  문장 제거 Warming Up!

**예제 1**  다음 글에서 전체 흐름과 관계없는 문장을 고르시오.   정답 ②

> A snowflake forms inside a winter storm cloud when a microscopic piece of dust is trapped inside a tiny drop of water. ① This happens in the atmosphere 10 kilometers above the earth. ② In Alaska, billions of snowflakes fall every winter. ③ The water freezes around the dust, and as this flake is blown by the wind, it collects more drops of water. ④ These drops freeze too. The snowflake becomes heavy enough to fall to the earth.

**해석**  눈송이는 미세한 먼지조각이 작은 물방울 안에 갇히게 될 때 겨울 폭풍 속에서 형성된다. 이것은 지상에서 10km상공에서 발생한다. (Alaska에서는 매년 겨울에 수십억 개의 눈송이가 떨어진다.) 그 먼지 주변에서 물이 얼어붙고, 이 눈송이가 바람에 날리면서, 그것이 더 많은 물방울을 모은다. 이 물방울들은 또한 얼어붙는다. 그 눈송이는 땅에 떨어질 정도로 충분히 무거워진다.

**해설**  글 전체적인 내용 '눈송이 형성 과정'과 내용상 거리가 먼 '알래스카에서 매번 겨울마다 수십억의 눈송이가 내린다.'로 해석이 되는 ②번이 정답이다.

**어휘**  snowflake 눈송이   microscopic 현미경

**예제 2**  다음 글에서 전체 흐름과 관계없는 문장을 고르시오.   정답 ④

> The domestic yak is so useful to the inhabitants of Tibet. ① From this animal, the Tibetans get milk and butter. ② They use its hair to make cloth, mats, and tent covering. ③ The flesh of the domestic yak is also useful, as it is often dried or roasted and used as food. ④ The yak is found at heights of 500 meters above sea level. The yak's skin is made into saddles and boots.

**해석**  가축인 yak는 Tibet지역 거주민들한테 너무 유용하다. 이 동물로부터, 티베트인들을 우유와 버터를 얻는다. 티베트인들은 옷감, 돗자리, 텐트 덮개를 만들기 위해서 yak의 털을 사용한다. yak의 살은 건조되어지거나 구워져서 음식으로 사용되기 때문에, 유용하다. (yak는 해발고도 500m 고도에서 발견되어진다.) yak의 피부는 안장이나 신발로 만들어진다.

**해설**  글 전체적인 내용 'yak의 유용함'과 내용상 거리가 먼 'yak는 해수면 기준 500미터의 고도에서 발견된다.'로 해석이 되는 ④번이 정답이다.

**어휘**  saddle 안장

**예제 3** 다음 글에서 전체 흐름과 관계없는 문장을 고르시오.　　　　　　　　　정답 ③

The rainforests are full of plants and animals that need each other and help each other. For example, the ant plants has tunnels in its stems which are just right for ants to live in. ① <u>The ants put bits of dead insects inside some of the tunnels, and then the ant plant uses them for food.</u> ② <u>The ants also look after a caterpillars which lives inside the ant plant and eats its leaves.</u> ③ <u>Because of this, the ants come out of the ground and attack the caterpillar.</u> ④ <u>In return, the caterpillar makes a special honey mixture which the ants eat.</u> In this way, these three all live together in harmony.

**해석** 열대우림은 서로서로 필요로 하고 도와주는 동식물로 가득 차 있다. 예를 들어, ant plants는 줄기 안쪽에 개미들이 살기에 딱 적합한 터널을 가지고 있다. 개미는 터널 안쪽 어딘가에 죽은 곤충 부스러기를 두고 ant plants가 그것들을 먹이로 사용한다. 개미들은 또한 ant plants 안에 살면서 그것의 잎들을 먹는 애벌레들을 돌본다. (이것 때문에, 개미는 땅밖으로 나와서 그 애벌레를 공격한다.) 그에 대한 보답으로, 애벌레는 개미가 먹는 특별한 꿀 혼합물을 만든다. 이런 식으로, 이 셋은 함께 조화롭게 살아간다.

**해설** 글 전체적인 내용 '열대우림에서 일어나는 동물, 식물 간의 공생관계'와 내용상 거리가 먼 '이것 때문에, 개미가 땅 밖으로 나와서 애벌레를 공격한다.'로 해석이 되는 ③번이 정답이다.

**어휘** caterpillar 애벌레

## 5 -2  문장 제거 Application

**예제 1**  다음 글에서 전체 흐름과 관계없는 문장은?                    정답 ③

Of the many forest plants that can cause poisoning, wild mushrooms may be among the most dangerous. ① This is because people sometimes confuse the poisonous and edible varieties, or they eat mushrooms without making a positive identification of the variety. ② Many people enjoy hunting wild species of mushrooms in the spring season, because they are excellent edible mushrooms and are highly prized. ③ Farming edible mushrooms at a reasonable cost is an important part to increase profit. ④ However, some wild mushrooms are dangerous, leading people to lose their lives due to mushroom poisoning. To be safe, a person must be able to identify edible mushrooms before eating any wild one.

**해석**  중독을 일으킬 수 있는 많은 산림 식물 중에서 야생 버섯은 가장 위험한 것들 중의 하나이다. 이는 사람들이 종종 독성이 있는 품종과 먹을 수 있는 품종을 혼동하거나 혹은 품종에 대해 확실한 확인을 하지 않고 버섯을 먹기 때문이다. 야생 버섯 종들이 훌륭한 식용 버섯이고 매우 귀하게 여겨지기 때문에 많은 사람들이 봄에 야생 버섯 종을 찾아다니는 것을 즐긴다. (합리적인 비용으로 식용 버섯을 재배하는 것이 이윤을 늘리는 데 있어 중요한 부분이다.) 그러나 몇몇 야생 버섯은 위험해서 그 독성으로 사람들의 목숨을 잃게 한다. 안전을 위해서 사람들은 야생 버섯을 먹기 전에 식용 버섯을 식별할 수 있어야 한다.

**해설**  ④번 문장 앞에 있는 대조와 반대의 내용을 이어주는 연결사 'However'가 ③번 문장보다는 ②번 문장과 연결된다. 따라서 그 사이에 있는 ③번이 정답이다.

**어휘**  edible 먹을 수 있는

**예제 2** 다음 글에서 전체 흐름과 관계없는 문장은?  **정답** ②

---

Since the concept of a teddy bear is very obviously not a genetically inherited trait, we can be confident that we are looking at a cultural trait. However, it is a cultural trait that seems to be under the guidance of another, genuinely biological trait: the cues that attract us to babies (high foreheads and small faces). ① Cute, baby-like features are inherently appealing, producing a nurturing response in most humans. ② Indeed, using baby-like images of teddy bear for commercial purposes was faced with severe criticism from animal rights activists. ③ Teddy bears that had a more baby-like appearance — however slight this may have been initially — were thus more popular with customers. ④ Teddy bear manufacturers obviously noticed which bears were selling best and so made more of these and fewer of the less popular models, to maximize their profits. In this way, the selection pressure built up by the customers resulted in the evolution of a more baby-like bear by the manufacturers.

---

**해석** 봉제 장난감 곰이라는 개념은 유전학적으로 물려받은 특성이 아닌 것이 아주 명백하므로 우리는 문화적 특성을 보고 있는 것이라고 자신할 수 있다. 하지만, 그것은 다른, 정말로 생물학적인 특성, 즉 우리를 아기 (높은 이마와 작은 얼굴)에게 이끄는 신호에 의해 유도되고 있는 것처럼 보이는 문화적 특성이다. 귀엽고 아기 같은 생김새는 선천적으로 사람의 마음을 끌어, 대부분의 인간 속에 있는 보살피려는 반응을 불러일으킨다. ( 실제로 상업적 목적으로 봉제 장난감 곰의 아기 같은 이미지를 사용하는 것은 동물 권리 운동가로부터의 심한 비판에 직면했다. ) 처음에는 아무리 사소했을지는 모르지만, 더 아기 같은 모습을 지닌 봉제 장난감 곰들은 그렇기 때문에 소비자들에게 더욱 인기 있었다. 봉제 장난감 곰 제조사들은 어느 곰이 최고로 잘 팔리고 있는지를 분명히 알아챘으며 그래서 자기들의 이익을 최대화하기 위해서 이런 것들을 더 많이 그리고 인기가 덜한 모델을 더 적게 만들었다. 이렇게 해서 소비자에 의해 고조된 선택 압력으로 제조사들은 더 아기 같은 곰을 점진적으로 발전시키게 되었다.

**해설** ③번에 있는 원인과 결과의 내용을 이어주는 연결사 'thus'가 ②번 문장보다는 ①번 문장과 연결된다. 따라서, 그 사이에 있는 ②번이 정답이다.

**어휘** guidance 안내, 지도

**예제 3** 다음 글에서 전체 흐름과 관계없는 문장은?　　　　　　　　　　　　　　　　　　　　**정답** ④

Most often, you will find or meet people who introduce themselves in terms of their work or by what they spend time on. These people introduce themselves as a salesman or an executive. ① There is nothing criminal in doing this, but psychologically, we become what we believe. ② People who follow this practice tend to lose their individuality and begin to live with the notion that they are recognized by the job they do. ③ However, jobs may not be permanent, and you may lose your job for countless reasons, some of which you may not even be responsible for. ④ In addition, identifying what we can do in the workplace is not enough to enhance the quality of our professional career. In such a case, these people suffer from an inevitable social and mental trauma, leading to emotional stress and a feeling that all of a sudden they have been disassociated from what once was their identity.

**해석** 아주 자주 여러분은 자신이 하는 일로 혹은 자신이 시간을 보내는 일에 의해 자기 자신을 소개하는 사람들을 발견하거나 만날 것이다. 이러한 사람들은 자기 자신을 판매원이나 경영 간부로서 소개한다. 이렇게 할 때 죄가 되는 것은 없지만, 정신적으로 우리는 우리가 (그렇다고) 믿는 존재가 된다. 이러한 관행을 따르는 사람들은 자신들의 개성을 잃어버리고 자신들이 하는 일에 의해 인식된다는 개념을 가지고 살기 시작하는 경향이 있다. 그러나 일은 영구적이지 못할 수 있으며 여러분은 무수하게 많은 이유로 인해 일자리를 잃을지도 모르는데, 여러분은 그 이유 중 몇몇에 대해서는 아무런 책임도 없을 수 있다. ( 게다가, 직장에서 우리가 할 수 있는 것을 확인하는 것은 우리가 하는 전문적 일의 질을 높이기에 충분하지 않다. ) 그러한 경우에 이러한 사람들은 피할 수 없는 사회적, 정신적 외상 때문에 고통을 받고 이것은 감정적 스트레스와 한때 그들의 정체성이었던 것과 자신들이 갑자기 단절되어 왔다는 느낌을 유발한다.

**해설** ④번 뒤 문장(마지막 문장) 앞에 있는 지시사 'such N / these Ns'와 문맥상 ④번 뒤에 있는 문장이 ④번 문장보다는 ③번 문장과 연결된다. 따라서, 그 사이에 있는 ④번이 정답이다.

**어휘** permanent 영구적인　enhance 향상시키다　disassociated 분리된

 **다음 글에서 전체 흐름과 관계없는 문장은?**    정답 ③

Most of the animal-training practices considered good and normal in our world do not take the animals' viewpoint into account. ① Animals should have the right to participate, and to have a say, in their training. ② The true goal of training should be to get animals to do something because they want and choose to, not because we force them to. ③ No matter what anyone says, we must believe that our animals can do whatever task they've set for themselves. ④ Instead, people typically get so involved in doing a program or getting a result-like winning a title in a dog show-or they worry so much about getting hurt, that they fail to listen to what their animals have to say. That's when I get calls about the dogs who are refusing to go in the show ring or the horses who are acting crazy.

**해석** 우리 세계에서 바람직하면서 정상적이라고 여겨지는 대부분의 동물 훈련 관행은 동물의 관점을 고려하지 않는다. 동물들은 자신들의 훈련에 참여하고 발언할 수 있는 권리를 가져야 한다. 훈련의 진정한 목적은 우리가 동물들에게 하도록 강요해서가 아니라 동물들이 원하고 선택해서 무언가를 하도록 하는 것이 되어야 한다. ( 누군가가 어떤 말을 하든지 간에, 우리는 우리의 동물들이 그 자신들을 위해서 설정한 어떤 과업이든지 해낼 수 있다는 것을 믿어야 한다. ) 대신에, 사람들은 일반적으로 어떤 프로그램을 완수하거나 애완견 대회에서 순위(타이틀)를 차지하는 것과 같은 어떤 결과를 얻는 데에 지나치게 몰두하거나, 그것이 아니면 그들이 다치는 것을 너무나 걱정한 나머지, 그들의 동물들이 하는 말을 듣지 못한다. 바로 그때 나는 대회장에 들어가지 않으려고 하는 강아지들이나, 비정상적으로 행동하는 말들에 대한 전화를 받는다.

**해설** ④번 문장 앞에 있는 앞부분의 대안적 행동을 유도하는 연결사 'instead'가 ③번 문장보다는 ②번 문장과 연결된다. 따라서, 그 사이에 있는 ③번이 정답이다.

**어휘** refuse 거절하다

**1  복합지문**

**기출 1**  다음 글을 읽고 물음에 답하시오.  정답 01. ②  02. ④

| noplasticjuly | × | + |

http://noplasticjuly.org

HOME    ABOUT US    CONTACT US    SEARCH

(A)

Each year in July people all over the world aim to exclude common plastic waste items from their daily life, opting instead for reusable containers or those made from biodegradable materials. We think this is a great idea and why not make it a year-round effort at home and in the workplace. The vision started in Western Australia in 2011 and has since moved across the world to help promote the vision and stop the earth becoming further saturated with plastic materials which are part of our convenience lifestyle.

Lots of items are designed to be used once and disposed of. They fill up bins in homes, schools, at work and on streets across the world.

You can assist in achieving the goal of having a world without plastic waste.

Choose what you will do
☐ Avoid single-use plastic packaging
☐ Target the takeaway items that could end up in the ocean
☐ Go completely plastic free

I will participate
☐ for 1 day                           ☐ for 1 week
☐ for 1 month                        ☐ from now on

**01. (A)에 들어갈 윗글의 제목으로 가장 적절한 것은?**

① Development of Single-Use Items
② Join the Plastic-Free Challenge
③ How to Dispose of Plastic Items
④ Simple Ways to Save Energy

**02. 윗글에서 캠페인에 관한 내용과 일치하지 않는 것은?**

① 2011년 서호주에서 시작되었다.
② 플라스틱 과다 사용을 줄이기 위해 전 세계로 확산되었다.
③ 실천할 활동을 선택하여 참여할 수 있다.
④ 최대 한 달까지 참여할 수 있다.

---

**해석** **플라스틱 없애기 챌린지에 참여하세요**

매년 7월, 전 세계 사람들은 일상생활에서 흔한 플라스틱 쓰레기 물품을 배제하고, 대신 재사용 가능한 용기나 생분해성 소재로 만든 물건을 선택하는 것을 목표로 합니다. 저희는 이것이 좋은 아이디어라고 생각하는데, 이를 가정과 직장에서 일년 내내 실천하는 것은 어떨까요. 이 비전은 2011년 서호주에서 시작되었으며, 이후 전 세계로 퍼져나가 이 비전을 홍보하고 편리한 생활방식의 일부인 플라스틱 재료로 지구가 더 포화되는 것을 막는 데 기여하고 있습니다.

많은 물건들이 한 번 사용되고 버려지도록 설계되어 있습니다. 이것들이 전 세계의 가정, 학교, 직장, 거리의 쓰레기통을 가득 채웁니다.

여러분도 플라스틱 쓰레기가 없는 세상을 갖는 목표를 달성하는 데 도움을 줄 수 있습니다.

무엇을 할 것인지 선택하세요
□ 일회용 플라스틱 포장 피하기
□ 결국에 바다에 버려질 수 있는 테이크어웨이 물품 겨냥하기
□ 완전히 플라스틱 없는 생활하기

참여하겠습니다
□ 1일 동안        □ 1주일 동안
□ 1개월 동안      □ 지금부터 계속

**해설** 01 플라스틱 쓰레기를 줄이기 위한 운동을 알려주고, 함께 플라스틱이 없는 삶을 살아가도록 유도하는 글이다. 따라서 글의 제목으로 가장 적절한 것은 ② '플라스틱 없애기 챌린지에 참여하세요'이다.
　　① 일회용품의 개발
　　③ 플라스틱 제품 처리 방법
　　④ 에너지를 아끼는 간단한 방법들
02 '참여하겠습니다' 항목에서 마지막에 '지금부터 계속'이라는 항목이 있으므로, 글의 내용과 일치하지 않는 것은 ④ '최대 한 달까지 참여할 수 있다.'이다.

**어휘** aim ~을 목표로 하다.　exclude 배제하다　reusable 재사용 가능한　biodegradable 생분해성의　year-round 일년 내내
promote 홍보하다　saturated 포화된　dispose of 처분하다, 버리다　single-use 일회용의　from no on 앞으로 쭉

**기출 2** 다음 글을 읽고 물음에 답하시오.



## Consular services

We welcome all feedback about our consular services, whether you receive them in the UK or from one of our embassies, high commissions or consulates abroad. Tell us when we get things wrong so that we can assess and improve our services.

If you want to make a complaint about a consular service you have received, we want to help you resolve it as quickly as possible. If you are complaining on behalf of someone else, we must have written, signed consent from that person allowing us to share their personal information with you before we can reply.

Send details of your complaint to our feedback contact form. We will record and examine your complaint, and use the information you provide to help make sure that we offer the best possible help and support to our customers. The relevant embassy, high commission or consulate will reply to you.

01. 밑줄 친 assess의 의미와 가장 가까운 것은?

① upgrade

② prolong

③ evaluate

④ render

02. 윗글의 목적으로 가장 적절한 것은?

① to give directions to the consulate

② to explain how to file complaints

③ to lay out the employment process

④ to announce the opening hours

**해석** **영사 서비스**

영사 서비스를 영국에서 받았든 해외의 대사관, 고등판무관 또는 영사관 중 한 곳에서 받았든 그에 대한 모든 피드백을 환영합니다. 저희가 서비스를 <u>평가하고</u> 향상시킬 수 있도록 저희가 잘못하는 점들이 있으면 알려주세요.

당신이 받은 영사 서비스에 대해 불만을 제기하고자 하는 경우, 저희는 가능한 한 빨리 문제를 해결하도록 도와드리고자 합니다. 다른 사람을 대신하여 불만을 제기하는 경우, 우리가 답변을 할 수 있기 전에 해당 사람의 개인 정보를 귀하와 공유할 수 있도록 하는 서명된 서면 동의서가 있어야만 합니다.

불만 사항에 대한 자세한 내용을 피드백 문의 양식으로 보내주세요. 저희는 당신의 불만 사항을 기록 및 검토하고 당신이 제공한 정보를 사용하여 고객에게 가능한 한 최선의 도움과 지원을 제공할 수 있도록 할 것입니다. 관련 대사관, 고등판무관 또는 영사관에서 답변을 드릴 것입니다.

**해설** 01 assess는 '평가하다'라는 뜻으로 쓰였으므로, 이와 의미가 가장 가까운 것은 ③ 'evaluate(평가하다)'이다.

① 개선하다

② 연장하다

④ 만들다, 되게 하다, 주다

02 영사 서비스를 개선하기 위해 서비스를 받은 고객들에게 불만 사항을 받고, 불만 사항 접수 방법과 주의사항을 안내하는 글이다. 따라서 글의 제목으로 가장 적절한 것은 ② '불만 제기 방법을 설명하려고'이다.

① 영사관 가는 길을 안내하려고

③ 채용 절차를 설명하려고

④ 영업시간을 알리려고

**어휘** consular 영사의   embassy 대사관   high commissions 고등판무관   consulate 영사관   assess 평가하다
complaint 불평, 불만   consent 동의, 합의

**예제 1** 다음을 읽고 물음에 답하시오.

정답 01. ② 02. ①

## Construction Set to Begin on Music Hall

March 25—Construction on the long-awaited Metro City Orchestra Center is set to begin next month. The music hall has been in its planning stages for over a year and residents have been eagerly awaiting information about the five-story building. Terrance Jacobs, who has been <u>overseeing</u> the design of the building, says construction will take up to one year. The building will feature four different concert halls, each with state-of-the art acoustics. Mr. Jacobs has stated that "the hall will provide a place for music lovers to enjoy their favorite musicians' and composers' works in a comfortable and elegant atmosphere." The music hall will be located directly across from the already greatly successful Metro City Convention Center. "We decided to build the music hall nearby the convention center because of the convenience of the location and also to solidify the location as a cultural hub," said Mr. Jacobs during the recent announcement of construction. Local residents are excited to see the opening of the music hall and attendance to musical events is expected to be high. "I have a great love for classical music and it will be great to finally have somewhere to see the performances that I want," said Tracy Diaz, a local music enthusiast. If you wish to stay up to date on the progress of the construction, you can visit the Metro City Orchestra Center Web site at www.mcocenter.com.

01. 위 글에서 언급된 Music Hall에 대해 추론할 수 있는 것으로 가장 적절한 것은?

① It will open next month.

② It will offer classical music.

③ It is nearing completion.

④ It will be next to the convention center.

02. 밑줄 친 "overseeing"의 의미와 가장 가까운 것은?

① supervising

② allocating

③ engineering

④ processing

**해석** **음악당 건설 시작**

3월 25일 – 오랫동안 기다려온 Metro City Orchestra Center의 건설이 다음 달에 시작될 예정입니다. 음익딩은 1년 이상 계획 단계에 있었고 주민들은 5층 건물에 대한 정보를 간절히 기다리고 있었습니다. 건물 설계를 <u>감독해</u> 온 Terrance Jacobs는 건설에 최대 1년이 걸릴 것이라고 말했습니다. 이 건물에는 최첨단 음향 시스템을 갖춘 4개의 콘서트 홀이 들어설 예정입니다. Jacobs 씨는 "이 홀은 음악 애호가들이 편안하고 우아한 분위기에서 좋아하는 음악가와 작곡가의 작품을 즐길 수 있는 장소가 될 것입니다."라고 말했습니다. 음악당은 이미 큰 성공을 거둔 Metro City Convention Center 바로 맞은편에 위치할 예정입니다. Jacobs 씨는 최근 건설 발표에서 "컨벤션 센터 근처에 음악당을 짓기로 한 이유는 입지가 편리하고 문화적 허브로서의 입지를 공고히 하기 위해서였습니다."라고 말했습니다. 지역 주민들은 음악당 개장을 고대하고 있으며 음악 행사 참석률이 높을 것으로 예상됩니다. "저는 클래식 음악에 큰 애정을 가지고 있고, 제가 원하는 공연을 볼 수 있는 곳이 마침내 생겨서 정말 기쁠 겁니다."라고 지역 음악 애호가인 Tracy Diaz가 말했습니다. 공사 진행 상황을 최신으로 알고 싶으시다면, www.mcocenter.com에서 Metro City Orchestra Center 웹사이트를 방문하세요.

**해설** 01 글의 후반부에 Tracy Diaz가 한 말 "저는 클래식 음악에 큰 애정을 가지고 있고, 제가 원하는 공연을 볼 수 있는 곳이 마침내 생겨서 정말 기쁠 겁니다"를 근거로 ②번이 정답이다.

① 다음 달에 오픈할 예정입니다.
② 클래식 음악을 제공할 예정입니다.
③ 완공이 임박했습니다.
④ 컨벤션 센터 옆에 위치할 예정입니다.

02 oversee는 '감독하다'의 뜻으로 쓰였으므로, 밑줄 친 overseeing과 의미가 가장 가까운 것은 supervise(감독하다)의 ing형태인 ① 'overseeing'이 정답이다.

① 감독하다
② 할당하다
③ 엔지니어링
④ 처리하다

**어휘** Construction 건설, long-awaited 대망의  ○○-story ○○층의  oversee 감독하다  feature 특징을 이루다, 특집기사 state-of-theart 최신식의  acoustics 음향학  convenience 편의  enthusiast 광팬, 광신자

## 2 글의 목적

**기출 1** 다음 글의 목적으로 가장 적절한 것은? 정답 ③

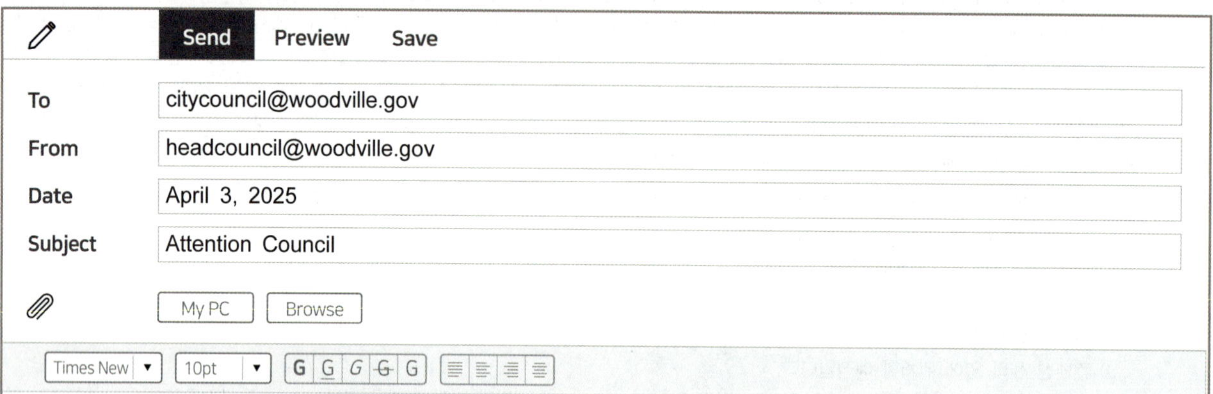

| | |
|---|---|
| **To** | citycouncil@woodville.gov |
| **From** | headcouncil@woodville.gov |
| **Date** | April 3, 2025 |
| **Subject** | Attention Council |

Dear Members of the Woodville City Council,

I am writing to inform you of several issues in our community that need attention. A resident, John Smith, of 123 Elm Street, has reported problems with the road conditions on Elm Street, especially between Maple Avenue and Oak Street. There are many potholes and cracks that have worsened after recent heavy rain, causing traffic disruptions and safety hazards. Even though temporary repairs have been made, the problems continue.

The resident is also concerned about poor lighting in Central Park, especially along Park Lane, because broken or missing streetlights have led to minor accidents and lowered property values. He requests that the Council repair Elm Street and improve the lighting in the park.

I urge the Council to address these issues for the safety and well-being of our community. Thank you for your attention to these matters. I trust we will work together to resolve these issues effectively.

Sincerely,

Stephen James
Head of Woodville City Council

① to express gratitude to the Council for their efforts
② to invite the Council to visit Central Park
③ to solicit the Council to deal with the community problems
④ to update the Council on recent repairs made in the area

**해석** 수신: citycouncil@woodville.gov
발신: headcouncil@woodville.gov
날짜: 2025년 4월 3일
제목: 시의회 주목해 주세요

Woodville 시의회 의원 여러분께,

저는 우리 지역사회에서 주의가 필요한 몇 가지 문제에 대해 알리고자 이 글을 씁니다. Elm가 123번지에 거주하는 주민 John Smith는 Elm가, 특히 Maple가와 Oak가 사이의 도로 상태에 문제가 있다고 신고했습니다. 최근 폭우 이후 많은 움푹 패인 곳과 균열이 심해져 교통 혼란과 안전 위험을 초래하고 있습니다. 임시 보수가 이루어졌으나 문제는 계속되고 있습니다.

또한 이 주민은 고장 나거나 (있어야 할 곳에) 없는 가로등으로 인해 작은 사고와 재산 가치 하락이 발생하였기에 센트럴 파크, 특히 Park길을 따라 조명 상태가 좋지 않은 것에 대해 우려하고 있습니다. 그는 시의회가 Elm가를 수리하고 공원의 조명을 개선해 줄 것을 요청합니다.

저는 저희 지역사회의 안전과 복지를 위해 시의회가 이러한 문제를 처리해 줄 것을 촉구합니다. 이러한 문제에 관심을 가져 주셔서 감사합니다. 이러한 문제를 효과적으로 해결하기 위해 저희가 함께 노력할 것이라 믿습니다.

진심을 담아,

Stephen James

Woodville 시의회 의장

**해설** 도로와 조명을 비롯해 지역사회에서 발생한 문제들에 대해 알리며 시의회가 이를 해결해 줄 것을 요청하는 글이다. 가장 적절한 것은 ③ '시의회에 지역사회 문제를 해결해 달라고 요청하려고'이다.
① 시의회의 노력에 감사함을 표현하려고
② 시의회를 센트럴 파크에 방문하도록 초청하려고
④ 시의회에 지역에서 이루어진 최근 수리에 대해 알려주려고

**어휘** resident 거주자   pothole 움푹 패인 곳   crack 금, 갈라지다   traffic disruptions 교통 혼란   hazard 위험
temporary 일시적인, 임시의   repair 수리, 보수   urge 촉구하다   address 다루다, 취급하다   resolve 해결하다

**예제 1** 다음 글의 목적으로 가장 적절한 것은?  정답 ④

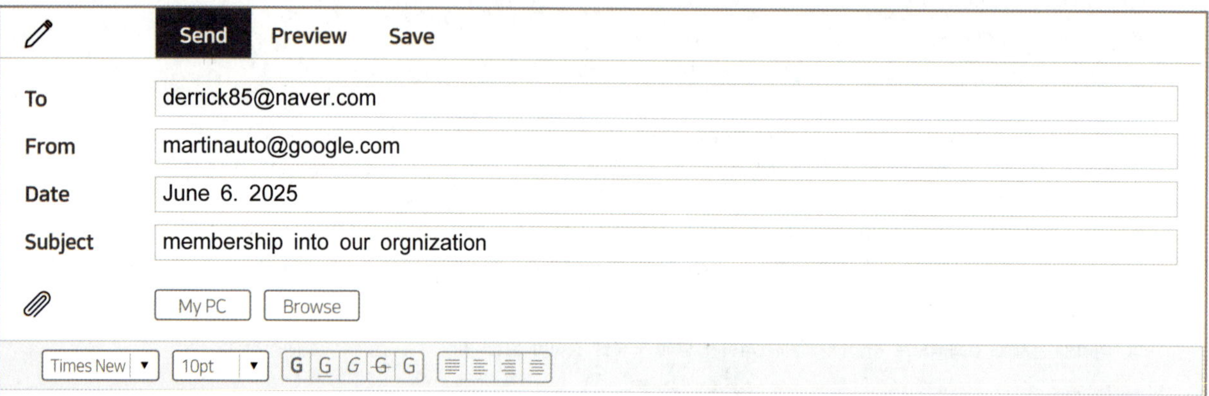



Dear Mr. Martin,

The Mechanics Association of America (MAA) would like to let you know that you are eligible for membership into our organization. As a professional mechanic, you have a lot to gain by joining us.

One of the benefits is that you will receive a free subscription to Mechanics Today, the official magazine of the MAA. This magazine, which is delivered monthly, has numerous articles and tips on how to improve your skills as a mechanic.

The MAA also sponsors special events all around the country. We put on seminars that explain how to repair some of the newest cars. One of them, incidentally, will be in Columbus this year. We also sponsor conferences and other events throughout the year.

If this sounds interesting to you, call me at 1-800-MECHANIC, and we can discuss your membership.

Sincerely,

Ray Brothers
Mechanics Association of America

① To encourage a person to purchase a magazine

② To make an invitation to a special seminar

③ To announce a special event to be held next month

④ To ask a person to become a member of a group

**해석** 데릭 마틴
마틴 자동차 정비소
헤밀턴 드라이브 53번지
콜럼버스, 오하이오 주
Martin 씨,
미국 정비공 연맹은 귀하가 저희 조직에 들어올 회원 자격 요건을 갖추셨다는 것을 알려드립니다. 전문 정비기사로서, 저희와 함께하시면 귀하는 많은 것을 얻을 것입니다.

혜택 중 하나는, MAA의 공식 잡지인 '메카닉스 투데이'의 무료 구독권을 얻게 된다는 것입니다. 매달 배송되는 이 잡지는 정비공으로서의 능력을 향상시킬 수 있는 방법에 관한 많은 기사와 조언을 담고 있습니다.

MAA는 전국의 특별 행사도 후원합니다. 저희는 최신 자동차를 수리하는 방법을 설명하는 세미나를 개최합니다. 우연히 올해는 그 중 하나가 콜럼버스에서 열립니다. 저희는 연중 내내 회의와 다른 행사들도 후원합니다.

이 내용에 흥미가 있다면, 1-800-메카닉으로 저에게 전화 주세요. 그러면 귀하의 회원 자격을 논의할 수 있습니다.
진심을 담아,

레이 브라더스
미국 정비공 연맹

**해설** 글의 전반부에 '귀하가 저희 조직에 들어올 회원 자격 요건을 갖추셨다는 것을 알려드립니다'와 글의 후반부에 '귀하의 회원 자격을 논의할 수 있습니다'를 근거로 ④번이 정답이다.
① 잡지를 구매하도록 부추기기 위해
② 특별 세미나에 초대하기 위해
③ 다음 달에 열리는 특별 행사를 알리기 위해
④ 단체의 회원이 될 것을 요청하기 위해

**어휘** association 연맹  be eligible for ~에 적합하다, ~의 자격이 있다  benefit 혜택  subscription to ~의 구독  put on 개최하다  incidentally 우연히  make an invitation 초대하다

**3**  내용 일치, 불일치

**기출 1** 다음 글의 내용과 일치하지 않는 것은?  정답 ④ 

---

## KIDS SUMMER ART CAMP 2025

Join the Stan José Art Museum (SJAM) for a week of fun!

Campers get behind-the-scenes access to exhibitions, experiment with the artistic process, and show off their own work in a student exhibition.

### WHO

For children ages 6 - 14

Each camper will receive individual artistic support, encouragement, and creative challenges unique to their learning style and skill level.

### WHAT

Join SJAM for a summer art camp that pairs creative exploration of art materials and processes led by our experienced gallery teachers and studio art educators. In addition, campers will engage in interpretive art and science lessons created by Eddie Brown, a STEM consultant.

### ART CAMP EXHIBITION

We invite families and caregivers to attend a weekly exhibition reception of campers' artwork to celebrate the artistic achievements of each participant.

### WHEN

All camps run 9 am - 3 pm, Monday - Friday.

Monday, June 9 - Friday, July 25 (no camp the week of June 30)

---

① Campers will have opportunities to display their work in a student exhibition.

② The camp includes individual artistic support for children ages 6 - 14.

③ A STEM consultant developed interpretive art and science lessons.

④ The camp runs with no break between June 9 and July 25.

**해석** **어린이 여름 미술 캠프 2025**

일주일 동안 즐겁도록 Stan José 미술관 (SJAM)과 함께 해보세요!

캠프 참가자들은 전시회의 숨겨진 장면들을 접하고, 예술적 과정을 실험하며, 학생 전시회에서 자신의 작품을 뽐냅니다.

**누구 (대상)**

6-14세 어린이 대상

각 캠프 참가자는 개별적인 예술적 지원과 격려, 학습 스타일과 기술 수준에 맞는 창의적인 도전을 받게 됩니다.

**무엇 (내용)**

경험이 많은 갤러리 교사와 스튜디오 미술 교육자가 이끄는 미술 재료와 과정에 대한 창의적인 탐구를 함께하는 여름 미술 캠프 SJAM에 참가하세요. 또한 캠프 참가자들은 STEM 컨설턴트인 Eddie Brown이 만든 해석적 미술 및 과학 수업에 참여하게 됩니다.

**미술 캠프 전시회**

매주 열리는 캠프 참가자들의 작품 전시회 리셉션에 가족과 보호자를 초대하여 각 참가자의 예술적 성과를 축하합니다.

**언제 (일정)**

모든 캠프는 월요일-금요일, 오전 9시-오후 3시까지 진행합니다.

6월 9일 월요일-7월 25일 금요일 (6월 30일이 포함된 주에는 캠프 없음)

**해설** 언제(일정)부분 마지막에 6월 30일이 포함된 주에는 캠프가 없다고 언급되어 있으므로, 글의 내용과 일치하지 않는 것은 ④ '캠프는 6월 9일부터 7월 25일까지 쉬는 날 없이 운영된다.'이다.

① 캠프 참가자들은 학생 전시회에서 자신의 작품을 전시할 기회를 갖게 될 것이다.

② 캠프는 6-14세 어린이를 위한 개별적인 예술적 지원을 포함한다.

③ STEM 컨설턴트가 해석적 미술 및 과학 수업을 개발했다.

**어휘** experiment 실험하다    show off 자랑하다, 뽐내다    exhibition 전시회    encouragement 격려    pair 짝 지우다, 결합시키다

exploration 탐구    material 재료    engage in 참여하다    interpretive 해석상의    caregiver 보호자    celebrate 기념하다, 축하하다

achievement 성취, 성과    participant 참여자

---

## Department of Health and Human Services

### Mission Statement

The mission of the Department of Health and Human Services (HHS) is to enhance the health and well-being of all individuals in the nation, by providing for effective health and human services and by fostering sound, sustained advances in the sciences underlying medicine, public health, and social services.

### Organizational Structure

HHS accomplishes its mission through programs and initiatives that cover a wide spectrum of activities. Eleven operating divisions, including eight agencies in the Public Health Service and three human services agencies, administer HHS's programs. While HHS is a domestic agency working to protect and promote the health and well-being of the American people, the interconnectedness of our world requires that HHS engage globally to fulfill its mission.

### Cross-Agency Collaborations

Improving health and human services outcomes cannot be achieved by the Department on its own; collaborations are critical to achieve our goals and objectives. HHS collaborates closely with other federal departments and agencies on cross-cutting topics.

---

① HHS aims to improve the health and well-being of low-income families only.

② HHS's programs are administered by the eleven operating divisions.

③ HHS does not work with foreign countries to complete its mission.

④ HHS acts independently from other federal departments and agencies to achieve its goals.

**해석**  **보건복지부**

**임무 진술(설명)**

보건복지부(HHS)의 임무는, 효과적인 보건 및 인적 서비스를 제공하고, 의학, 공중 보건 및 사회 서비스의 기반이 되는 과학의 건전하고 지속적인 발전을 만들어냄으로써, 국가 내 모든 개인의 건강과 복지를 개선하는 것입니다.

**조직 구조**

HHS는 넓은 활동 범위를 아우르는 프로그램과 계획을 통해 임무를 성취합니다. 공중 보건서비스의 8개 기관과 3개의 인적 서비스 기관을 포함하여 11개의 운영 부서가 HHS의 프로그램을 관리합니다. HHS는 미국 국민의 건강과 복지를 보호하고 개선하기 위해 노력하는 국내 기관이지만, 전 세계의 상호 연결성은 HHS가 임무를 완수하기 위해 전 세계적으로 참여할 것을 요구합니다.

**기관 간 협력**

보건 및 인적 서비스의 성과를 개선하는 것은 이 부처 단독으로는 성취될 수 없으며, 우리의 목표와 목적을 달성하기 위해서는 협력이 매우 중요합니다. HHS는 다른 연방부처 및 기관과 공통적인 주제에 대해 긴밀히 협력합니다.

**해설**  두 번째 문단에서 공중 보건 서비스의 8개 기관과 3개의 인적 서비스 기관을 포함하여 11개의 운영 부서가 HHS의 프로그램을 관리한다고 언급하고 있으므로, 글의 내용과 일치하는 것은 ② 'HHS의 프로그램은 11개의 운영 부서에서 관리한다.'이다.

① HHS는 오직 저소득 가정의 건강과 복지 향상을 목표로 한다.

③ HHS는 임무를 완수하기 위해 외국과 협력하지 않는다.

④ HHS는 목표를 달성하기 위해 다른 연방 부처 및 기관과 독립적으로 행동한다.

**어휘**  statement 말, 진술   enhance 향상 시키다, 높이다   foster 촉진시키다, 조성하다   sustained 지속적인   initiative 계획   administer 관리하다, 경영하다   domestic 국내의   interconnectedness 상호 연결성   fulfill 충실히 이행하다   collaborations 협력   objective 목표, 목적

**예제 1** 다음 글의 Hotel Andromeda에 대한 내용으로 가장 적절한 것을 고르시오.  **정답** ④

## Hotel Andromeda

We are located in the downtown area, right next to Lakeshore Boulevard. Being only 10 minutes from both baseball stadium Eaton's Center and Exhibition Place, Hotel Andromeda is an ideal place for your weekend of business or pleasure. It is only 20 minutes to the region's only international airport and just minutes from multiple subway stations and bus lines. All of our rooms include mini-fridges, Wi-Fi access, cable television, and desk space. The swimming pool is available to all guests, and for no extra charge anyone staying at least two nights can enjoy our state-of-the-art fitness center.

The meeting chambers throughout the left wing of the hotel can accommodate groups from 10 to 400 people. Hotel Andromeda is an ideal venue for corporate events. Our event planner can aid your company in setting up conferences, meetings, and other events.

To book rooms of any size, please contact us at 123-458-7430, or e-mail us at andromedares@hotel.net. To contact our corporate event planner, please call 123-458-7222. You can find more information about the Andromeda Hotel, including directions to the premises, on our Web site at www.andromeda@hotel.net.

① It does not have any mass transit access.
② It has been in business for over 10 years.
③ It specializes in wedding and anniversary parties.
④ Its meeting rooms can accommodate up to 400 people.

**해석** **안드로메다 호텔**

우리는 시내에 위치해 있고, 레이크쇼어 대로 바로 옆에 있습니다. 야구 경기장인 이튼스 센터와 전시징으로부터 10분밖에 걸리지 않는 안드로메다 호텔은 주말에 업무를 보거나 즐거운 시간을 보내기에 이상적인 장소입니다. 지역의 유일한 국제공항으로부터 20분밖에 걸리지 않으며, 몇 분만 가면 다수의 지하철역과 버스 노선이 나옵니다. 우리의 모든 객실에는 미니 냉장고와 와이파이 접속, 케이블 텔레비전, 그리고 책상 공간이 포함되어 있습니다. 모든 투숙객은 수영장을 이용할 수 있고, 2박 이상 머무시는 분들은 추가 요금 없이 최신 헬스클럽을 즐기실 수 있습니다.

호텔의 좌측 부속건물에 있는 모든 회의실은 10명에서 400명의 단체를 수용할 수 있습니다. 안드로메다 호텔은 기업 행사를 하기에 이상적인 장소입니다. 우리 행사 기획자가 여러분의 회사를 도와 학회와 회의, 그리고 다른 행사 준비를 도울 것입니다.

모든 크기의 방을 예약하시려면 123-458-7430로 연락하시거나 andromedares@hotel.net으로 이메일을 보내세요. 우리의 기업 행사 기획자에게 연락하시려면 123-458-7222로 전화하세요. 안드로메다 호텔에 관한 보다 많은 정보와 오시는 길안내에 관한 정보는 저희 웹사이트인 www.andromeda@hotel.net.에서 찾으실 수 있습니다.

**해설** 두 번째 문단에서 '호텔의 좌측 부속건물에 있는 모든 회의실의 10명에서 400명의 단체를 수용할 수 있습니다'를 근거로 ④번이 정답이다.
① 대량 수송 수단에 접근할 수 없다.
② 10년 이상 사업을 해왔다.
③ 결혼식과 기념 파티를 전문으로 한다.
④ 회의실들은 사람들을 400명까지 수용할 수 있다.

**어휘** be located in ~에 위치하다    right next to ~의 바로 옆에    at least 적어도, 최소한    state-of-the-art 최신식의
throughout ~의 전체에, 도처에    wing 부속건물    accommodate 수용하다    venue 장소    corporate 기업의    aid 돕다
set up 설치하다    book 예약하다    premises 부지, 구내    mass transit (지하철, 버스 등의) 대량 수송 수단
specialize in ~을 전문으로 하다    up to ~까지    complimentary 무료의

CHAPTER 05

# MEMO

장대영

**주요 약력**

중앙대학교 사범대학 졸업 (영어교육, 교육학 전공)
정교사 2급 자격증
전) 메가 공무원 온라인 오프라인 강사
전) 메가 스터디 러셀 수능 강의
전) 메가 스터디 노량진 단과 강의
전) 대치 명인학원
현) 박문각 공무원 온라인 오프라인 강사

**주요 저서**

박문각 공무원 장대영 영어 Graphic 독해
박문각 공무원 장대영 영어 Graphic 구문
박문각 공무원 장대영 영어 Graphic 문법
Polaris 문법 / 구문 / 독해 시리즈
INPUT 문법 / 구문 / 독해 시리즈
Polaris 기출 문법 / 기출 독해
문법의 재구성
독해의 재구성
어휘의 재구성


# 장대영 영어 Graphic 독해

**초판 인쇄** 2025. 6. 25. | **초판 발행** 2025. 6. 30. | **편저자** 장대영

**발행인** 박 용 | **발행처** (주)박문각출판 | **등록** 2015년 4월 29일 제2019-000137호

**주소** 06654 서울시 서초구 효령로 283 서경 B/D 4층 | **팩스** (02)584-2927

**전화** 교재 문의 (02)6466-7202

저자와의
협의하에
인지생략




정가 20,000원
ISBN 979-11-7262-934-2